MW00975570

12 SECRETS TO CASHING OUT

How to Sell Your Company for the Most Profit

ROBERT L. BERGETH

PRENTICE HALL
Englewood Cliffs, New Jersey 07632

Prentice-Hall International (UK) Limited, *London*
Prentice-Hall of Australia Pty. Limited, *Sydney*
Prentice-Hall Canada, Inc., *Toronto*
Prentice-Hall Hispanoamericana, S.A., *Mexico*
Prentice-Hall of India Private Limited, *New Delhi*
Prentice-Hall of Japan, Inc., *Tokyo*
Simon & Schuster Asia Pte. Ltd., *Singapore*
Editora Prentice-Hall do Brasil, Ltda., *Rio de Janeiro*

©1994 by
Robert L. Bergeth

All rights reserved. No part of this book may be reproduced in any form whatsoever, by photograph or xerography or by any other means, by broadcast or transmission, by translation into any kind of language, nor by recording electronically or otherwise, without permission in writing from the author, except by a reviewer, who may quote brief passages in critical articles or reviews.

This book is designed to provide information in regard to the subject matter covered. It is sold with the understanding that the publisher and author are not engaged in rendering legal, accounting or other professional services. If legal or other expert assistance is required, the services of a competent professional should be sought.

Every effort has been made to make this book as complete and accurate as possible. However, there **may be mistakes** in both typography and content. Therefore, this text should be used only as a general guide and not as an ultimate source of information. Furthermore, this book contains information on the sale or merger of a company that is current only up to the publication date.

The purpose of this book is to educate. The author and the publisher shall have neither liability nor responsibility to any person or entity with respect to any loss or damage caused, or alleged to be caused, directly or indirectly by the information contained in this book.

10 9 8 7 6 5 4 3 2 1

Library of Congress Cataloging-in-Publication data

Bergeth, Robert L.
    12 secrets to cashing out : how to sell your company for the most profit /
Robert L. Bergeth
        p.   cm.
    Includes bibliographical references and index.
    ISBN 0-13-176454-3. — ISBN 0-13-176462-4 (pbk.)
    1. Sale of business enterprises—United States.   I. Title.
HD1393.4.U6B47   1994
658.1'6—dc20   93-37957
                                                                 CIP

ISBN   ISBN 0-13-176454-3

                    ISBN 0-13-176462-4 paper

PRENTICE HALL
Career & Personal Development
Englewood Cliffs, NJ 07632

Simon & Schuster, A Paramount Communications Company

Printed in the United States of America

ACKNOWLEDGMENTS

I would like to thank several people whose help, support, and encouragement I greatly appreciate.

This book is dedicated to the memory of my mother, Agnes Bergeth. Her lifetime love of books and positive attitude, and the poetry she wrote, have been a great inspiration to me. Her example of love, honesty, and humor has been cherished.

A special thanks to my beautiful wife, Beth, for her support, encouragement, and important editorial assistance in the early stages of the book.

My thanks to Dr. Greg Zeck, creative consultant, for his evaluation, proofreading, and editing.

Lana Harris is a great typist, and her moral support and typing of the manuscript were greatly appreciated. My thanks to Ralph Scorpio, whose editorial skill was greatly appreciated and who made this book user-friendly.

Last, to my editor, Tom Power, who has supported and encouraged the development of this manuscript and who insisted on quality at every step. A special thanks to Simon & Schuster for publishing this book.

One editorial note: Rather than use the words his/her throughout the book, for the sake of simplicity and reader friendliness, I have used the words he and his.

ABOUT THE AUTHOR

Robert Bergeth, Ph.D., is a merger and acquisition consultant in Minneapolis, Minnesota. His expertise is in assisting owners of middle-sized manufacturing and distribution companies analyze, prepare, and sell their companies.

Bob brings a senior management perspective to the process of acquiring and divesting businesses. He has over 20 years of experience as an owner, CEO, and/or senior manager of both manufacturing and distribution companies. As a former business owner and CEO, he knows from firsthand experience the problems owners of closely held businesses face when they want to cash out for the most profit. Bob has also been vice president of sales for two medium-sized manufacturing companies, most recently Mackay Envelope Corporation. Bob speaks to industry groups and writes on the subject of valuing, structuring, and selling a business.

Dr. Bergeth has an undergraduate degree in mathematics from Jamestown College, a masters degree from Northern Arizona University, and a Ph.D. from the University of North Dakota. He is married and lives in Minnetonka, Minnesota.

His book *12 Secrets to Cashing Out: How to Sell Your Company for the Most Profit* is a savvy, street-smart, practical, one-of-a-kind reference that all entrepreneurs and merger and acquisitions professionals should have in their reference library.

CONTENTS

INTRODUCTION

There are over 16 million businesses in the United States, and 95 percent of these companies have fewer than 50 employees. These firms with fewer than 50 employees employ almost half the work force and are the lifeblood of the American economy. There also are approximately 800,000 companies that have more than 50 employees. About 13,000 of all companies are publicly owned.

There are many forces at work that cause an owner of a closely held company to consider selling his or her business. The following paragraphs address five important forces that are contributing to the decision to cash out.

1. Consolidation

Industries such as banking, health care, computers, information systems, business services, and insurance are dominated frequently by larger companies. There are fewer and fewer small companies as the larger companies continue to buy companies that enhance their position in particular industries. This consolidation will continue forcing smaller companies to sell because of the intense competition caused by larger companies that are well financed and benefit from economies of scale.

2. Globalization

In the 1960s about 7 percent of the American economy was subject to global competition. Today, 70 percent of our economy is affected by globalization. As competition heats up in the global marketplace, consolidation speeds up in industries influenced by the global competitive economy. Consider the consolidation that has already taken place by the world's auto, airline, banking, home electronics, and textile companies, and you can see the impact of globalization on consolidation.

Because of globalization, we will be seeing consolidation of industries in financial services, electrical equipment, foods, packaged consumer products, pharmaceutical, telecommunications, energy, and the media. Some consolidation is already going on, but the trend will continue and accelerate. This will force many companies both in the United States and abroad to join forces with companies who will survive the shake out in these industries.

3. Tight Financing

Smaller companies do not have access to the financing that larger companies have. However, smaller companies that are well managed, have a good market position, and record consistent earnings will not have difficulty obtaining the capital needed to operate and grow their businesses.

Financing a business causes huge problems for the entrepreneur. Smaller privately held companies can't sell long-term bonds with low interest rates as the big companies can. They don't have access to huge pools of funds from capital sources controlled by institutional investors such as pension funds and insurance companies. Smaller companies can't issue new stock to raise capital as the public companies can. Big companies can take advantage of tax breaks written by Congress with big-company specifications. The inability to raise capital and provide for the financing needs of their companies will force many entrepreneurs to cash out.

4. Relaxed Regulation

Relaxed antitrust policy encourages deal making in consolidating industries. The Federal Communication Commission (FCC) now allows radio and television companies to own more stations. This relaxed regulation will increase acquisitions in those industries. When the FCC relaxes its antitrust policies in other industries, the same consolidation of industries as in the radio and television industries will take place. Smaller companies are vulnerable in those industries where relaxed antitrust policies are in force.

5. Restructuring and Sell-offs

For many companies, the best strategic bet will be to sell product lines and divisions and concentrate on core businesses or sell the whole company. Being overleveraged is not a good place to be in the 1990s.

Many business owners want to sell and cash out for reasons other than those discussed. Boredom is a common reason. Competition may be intensifying. The market or industry may be shrinking. Perhaps the entrepreneur doesn't want to sign personally on the loan documents required to obtain a bank loan.

Because of his age, experience, and accumulated wealth, the business owner becomes less willing to take the risks needed to expand and grow his company. Besides he knows it isn't good to have so much of his personal wealth tied up in his business. For these reasons, he decides to cash out. Can you blame him?

This book was written for the entrepreneur of a closely held business who has decided he wants to cash out and take the money out of his business. Cashing out is the biggest, most important, and toughest business decision of his business life. When it comes time to sell, it's the first time he has ever done something like this. He has no training or experience at a time when he needs it most. He gets only one chance. Because he can't practice, he needs to do it right the first time.

This book meets the information vacuum an entrepreneur needs to cash out successfully. It provides the business owner with all the latest deal-doing knowledge, techniques, and strategies needed to sell his company for the most profit possible . . . and retire in leisure without worrying. The successful, proven strategies and techniques needed for the business owner to cash out for a ransom are all included.

Whether you have a few employees or several hundred, the information and techniques contained in this book will be worth thousands of dollars. All you have to do is take the time to learn and use them.

This book was also written for the thousands of professional advisers and financing and business intermediaries who will be needed to help the entrepreneur. Companies and individuals on the acquisition trail will also find the information helpful.

Good luck!

CHAPTER 1

12 SECRETS TO CASHING OUT

How to Sell Your Company for the Most Profit

Selling your company or business for the most cash will prove to be one of the greatest challenges you will experience in your business life. If you're like most business or company owners, you started your company in the 1960s or 1970s and have been in business for 15 to 25 years. You are between 55 and 65 years of age and have most of your personal net worth tied up in your business.

You loved your business in the early years and gave it all the energy and enthusiasm you had. Now, years later, after having done the same things repeatedly, you are bored and burned out. Oh, you go to work every day, but it has become a chore. The fun is gone. All you really enjoy now are the golf outings with your suppliers and customers. It has become harder for you to go to work. You are tired of the business and the same old problems and complaints. They have become like a broken record to you, and you know the problems your employees will bring up almost before they open their mouths.

You are emotionally attached to the business. After all, you have lived and spent more time with it than you have with your own family. It is your child, who wants to part with his child, even a difficult one.

Your company has grown over the years, and you now employ 50 or maybe even 500 employees. You have become friends with many of your employees. You know their families. You've been to their weddings. You go to church with them. You may even be the godfather of several of their children. You have made loans to several when they were down on their luck.

It won't be easy to tell these people that you have sold or plan to sell your business. Worse yet, if they find out that your company is for sale, the word will spread like wild fire. No, sir. It won't be easy.

Your company's recent earnings have been flat or declining, and the business is not glamorous. However, you have little debt and your business is still a source of great pride.

Your two kids are through college and both have good jobs. Todd is a sportscaster and loves his work but has no interest in running your company or taking over for you. Your daughter, Stacey, is married and lives in Atlanta. Neither your daughter nor son-in-law has an interest in the business. Stacey has a good job and your son-in-law is moving up the executive ladder for a large company. Besides, while you love them both, you aren't sure they could run the company.

You started your business because you had a technical background, and you most enjoyed the production end of the business. However, the excitement of seeing new products developed has long passed.

You initially went into business for the independence, freedom, and financial rewards. Now it is time to cash in and take your equity out of the company.

You may be burned out and bored with the business. These are the main reasons many business owners decide to sell their business. You may want to sell out for other reasons as well. Perhaps your health needs some attention. Maybe you have several partners in the company and the relationship has soured. You could be having family problems. Your spouse doesn't want to personally guarantee the loan you need to expand the business. Perhaps you don't want to put your neck on the line anymore, either. Maybe you are just worried about the competition and the future is uncertain.

Whatever your reasons for selling, you want to cash out and become more liquid. You know it's not wise to have so much of your personal wealth tied up in your company.

What worries you more than anything about selling is that word will get on the street. You know when that happens your employees will start preparing resumes and you know where they will look first. Your most employable people are your best people, and your competitor will enjoy interviewing your star salesperson or your best technical person. You know your best employees could walk out with your company's trade secrets, contacts, and customers. Your competitor will have a field day interviewing them. Morale will nosedive because of fear of the unknown.

You also worry that your customers will hear your company is for sale. These are the loyal customers you have known for years who have kept you in business by paying their invoices on time. You know they even ordered more than they needed just to help you out during some tough times. You played golf yesterday with Tom, your best customer. He asked whether the rumor is true that your company is for sale. As a result, when Tom returns to work, he directs his purchasing agent to look around for another supplier because you are cashing out.

Your customers, employees, and suppliers fear the unknown. What will happen? Because Tom tells his purchasing agents to be safe and cut back on his company's purchases to you, your company becomes a secondary, rather than a primary, supplier. Further, Tom tells the billing department to pay you in 45 days, not the usual 30. Stretched for cash flow, Tom may even tell his payables department to pay in 90 days.

The rumor on the street might be that your company is in trouble and you are liquidating, not selling, it. Recourse now is the issue. If you aren't there, who is going to pay the invoices?

Your suppliers will have heard the rumors as well. They won't understand that you just are bored and want to do something else with your life. They have been giving you credit for years and have helped you in difficult times by extending the terms. Now they take a close look at your account to see how much you owe them. The credit manager changes the terms from 45 days to 30 days and places a credit limit cap on your account.

If you are considering liquidation and the word gets on the street, it is not unusual for suppliers to make you pay C.O.D. Further, you'll cease being a preferred customer. When your supplier is low on stock, your competitor will receive first choice, not you.

Normally, it will take about a year to sell or liquidate your business. The shorter the liquidation period, the less the business is worth. Liquidation is a much riskier option than selling because it exacerbates each scenario just described with your employees, customers, and suppliers. Your main enemies, therefore, are time and confidentiality.

The good news is that privately owned companies are sold every day and the process is kept confidential when required. After the sale, you are going to be around for a few months to make sure that your customers, suppliers, and employees are happy and that there is a smooth transition. This should be your objective, and you can achieve it once you become knowledgeable and informed about the selling process. A seller will typically be required to stay with the business by contract for a reasonable transition period.

You are also concerned about valuing your company: How much is it worth? Am I over- or undervaluing it? You have heard that many companies sell for less than true value. Why? You want to maximize the value you receive for your company. How do you do that?

Is this the best time to sell? If not, when is the best time to sell? How can you be assured of receiving the most money for your company? To whom do you sell? Who will pay you the most? How do you find them?

What advisers do you need, and when do you need them? How do you prevent the tax man from having a field day? How do you structure the deal? What are the financing and main legal issues involved?

I wrote this book to help you understand the intricacies of when and how to sell your business for the most profit. You need to know how to avoid the sharks so you can continue to run your business without the emotional trauma that can take place.

The most successful buyers, the ones you want, have an advantage over you in negotiating a deal. They know the ropes; they've completed several deals and are experienced. They also have the option of walking away from the deal. Therefore, it is very important that you gain the knowledge you need to do the deal so you are on an even footing with the buyer.

This is probably your first and only opportunity to sell your business. You can't practice by selling one or more other companies. If you understand the ideas found in this book, you can go eyeball-to-eyeball with the most experienced buyers.

You need to see your company's business from the buyer's perspective. The buyer will focus on the future of your company, not the past. So the buyer will want to keep you focused on the past. If you let this happen, you'll be paid for the past and will not share in the rewards for future growth of your company. It is not a bad past that will hurt you, but a bad future.

Take a few hours to read, study, and understand the ideas outlined in this book. You'll be glad you did. There are 12 secrets involved in the successful sale of your company for the most cash possible. Each is important. Become thoroughly acquainted with each secret.

The toughest decision is the first one. Do you really want to sell your business? Will you be fully committed to seeing it through to a successful conclusion? If you answer yes, then this book is written for you. Plunge in! Are you vacillating and not sure what to do? Dive in! You'll become armed with the latest information you'll need to make a sound decision. Are you thinking of selling in three to five years? You'll also benefit by reading this book because you'll begin immediately to build value into your company. Now is the time you can still do something about it.

This book is written for the entrepreneur who is considering or wants to sell his company or business and wants to sell for the highest possible dollar amount. It is also written for the financial, legal, accounting, and merger and acquisition professionals who will help him.

This book could also fall into the hands of a wily buyer. Should this misfortune happen, the buyer will better understand the seller's needs and probably can fill them. The result will be a satisfactory merger or sale, where there are no victors or losers, only a situation where both sides win.

The 12 secrets involved in a successful sale or merger are as follows:

TWELVE SECRETS TO CASHING OUT

Secret 1: Recognize That Timing Is Everything. Is now the right time to sell? It's a tough decision, but one that only you can make. When you become fully informed about the selling process and can identify and evaluate the various options available, you'll know what to do. Read the book step by step until the answer is clear. The best time to sell is discussed in Chapter 3.

Secret 2: Determine How Much Your Company Is Worth. There are more than 25 vital factors that can have a positive or negative impact on the value of your business (see Chapter 3). You can fix some negative factors. The buyer and his advisers will examine each factor, and so must you. Your buyer will use the negative factors to drive your price down. Conversely, he'll ignore those positive factors that will drive up the price. Get in the driver's seat and make sure the buyer understands those factors that enhance the value of your company. Chapter 4 describes the methods that professionals and smart companies use to arrive at a range of value for a company. This is tough reading, but you'll know what your company is really worth when you are done. A major reason sellers don't receive full value for their company is they don't know how to figure out the maximum value. Don't let that happen to you.

Secret 3: Hold the Tax People at Bay. No one can do it entirely or forever. You can pay more than 60 percent of the consideration you receive from the buyer for your company in taxes. You can also pay none. Chapters 5, 6, 12, and 13 are loaded with tax-saving ammunition. Load your guns and go on the offensive. Should you sell assets or stock? Don't skip Chapter 5 because lack of knowledge will cost you much money. An asset or stock sale is heavily influenced by tax laws. This chapter is a tax primer for you. An asset or stock sale is also one of the first decisions you'll make.

Secret 4: Engage the Necessary Advisers to Help You with the Transaction. To go it alone would be foolhardy. Read Chapter 2. You'll learn what to look for in a good professional adviser. You'll learn when you need him and when you don't. You don't go to a general practitioner when you have a heart attack. The same applies in the specialized world of mergers and acquisitions. Read about whom you need, when you need him, and how much to pay him.

Secret 5: Know How to Prepare Your Company for Sale. Chapter 7 reveals eight winning moves to make before selling. You must take action on some important issues before you put your company up for sale. You'll raise the ante for your company if you do and simplify the selling process simultaneously.

Secret 6: Acknowledge That the Buyer Will Be the Biggest and Most Important Customers You'll Ever Sell. Chapter 8 shows how to hook the big one. To hook him, you'll need the best and most persuasive selling tools you have ever produced. This chapter will give you the methods needed to bring that elusive, right buyer into your corner.

Secret 7: Show Your Company's True Earnings. You manage your company to suppress earnings and pay as little tax as possible. However, now that you are selling your company, you'll want to show the maximum earnings power of your company. You will want to recast your financial statements to maximize, not minimize, earnings. Chapter 9 shows you how to do it. The buyer will pay for the earnings of your company. Generally, the greater those earnings, the more he'll pay.

Secret 8: Where to Find the Best Buyers. Who are they? They are always the most elusive and toughest catch of all. Since you want the best buyers, you'll want to read all about it in Chapter 10. Don't ignore this chapter because you'll be in for some big surprises. What looks like the best prospect for your company isn't necessarily so. Chapter 10 tells you how the pros do it. You'll learn the risks and opportunities involved when you sell to competitors, employees, investors, large companies, and others. Chapter 12 shows how to finance the deal. Sometimes you have a good buyer, but he isn't sophisticated in the world of finance. Why let a deal fall through because of lack of knowledge about how to finance the deal? Chapter 12 is loaded with tips and ideas about how to help the buyer finance the deal.

Secret 9: Outsmart the Sharks by Negotiating Price and Terms the Right Way. You'll be the one who negotiates price and terms, so you'll need all the knowledge you can get. You'll be going nose-to-nose against smart, savvy buyers and deal-doing advisers who are the best money can buy. Chapter 11 is loaded with the latest negotiation techniques you'll need to win. Chapter 11 also discusses 17 mistakes some buyers make and suggests ways in which you can capitalize on their mistakes.

Secret 10: Learn Surefire Deal-Structuring Methods. Chapters 13 and 14 show how the pros do the big deals. It explains 16 solid, proven, and winning deal-structuring techniques. Each technique can put money in your pocket and leave the tax man high and dry.

Secret 11: Avoid the Inevitable Legal Traps. Chapter 15 discusses two blockbuster legal pitfalls you must avoid at all costs. Once you finish the deal, you don't want the shark to come back and bite you. He can and will if you let him. Chapter 15 also discusses the main legal issues involved in a letter of intent and purchase agreement.

Secret 12: Anticipate the Buyer's Due Diligence Investigation of Your Company. You'll want to know what the buyer will be looking for. By seeing your company's strengths and weaknesses from the buyer's perspective, you can take action on the problem areas and fix them. You'll also want to stress your strengths. Chapter 16 provides you with the opportunity to see your company through the eyes of the buyer.

You'll feel success, jubilation, elation, fatigue, sorrow, and exhaustion when you have finished signing all the papers and have a certified check in hand. The deal is done. What now? Chapter 17 will bring you down to earth.

The 12 secrets to cashing out are what this book is all about. It's a practical, step-by-step guide loaded with tools, techniques, and ideas that should make you a bundle of money when you put them to good work. It is a blueprint for you to sell out for a ransom. I have attempted to cover the key legal, tax, structuring, and valuation issues. Everything you'll need to know about selling your company for the most profit is contained in this book. Dive in!

2

WHICH ADVISERS ARE NEEDED?

Are They Right for the Job?

Most entrepreneurs dislike paying professional fees for accountants and attorneys. Entrepreneurs thus employ professional services only when they absolutely need to. Selling your company is not an easy task. This is one of those absolutely necessary times when you need the best tax adviser and deal-doing attorney you can employ.

All too often the principals involved in the sale of a company have the misconception that negotiations are pretty well completed when the issues of price and terms are resolved. There are many different ways to structure a deal and many tax and legal issues that can influence the price and terms of the deal. The purchase price of the deal will vary depending on those issues.

Generally, one structure or contractual clause will give an advantage to one party over the other. Both buyer and seller invite serious conflict when they settle price and terms without giving simultaneous attention to the tax and legal aspects of the deal.

For example, assume you and the buyer have negotiated the price and the buyer agrees that you will be paid $5 million in cash at closing for your company. At this point, both of you agree to leave the remaining details to your respective lawyers and accountants to work out. Let's see what issues remain unresolved. First are the nontax issues:

1. Is the transaction structured so that the buyer inherits all your company's liabilities, revealed and undisclosed? Or will the deal be structured in a way that the buyer assumes only specified liabilities and the remainder are left with your company or inherited by your shareholders?

2. Will your contractual representations, warranties, and indemnifications allow the buyer to recover from you part of the purchase price, if after the deal is completed, the buyer discovers that you have undisclosed liabilities. Undisclosed liabilities can include environmental cleanup, unpaid taxes, employment discrimination, product liability, patent or trademark infringement, and the like. Another undisclosed liability could be that your company lacks good title to part of its assets; another might be that part of your receivables are not collectible or that part of your inventory is not salable; it could be that your financial statements are inaccurate.

3. Will some of your employees receive employment contracts and severance agreements? Or, instead, will they receive no protection? Will the buyers want covenants not to compete from key executives?

Then several important tax issues need to be resolved:

1. Is the deal structured so that the buyer receives a new basis in your company's assets? Generally, the new basis is higher than the old. The basis is figured out by adding the purchase price paid by the buyer, and any liabilities the buyer assumes, and the buyer's expenses of getting your company. Or will the buyer take a carry-over basis in your company's assets. Generally, the carry-over basis is much lower and results in fewer tax advantages for the buyer.

2. Will the transactions cause your company to pay a corporate-level tax on all appreciations of its assets? If so, will the tax burden fall on you or the buyer?

3. Will your shareholders pay tax on the appreciation inherent in their stock? Can the capital gain of the stock be deferred by the installment method or a tax-free exchange?

As an example, let's assume that your buyer wants to purchase your company's assets to obtain a stepped-up basis without additional tax cost to him. The buyer's attorney, also, wants language in the purchase agreement that specifies particular liabilities the buyer will assume. Thus the buyer avoids assuming any undisclosed liabilities.

Your attorney advises you to sell stock and not assets when you are a C corporation so that you avoid the double tax. Further, he wants you to shift the economic burden of all disclosed and undisclosed liabilities to the buyer. Your lawyer also wants you to make no representation concerning undisclosed liabilities.

Thus you and the buyer are at a complete impasse because important tax and legal considerations were not accounted for when price and terms were agreed to. These tax and legal considerations will now result in renegotiating the price you receive and how you'll be paid. Because the manner in which the purchase is structured and the terms of the contract have major economic consequences, it is important that you are properly advised early in the negotiations. That doesn't mean that your advisers sit at your side from the first contact with the buyer. It does mean, however, that you are properly informed about the major tax and legal issues involved and can negotiate these to your advantage. See Chapter 11 on negotiations so you will know when to bring your legal and tax advisers into the negotiations. Bringing advisers into the picture too early can be costly, just as waiting too long can be a costly mistake. There is a right and wrong time.

You must be aware of two important points when employing advisers to help sell your company. First, employ advisers who are experienced deal-doers. Don't skimp here. You'll pay repeatedly if you use an attorney or tax adviser who isn't experienced in this type specialty. You don't go to a pediatrician when you have a heart attack. The same applies here. You want specialists.

Second, carefully consider the motivation of your current legal and accounting advisers. These advisers are often road blocks to putting together a successful deal. Both your attorney and accounting firms have been billing your company handsomely for years; they face losing you as their customer once you sell your company. It's not in their best interests to lose your business. This explains why they can find all sorts of reasons why a buyer isn't right for the deal or why they'll nitpick the deal to death. They'll drag their heels when it comes to timely production of important documents and reports and frustrate your potential buyer.

If you do decide to use your current legal and accounting firms, be aware of their motivations and closely supervise their activities. Their job is to provide you with the options and help you evaluate those options. It is not their job to tell you what to do.

Your current accounting firm should prepare the necessary accounting reports for your buyer. Your firm should help with the information as needed. If they are experienced merger and acquisition tax advisers, then continue to have them advise you on tax matters.

The same applies to your legal advisers. If they have someone on staff who is an experienced, deal-doing attorney, you'll want to use him. When not, look for someone else.

MERGER AND ACQUISITION INTERMEDIARIES

The third adviser you will need is a successful merger and acquisition consultant. "Intermediary" is a term that is often used to describe this individual also. A business broker is another adviser that is involved in a merger and acquisition. The distinction between business brokers and intermediaries isn't always evident. Generally, a business broker is involved with smaller companies, whereas merger and acquisition consultants and intermediaries are involved with larger deals. Intermediaries generally won't be involved with a company valued at under $1 million while a business broker will. However, there is much overlapping of the two. What is important is not his title, but his experience and expertise.

Your merger and acquisition intermediary will be the person who will find the one right buyer for your company. He'll help you in evaluating the buyer and negotiating and properly structuring the deal.

Industry Research

A good merger and acquisition consultant knows how to research your industry and related industries to find the right buyer for your company. He should have extensive contacts with other merger and acquisition professionals throughout the United States, Canada, Mexico, and Europe. These extensive contacts will help him find the right buyer for a deal when required. He should also be an experienced businessperson who will identify and understand your needs and know how to fill them.

A merger and acquisition consultant should first do an in-depth evaluation, and for your eyes only, of the key information needed for the most professional and profitable sale. This evaluation will include

1. The strengths of your business and how to maximize them.
2. The earnings potential of the business, based on a thorough evaluation of the market.
3. The fair market value of your business and its potential returns to the buyer.

You should see the company the way a prospective buyer wants to see it. The mergers and acquisition's adviser should help recast your financial statements to maximize your earnings.

From this evaluation, he'll develop a well-documented evaluation report that will show to the buyer the value of your business. You'll need to review and approve this report. Only you should authorize its release.

You will want someone you trust, respect, and like because it may take a year or more to sell your business. Your merger and acquisition consultant/broker will be a key player during this time. He'll be responsible for bringing a qualified buyer to the table so that confidentiality is maintained throughout the selling process.

CONFIDENTIALITY AGREEMENT

You'll want to discuss the subject of confidentiality with your broker. You'll want to know which procedures are in place to protect the fact your company is for sale. Because he'll be contacting many companies, you'll need to know how he plans to contact prospective buyers and still ensure confidentiality.

There are many different kinds of confidentiality agreements that can be used in a transaction. When you are approached by a broker or company investigating the possibility of acquiring your company, the first thing you will need from them before you provide any information is a confidentiality agreement. This agreement puts the buyer on notice that he must be very careful with any information you provide him. This agreement can be short and consist of one page or be as long as five or more pages. The confidentiality agreement presented here is typical.

Confidentiality Agreement

This Agreement is made between the undersigned individually and for the referenced business entity, its officers, directors, partners, employees, agents, and advisory (Buyer) and International Mergers and Acquisitions (IMA) for the benefit of IMA and a presently undisclosed prospect (Prospect).

Whereas: The Buyer has requested information from IMA and Prospect for purposes of investigating a possible acquisition, merger, financing, or joint venture involving all or part of the business interests owned by Prospect, described as: XXXXXX

Now Therefore: To induce IMA to identify the Prospect and provide such information, Buyer agrees as follows:

1. Buyer will not disclose any information obtained hereunder, or during its investigations, to any other person or organization not herein authorized or make known to others, by disclosure or confirmation, that this company, division, or product line is for sale or that financing is wanted, either before or after termination of investigations or negotiations.

2. Without the specific *prior written approval* of IMA or Prospect, Buyer shall not reveal this information to any broker, intermediary, lending institution, prospective equity partner, syndication member, or other financing source. In the event disclosure to such parties is deemed desirable, IMA and Prospect may require the execution of a document similar to this Agreement.

3. This Agreement applies to all information received by Buyer from IMA or Prospect now and during future investigations that is not available to the general public. All information provided pursuant to this Agreement shall be deemed confidential and valuable. Without specif-

ic written agreement to the contrary, it shall be deemed proprietary. Unauthorized disclosure of said information, even without intent to harm, could cause substantial and irreparable damage to IMA and Prospect.

4. All information provided shall be used for the sole purpose of evaluating the acquisition or financing decision and shall not at any time, or in any manner, be utilized for any other purpose. The buyer shall promptly advise IMA when its investigations or negotiations are ended and will return all information furnished, in whatever form, without retaining copies, summaries, or extracts.

5. Buyer will not contact the Prospect's banker, accountant, attorney, employees, suppliers, competitors, customers, or others who might have information concerning Prospect without written permission of IMA or Prospect. Buyer will not contact Prospect directly until authorized by IMA.

6. IMA makes no representation or warranty, express or implied, as to the truth, accuracy, or completeness of any information provided, or not provided, to buyer under this Agreement. Buyer assumes full responsibility for its reliance upon such information and expressly waives all rights of recourse, if any, against IMA for Buyer's reliance thereon.

7. This letter of agreement shall be governed and construed in accordance with the laws of the State of Minnesota. It is understood that there are two pages to this Agreement.

8. If you agree with this, please sign and return one copy of this letter. This will constitute our Agreement with respect to the subject matter of this letter.

Sincerely,

Robert L. Bergeth

ACCEPTED AND AGREED TO:

Company:_____

By: _____

Title: _____

Date: _____

What happens if there is a breech of the confidentiality agreement? How do you prove a breech? If you can prove it, how much should the monetary damages be? These are legal questions beyond the scope of this discussion and should be discussed with your attorney. Do not release any information to a broker or his client without having both of them execute a confidentiality agreement. It is a good idea to insist that bankers, accountants, attorneys, and others who may be involved in the deal sign a confidentiality agreement too.

MERGER AND ACQUISITION FEES

Most merger and acquisition consultants are paid a success fee when the deal closes and nothing when it doesn't. The fee usually is a percentage of the total selling price and varies depending on the selling price. When total consideration is under $1 million, fees can range from 12 percent on the high end to something considerably less. Fees are generally negotiable. When companies are sold for several millions of dollars, consultants sometime use the Lehman fee arrangement. This formula provides for 5 percent on the first $1 million of the selling price, 4 percent of the second million of sales price, 3 percent of the third million of sales price, 2 percent of the fourth million of sales price, and 1 percent on the sale price over $4 million. Other fee arrangements are 8 percent on the first $1 million of consideration, 6 percent of the second million of consideration, 4 percent of the third million, and 2 percent of the remaining consideration. When the selling price is in the millions, it is not unusual to see a fee arrangement that specifies 2 percent of the first $25 million of consideration and 1 percent on the consideration more than $25 million.

Fee arrangements can include a flat fee, such as 5 percent, which is paid only when the deal is done. Fees vary widely just as accounting and legal fees vary. Some consultants/brokers have their expenses paid and receive a monthly fee that is offset against the final fee they'll earn when the deal closes.

There are two basic fee agreements. The first is a situation where the buyer pays the intermediary and the seller is not responsible for the broker's fee. In this instance the broker represents the buyer in the transaction. The second agreement is one where the seller retains an intermediary to sell his business and is responsible for paying the fee. The intermediary represents the seller. First let's look at a typical fee agreement that a buyer might have with a broker or intermediary

Success Fee Agreement—Nonexclusive

This letter confirms our agreement that International Mergers and Acquisitions, 2109 Indian Road West, Minneapolis, MN 55305 (hereinafter IMA) will receive a success fee from XXXX (hereinafter Company) for professional services rendered upon the completion of any sale (or lease, merger or consolidation, exchange, transfer, assignment, or other disposition of the business or its assets or any part of it or interest therein, all of which will throughout this Agreement shall be deemed a Sale) entered into by the Company or any of its divisions, subsidiaries, or affiliates with any person, partnership, corporation, or other entity that IMA has introduced or referred to it in writing.

If Company, through its authorized representative, reaches agreement to acquire a business property that results in a change of ownership, Company guarantees that IMA, irrespective of any specific involvement by IMA, will be compensated according to the schedule titled FEES. IMA shall assist the Company or its shareholders in its or their negotiations with any party introduced, directly or indirectly, by IMA to the extent that the Company or its shareholders request us to do so.

If a transaction is consummated or if Company acquires any business interest of a party introduced to Company by IMA, Company shall pay IMA a fee based on the total face value of consideration paid by Company or Affiliates (Consideration), directly or indirectly, regarding the transaction. Consideration may include, but is not limited to, payments in cash, stock, real and personal property, warrants and options, fees, notes, debentures or other debt, assumption or relief of any debt (including guarantees), the total amount of noncompeting, employment, consulting and lease agreements or amendments thereto, earnouts, and all other elements or value exchanged, or to be exchanged concerning the Transaction.

No fee shall be paid under this Agreement if on the date of closing the seller is obligated to pay IMA a fee or commission pursuant to a written agreement between the seller and IMA.

FEES: The amount of the fee shall be calculated from the following schedule on the total Consideration:

Five percent of the first one million dollars of Consideration, or any part; plus 4% of the second one million dollars of Consideration, or any part; plus 3% of the third one million dollars of Consideration, or any part; plus 2% of the fourth one million dollars of Consideration, or any part; plus 1% of the fifth one million dollars of Consideration or more than five million dollars.

IMA's fee is payable in certified funds at the earlier of settlement or closing. If part of the Consideration is incalculable at closing, such as royalty or earnout, the portion of IMA's fee relating to such Consideration will be paid to IMA when Company pays the acquired company. In any event, when the consideration paid is more than $500,000, the total fee paid to IMA at closing shall not be less than $50,000. Any forfeited option or earnest money is to be divided equally between Company and IMA.

IMA makes no representation or warranty, express or implied, as to the truth, accuracy, or completeness of any information provided, or not provided, to Company under this Agreement. Company assumes full responsibility for its reliance upon such information and expressly waives all rights of recourse, if any, against IMA for Company's reliance thereon.

Company will include language in the Transaction documents describing Company's fee responsibility to IMA. Upon request, Company will provide IMA with copies of all Transaction documents and will provide IMA with advance notice of the time and place of closing. IMA shall have the right to attend.

In the event IMA prevails in any action to enforce collection of amounts due or other rights under this Agreement, Company agrees to pay IMA's legal and other collection costs plus interest at 1 percent per month on any unpaid balance from the original due date until the date paid.

This Agreement shall remain in effect for 12 months from this date and shall continue after that until canceled by either party upon 30 days prior written notice. Within 72 hours of expiration of this Agreement, IMA will furnish Company a written list of persons, partnerships, corporations, and other entities IMA has introduced or referred to it in writing. The fee shall be due and payable in case of a sale or merger entered into by the Company or any of its divisions, subsidiaries, or affiliates, with any person, partnership, corporation, or other entity contained on the list for one year after the date of termination of this Agreement.

The attached Standard Terms and Conditions are incorporated into this Agreement. It is understood there are three pages to this Agreement.

Entire Agreement: This is the entire Agreement between the parties about its subject matter and supersedes all prior agreements, representations, and understandings of the parties. No modifications of this Agreement shall be binding unless agreed to in writing by the parties.

Please confirm that this is according to your understanding by signing and returning to IMA the duplicate of this letter attached.

Sincerely,

Robert L. Bergeth

ACCEPTED AND AGREED TO:
Company: _____
By: _____
Title: _____ Date: _____

Standard Terms and Conditions to Fee Agreement

The following Standard Terms and Conditions are incorporated into the agreement (Agreement) dated _____, 199X.

Services: IMA is an independent contractor and will identify and present to Company parties that IMA deems suitable for the intended transaction. IMA will prepare documents for describing and presenting information used for possible transactions; will participate in plant visits, discussions, and negotiations where Company deems appropriate; will work with Company's attorney and accountants under the direction of Company; and will otherwise help Company to bring Transaction to a close. In performing these services, IMA will obtain Company's prior approval of information to be released and will employ the resources of the International Mergers and Acquisition's network to the extent appropriate. However, IMA makes no representation, express or implied, that it will effect a Transaction because of the services furnished under this Agreement.

Authority: The person executing this Agreement on Company's behalf hereby warrants and represents, knowing that IMA will rely thereon, that the signature is duly authorized to bind the Company to the Agreement.

Information: Company shall furnish IMA complete and accurate current and historical business information, and shall promptly inform IMA of any changes that may materially affect its business or IMA's services under this Agreement. Company warrants the accuracy of all information provided by Company to IMA in the course of activities under this Agreement.

Indemnification: Recognizing that transactions of the type contemplated by this Agreement sometimes result in litigation and that IMA's role is advisory, Company agrees to indemnify IMA and its officers, directors, employees, agents, and affiliates against any suits, losses, claims, damages, or liabilities, joint or several, including shareholder actions, to which the indemnified parties may be subject concerning the services provided, and to reimburse the indemnified parties for any legal or other expenses reasonably incurred by them in connection therewith. However, company shall not be responsible for any loss, claim, damage, or liability resulting from the willful misfeasance or gross negligence of an indemnified party.

Arbitration: Any controversy, dispute, or claim between the parties to this Agreement shall be resolved by binding arbitration according to the rules of the American Arbitration Association.

Consideration: Any portion of the Consideration to be decided after closing shall be considered additive to Consideration paid at closing for applying the schedule of fees. The value of all Consideration shall be its face value, without discount for the timing of receipt.

Disclosure of Fee: IMA shall have the right, but not the obligation, to disclose to any party to the transaction, Company's fee responsibility to IMA.

Successors and Assigns: This Agreement shall inure to the benefit of and be binding upon the parties hereto and their respective assigns and representatives.

Jurisdiction: This Agreement shall be interpreted under and be governed by the laws of the State of Minnesota.

The Nonexclusive Success Finder's Fee Agreement just presented is typical of that which a buyer may sign to induce the broker or intermediary to bring deals to him. The buyer pays a success fee only when a deal is successfully closed. This is called a contingency fee and is commonly used. As noted earlier, the fees due under the terms of this agreement are called Lehman fees.

Everything in a fee agreement is negotiable. In this case, the agreement pretty well protects the broker. If a deal is consummated, it is fairly certain that the buyer will have to pay a fee to the broker. In some states the broker must have a real estate license to legally enforce the collection of a fee. Should the broker not have a license, a judge may deny him a fee and the buyer would have no legal obligation to pay a fee. Many states, however, have no licensing laws, and brokers are not regulated because there is no regulatory authority.

One last point that should be noted about this agreement: the buyer is obligated to pay the broker a fee on any debt that is assumed. When the seller wants the buyer to pay him $1.5 million and assume debt of $1 million, the broker will be paid a fee based on the purchase price plus any debt assumed. Then the total fee will be based on $2.5 million.

The following is an example of the type of agreement that the seller and broker might have.

Seller's Authorization and Exclusive Fee Agreement

The party signing below as Company engages the undersigned International Mergers and Acquisitions, 2109 Indian Road West, Minnetonka, MN 55305 (hereafter "IMA") to provide professional brokerage services to Company and/or its shareholders, principals, subsidiaries, partnerships, and other related parties (affiliates) to accomplish a sale, merger, exchange, capital investment, loan, joint venture, or other such transaction involving all or part of the business interest of Company, including, but not limited to, stock and assets owned directly or indirectly by company or Affiliates described generally as follows: XXXXX (Transaction).

Company engages IMA on an "exclusive right to sell" basis and agrees to forward to IMA all inquiries from any party during the term of this Agreement. Company's obligations to IMA shall arise regardless of any specific involvement by IMA. IMA shall assist the Company or its shareholders in its or their negotiations with any party introduced, directly or indirectly, by IMA to the extent that the Company or its shareholders request IMA to do so.

Company shall have the sole right to accept or reject any offer received.

If a transaction is consummated or if Company acquires any business interest of a party introduced to Company by IMA, Company shall pay IMA a fee based on the total face value of consideration paid by Company or Affiliates (Consideration), directly or indirectly, regarding the transaction. Consideration may include, but is not limited to, payments in cash, stock, real and personal property, warrants and options, fees, notes, and debentures or other debt; assumption or relief of any debt (including guarantees); the total amount of noncompeting, employment, consulting, and lease agreements or amendments thereto; earnouts; and all other elements or value exchanged, or to be exchanged concerning the Transaction.

The amount of the fee shall be calculated from the following schedule on the total Consideration:

Five percent of the first one million dollars of Consideration, or any part; plus 4% of the second one million dollars of Consideration, or any part; plus 3% of the third one million dollars of Consideration, or any part; plus 2% of the fourth one million dollars of Consideration, or any part; plus 1% of the fifth one million dollars of Consideration or more than five million dollars.

IMA's fee is payable in certified funds at the earlier of settlement or closing. If part of the Consideration is incalculable at closing, such as a royalty or earnout, the portion of IMA's fee relating to such Consideration shall be paid to IMA upon receipt of this Consideration by Company or Affiliates. In any event, the total fee to be paid to IMA at closing shall not be less than $75,000.

Company agrees to reimburse, within 30 days of invoice, the out-of-pocket expenses incurred on behalf of Company by IMA. Such expenses shall be documented by IMA and shall not exceed $1,000, in total, without specific authorization by Company.

To cover planning, research, and the preparation of marketing documentation, an initial payment of $5,000 is payable to IMA upon execution of this Agreement and shall be credited against the total fee that may ultimately be due IMA.

Company will include language in the Transaction documents describing Company's fee responsibility to IMA. Upon request, Company will provide IMA with copies of all Transaction documents and will provide IMA with advance notice of the time and place of closing. IMA shall have the right to attend.

In the event IMA prevails in any action to enforce collection of amounts due or other rights under this Agreement, Company agrees to pay IMA's legal and other collection costs plus interest at 1 percent per month on any unpaid balance from the original due date until the date paid.

This Agreement shall remain in effect for 12 months from this date and shall continue after that until canceled by either party upon 30 days prior written notice. Within 72 hours of expiration of this Agreement, IMA will furnish Company a written list of persons, partnerships, corporations, and other entities IMA has introduced or referred to it in writing. The fee shall be due and payable in case of a sale or merger entered by the Company or any of its divisions, subsidiaries, or affiliates, with any person, partnership, corporation, or other entity contained on the list for one year after the date of termination of this Agreement.

Entire Agreement: This is the entire Agreement between the parties about its subject matter and supersedes all prior agreements, representations, and understandings of the parties. No modifications of this Agreement shall be binding unless agreed to in writing by the parties.

Please confirm that this is according to your understanding by signing and returning to IMA the duplicate of this letter attached.

Sincerely,

INTERNATIONAL MERGERS & ACQUISITIONS
Robert L. Bergeth
Accepted and Agreed TO:
Company: _____
By: _____
Title: _____ Date: _____

Certain parts of this contract should be noted. The agreement has a several paragraphs that were not included in the buyer's fee agreement. First, the seller agrees to pay the broker his out-of-pocket expenses. Any expenses beyond $1,000 are to be agreed to in writing. Second, the seller makes a $5,000 payment up front to cover the broker's costs of planning, research, and preparation of marketing documentation such as a selling memorandum. The $5,000 will be subtracted from the Lehman fee due at the successful conclusion of the transaction. The third difference between the contract shown here and the one between the broker and buyer is that the agreement stipulates a minimum fee that must be paid whatever the purchase price.

The practice of paying a broker's out-of-pocket expenses and a retainer is becoming more frequent and varies by size of deal and competition in any given market. Some very talented merger and acquisition firms will not proceed with a transaction unless a retainer is paid either in advance or monthly. Again, there are no strict rules. Fees can be negotiated like everything else.

Another important point made in the contract is that it stipulates an "exclusive right to sell" basis. This means that should the seller find a buyer on his own, with or without the knowledge of the broker, the seller is liable for the brokerage fee to the broker. Brokers and intermediaries want this clause in the contract. This ensures that the seller can't go around the broker and thus avoid the fee. Intermediaries want to be compensated for the time and money they have put into a deal.

WHY YOU MUST ENGAGE SPECIALISTS AND NOT GENERALISTS

The world is more complicated than ever. Take the case of attorneys. There are attorneys in small practices who are generalists. These attorneys have little, if any, experience with buying and selling businesses even if they practice some corporate law. Attorneys specialize in various parts of the law just as physicians specialize in various parts of medicine. Some specialize in bankruptcy law, criminal defense, or family law. Others specialize in labor and employment law, personal injury, real estate, environmental law, and other areas.

You want an attorney who specializes in corporate law and has a major part of his practice devoted to mergers and acquisitions. Some corporate lawyers specialize in corporate finance, leveraged buyouts, and securities regulations. Be sure your attorney specializes in mergers and acquisitions and has experience in your industry if possible. How many deals of your size and your industry has he done over the last five years? One year?

Most larger law firms have tax specialists who concentrate on corporate tax and partnerships. Be sure your tax adviser is competent and experienced in tax matters relating to the sale of a company. Sometimes you can get double your money's worth by employing an attorney who specializes in both mergers and acquisitions and the tax law related to it.

To help you identify the best merger and acquisitions lawyers, I have listed in the appendix selected attorneys who specialize in mergers and acquisitions. These people will serve as a good starting point for selecting a top-flight attorney or tax specialist to advise you. They will also be a good referral source for other attorneys if you don't like them or they are too busy.

Many people will claim they can sell your company. Just remember: you want someone who does this for a living, a specialist who will work full time for you. Once you have selected your merger and acquisition firm, understand that usually not more than two and usually only one person will be assigned to sell your company. A senior adviser may be the one who puts the close on you, but you can bet it will be the junior guy who will do the work.

The best people in the industry are experienced businesspeople with multiple talents and contacts. They can pick up the telephone and contact a merger and acquisition firm in another part of the country and have instant access to that firm's contacts.

Some merger and acquisition firms have membership in an association made up of consultants or brokers like themselves. This gives them the ability to have contacts throughout the United States and the world as well. Other firms may subscribe to a national listing service or directory.

First List and World M&A Network are both examples of a listing service. They provide its subscribers access to a brief synopsis of merger and acquisition buyers and lists their acquisition criteria. It's not unusual for one of these listing services to have 500 or more companies actively seeking acquisitions in all industries. Most of these buyers will be represented by intermediaries. These buyers are seeking acquisitions with purchase prices less than $1 million to more than $50 million. First List and World M&A Network are just two examples of the contacts a top-flight merger and acquisition firm has. First List can be reached at 1-800-999-0920 or by writing First List, Vision Quest Publishing, Inc., 655 Rockland Road, Suite 103,

Lake Bluff, IL 60044. World M&A Network can be reached at: 7170 Street, N.W., Suite 300, Washington, D.C. 20004. (202) 628-6900. The last section of this chapter shows a checklist of criteria that will help you select a high-quality adviser.

ADVISER CHECKLIST

The following is a checklist of the most important criteria that you should consider when selecting trustworthy and competent legal, tax, appraisal, and merger and acquisition advisers:

Ask These Key Questions

_____ How many years of experience does he or she have?

_____ How much experience does he or she have in this area?

_____ How much experience in your type of business?

_____ Would he feel comfortable representing your particular view?

_____ Why would he or she be a good adviser for you?

_____ What fees does he or she charge?

_____ What is his or her work load right now? Heavy? Light?

_____ Are you comfortable with the prospective adviser and do you trust him?

Determine the Fees and Expenses

Fees vary considerably from firm to firm. Usually, an adviser can give you an estimate or range as to the cost, although it is often impossible to do more than this. Find out what would not be covered and what the charge would be for those matters; for example:

_____ Are telephone and fax costs charged to you?

_____ What about travel costs?

_____ What about duplicating and copying costs?

_____ What is the hourly rate?

_____ If a retainer is charged, what services will be performed for the retainer and how will you be charged once the retainer has been used up?

_____ How are bills itemized? Insist on detailed itemization and monthly billing.

_____ Does billing/itemization add to costs?

_____ Can you make monthly payments instead of paying off the entire bill each month?

_____ Can fees be delayed and not paid until the transaction is closed?

_____ Will an interest charge be assessed on the unpaid balance?

_____ Is there a written retainer agreement incorporating how fees will be billed and computed?

_____ Do you know what you are being billed for and how much you are being billed?

What You Should Expect from Your Adviser

_____ How will you be kept informed about the progress of your deal?

_____ How will confidentiality be maintained?

_____ Will you be advised of the law, the alternatives, and their consequences?

_____ Do you both understand what important decisions you want to make and those decisions that concern detail that your adviser should make?

_____ How can your agreement be ended?

What Your Adviser Can Expect from You

_____ You will be honest with him and will discuss every fact concerning your situation whether favorable or unfavorable to your situation. Do not be caught by the other side producing information you withheld.

_____ Come prepared for meetings with the necessary information, documents, and questions. The more legwork you can do, the less you must pay someone else to do it for you.

_____ Bring any dissatisfaction you have with your adviser's work to his attention immediately.

3

FACTORS THAT IMPACT VALUE

How to Build Value That a Buyer Will Pay For

There are many factors, both internal and external, that can significantly affect the purchase price of a selling company. Buyers are looking for a cash cow—a cash machine, an income stream. The larger the income stream and the more predictable the future of that income stream, the more buyers will pay for your company. Buyers want return on investment. The greater the return, the more they will pay. Income that is predictable has less risk than does income that isn't predictable. Therefore, the greater the predictability and the less risk involved to the buyer, the more your company will be worth. Any factor, whether internal to the company or beyond the company's control, that can influence the future earnings of the company will affect the value of the company.

First, let's explore those factors outside the control of the company.

EXTERNAL FACTORS

Low inflation, maybe even falling prices, not inflation, will be a businessperson's greatest concern during the 1990s. Here is why:

The Federal Reserve has kept the lid on money growth since 1987. Excess credit won't be as available because of the credit crunch of the early

1990s and the crisis in the banking system. The two prime causes of inflation are excess money growth and credit expansion. When credit limits have been reached and debt service becomes a significant portion of expenses (as it is today), businesses and consumers lose their ability to make additional purchases. The corresponding decrease in demand contributes to falling prices, or deflation.

Today, total credit market debt is 242 percent of the gross national product. Only in the 1920s and 1930s was it higher. In the early 1990s, business bankruptcies were six times historical averages and totaled over 100,000, according to figures released by Dun & Bradstreet. Insurance, finance, and real estate companies took a beating. Falling real estate prices, debt-burdened businesses, stingy banks, and bankruptcy from failed leveraged buyouts contributed to their demise. Personal bankruptcies were eight times historical averages.

A decade ago, when credit was easier to come by and rising real interest rates boosted the tax-deductible value of debt payments, it made sense for companies to increase leverage and whittle down equity. But things are different today. The real estate debacle has deflated property values and undermined the nation's banks. Cash-rich real estate buyers are snapping up real estate at bargain values.

The resulting credit crunch has drastically reduced the flow of capital to business. A slow-growth economy and corporate interest expense—nearly 56 percent of pretax profits—have caused the market to reassess the risks of leverage.

Investors and the business community are now bidding up the prices of companies that have avoided heavy debt. Today's market wants equity, not debt. The real story of the 1990s will be the selling off corporate assets. Decapitalization, not deleveraging, will be the theme of the 1990s.

What does this mean to you as the owner and chief executive officer of your company? Your company is in good shape if it has a strong balance sheet with little long-term debt. Bank loans will continue to be difficult for small companies and those that are highly leveraged.

Sales increases must come from increases in units and not price. If you are in a mature industry, you must take market share from your competitors more than ever. This will keep prices down. However, your fixed costs will continue to increase, and this will squeeze your profits.

Competition will increase and become more fierce as companies strive to maintain and grow unit sales. Low inflation and, in some industries, deflation will cause erosion of what price you can command for your product. As a result, many companies will be forced to sell to larger companies.

Low returns will plague personal and company investments. Short-term Treasury bonds are under 3 percent. Long-term bonds are 6 percent. The days of good returns with little risk are almost gone.

These are the problems that falling prices present. However, opportunities will be plentiful for the astute businessperson who has a strong management team attuned to the new reality.

Companies with strong balance sheets and little long-term debt should not have banking problems. Companies with a strong, proven management team and ability to market their product will do fine. A company with a dominant market share or niche will thrive. Companies with proprietary products that are less vulnerable to competition will grow and expand, provided the markets they are in are growing and expanding.

Businesses that are in fragmented industries will be in demand by buyers as well. The big problem with a concentrated industry with one or two big players is that the big companies decide the price smaller companies can charge for their products. Buyers prefer companies in a fragmented industry made up of hundreds of smaller players. When you see an industry consolidating, those companies that sell early in the consolidation process receive a lot higher price than do those at the tail end.

Deflation or inflation? We have had inflation for so long (since the beginning of 1968) that most of us have forgotten how to thrive and survive in low-inflation times. The 1990s will be an interesting and exciting time for the companies that understand how to play the low inflation game.

When your operating profits are marginal or your assets are overstated, you will receive a lower selling price and will not receive an all-cash offer. You'll have to take back paper and help finance the deal or allow the buyer to use the company's assets for a loan to purchase the company. Outside factors such as interest rates, inflation/deflation, and taxes all can reduce a company's profits, which in turn will reduce its value when it comes time to sell.

Importance of Timing

Timing, whether it is in music, lovemaking, or selling a business, is everything. It greatly affects the amount of money an experienced buyer will pay for your company.

As late as 1989, it was not unusual for a privately owned company to receive a purchase price of seven to ten times earnings before interest and

taxes (EBIT). Today, the seller is getting a triple whammy. First, his earnings are down. Second, buyers aren't willing to pay more than three to
seven times EBIT. And, third, buyers are fewer, and those who are looking
definitely aren't paying premiums; they are bargain hunters. As a result, sellers are receiving less for their companies than in the decade just past.

An ideal time to sell your business is when the economy is growing
and your market or industry is expanding. In turn, sales and profits are up
and the next year looks like another banner year. Lots of buyers are out in
good times looking for companies in a fragmented market whose sales and
profits are growing.

Sell when the future is rosy. Buyers don't mind a bad past; what they
don't like is a bad or uncertain future that increases risk. The more predictable those future profits, the less risk to the buyer, the more he's willing to pay. When profits are negligible, a buyer will significantly discount
any projections of future profits; thus a seller receives less for his business.

A rule of thumb for someone who wants to maximize the sales price
of his company is to sell when he is having a record sales and earnings year
and when next year looks just as good.

The 1990s will be outstanding years for both sellers and acquisition-
minded companies. The place of action will be with middle-market companies, those with sales between $1 million and $100 million. Many cash-
rich buyers will want to enter these industries and buy companies like
these. These are the buyers who will pay most for your company.

Today's cash-rich companies like privately owned middle-market companies because they are smaller and more easily digestible, and give them
less financial exposure. Buyers prefer doing several deals versus betting
everything on a single acquisition. These buyers want private midsized
companies in a growing or mature industry that have good cash flow, are
performing well, and have little debt. If that is your company, you will reap
a bonanza when you sell.

Usually, the seller will receive the highest purchase price from someone trying to enter his market. So maximize the value you'll receive for your
company by selling to a larger company that wants to enter your market.

The ability of a company to finance debt also significantly affects
value, and most buyers will need financing to acquire your company.
Lending institutions in the 1990s are much more conservative in their lending practices than they were in the 1980s. Lenders of the 1990s have
returned to the more conservative lending practices of the 1970s. This

renewed conservatism will influence and reduce the selling price you'll receive for your company. In 1955, Dr. Geoffrey Moore, a well-known economist, described the evolution of a period of troubled credit in this manner: "First and foremost is a rapid increase in the volume of credit or debt; second, a rapid speculative increase in the prices of the assets that are bought with the rapidly expanding credit; third, there is vigorous competition among lenders for new business; fourth, relaxation of credit terms or standards; and fifth, a reduction in the risk premiums sought or obtained by lenders."

Dr. Moore described the 1980s exactly. Plenty of money was available, and it was easy to get. Buyers' equity requirements were low. It was common in the 1980s for sellers to receive seven to ten times EBIT. If you had sold then, you would have received a much higher multiple of earnings for your business than you will today.

As the merger boom peaked and the slowdown began in late 1989 and continued into the 1990s, the excesses of the prior decade contributed to unprecedented levels of nonearning loans and write-offs for lenders. Lenders' problems today are compounded because of tougher standards that regulators have imposed on banks for making loans and maintaining adequate capital.

Lenders are still making loans, but not at the previous high multiple of earnings that companies sold for. Availability of lending capital directly affects what a seller will receive for his or her company. Lenders won't help a buyer when the lender thinks the buyer has paid too much.

INTERNAL FACTORS

Manufacturers of nonproprietary products and distribution companies are worth the least to a buyer. Nonproprietary products are those products with no patent protection or no recognized brand name. The multiple a buyer will pay for earnings (EBIT) will be in the four to five times ranges. The more value these companies add to raw materials, the more rapid their sales and earnings growth, the stronger their management team, and the more diversified and larger their customer base, the more sellers will receive for their business.

Audited financials increase a buyer's confidence in the numbers and generally will result in a better selling price. Audited financials reduce the perceived risk to the buyer, and a seller with audited financials brings more credibility to the table.

A buyer who can see a synergistic relationship with a seller's company will pay more for that company than one with no synergy. Synergy occurs when the acquiring company sees a strength in a seller that the buyer doesn't now have. It could be market, marketing, production, distribution, product line, research and development, technical knowledge, or management capability. The more synergies, the more value added to the selling company.

A seller can enhance his company's value by preparing a carefully documented sales memorandum that presents the strengths of his company in a positive way.

The seller will most likely obtain the highest price for his company if he cooperates with the buyer and tries to structure as much of the purchase price as tax-deductible payments for the buyer.

A seller who is willing to be patient and devote up to one year to complete a sale will receive more for his company than will an owner who is feeling forced to sell because of death, poor health, divorce, or lease expirations.

Management

Generally, companies with a well-rounded management team and a good secondary backup for the chief executive are worth more than comparable companies that are more of a one-person operation. The buyer reduces price when he sees a risk of buying one person and possibly losing his investment if this person becomes ill, dies, or decides to take his profits and retire. A seller will find his company more marketable and appealing to more acquirers if he has taken the time to develop management under him so that the company's operations are not solely dependent on one person.

When the selling company's owner is a key management person, and if his services are required after the sale, it is extremely important for the seller to express very clearly his reasons for selling. Such information about whether the seller wants to retire or continue to manage can cause the buyer to reject the purchase or serve as a framework in structuring the deal.

Proprietary Products

Generally, a company that sells its products under its own brand names is more valuable than one that sells products to other companies that add their own labels. A buyer knows that the process of developing brand names is time consuming and costly in both consumer and industrial markets.

Trademarks and patents are very important to some buyers and not so much to others. The key is whether someone can develop a better mousetrap and not infringe on the patents.

A seller who can prove to a buyer a knowledge of the strengths and weaknesses of his competitors' products and how he can compete by being better, faster, or cheaper is more valuable to a buyer than is a seller who can't provide that information. Anytime a seller can reduce the unknown, it reduces risk and makes his company more attractive and more valuable.

You will also need to find out profitability by product line because one or two product lines frequently generate most of the profits for a company. A company whose sales and profits are based on one or two product lines poses a significant risk to the buyer. The product life cycle is also important. If a company is generating its profits from a product line whose life cycle is limited because of competition or technology, there exists a negative factor that must be considered in deciding the price a buyer will pay.

Customers' Impact

A company that has one customer who contributes 40 percent of a company's sales is worth less than a company whose sales are diversified in many industries with no customer having more than 5 percent of a company's sales.

In cases where sales are concentrated with a few customers or when customer turnover is high, the only way most buyers will acquire such a company is if the seller agrees to an earnout or guarantees earning levels or another deferred payment. A balloon payment is an example. The seller has to sweeten the deal to entice the buyer.

You need to find out profitability levels of those customers whose sales make up 80 percent of a company's sales. A buyer wants to learn if sales to customers have been profitable. If profit trends are down, it may be that the seller's margins are slipping and profits can't be maintained.

Industry Status

A company is worth more when its industry is expanding and when its share of the market has been growing. The business whose industry is shrinking and whose market share is slipping is worth a lot less.

A buyer will pay more for a company whose industry has an uptrend over the next five years. The industry should be well established with companies tending to be smaller and medium-sized than concentrated with one or two large firms. In a consolidated industry, you have the problem of industry leaders establishing pricing. Leaders also determine turnover of products, product life cycles, and a host of other factors. Smaller companies in a consolidated industry are worth far less than are companies with dominant niche positions in a fragmented market.

Expansion of Facilities

Many buyers are not interested in immediately expanding the capacity of a company because of the risk involved in moving a business or because of the additional capital required. Therefore, a seller who can operate profitably at 70 percent of capacity will be more attractive to a buyer than will a company that is near capacity and faces moving to larger facilities or expanding existing facilities.

Geographic Location

Companies that have a strong sales presence in their local market are more valuable than are those with poor local presence. This is true whether the company's market is regional or national. This is because mature or saturated local markets limit the expansion of many companies. There is nowhere to go. A company in Chicago wanting to expand into Minneapolis will find great costs associated with acquiring, building, or establishing facilities and developing sales in the new market. It can buy a company in Minneapolis cheaper, faster, and easier than it can develop the market from scratch. The Chicago buyer would want a company to have a strong sales position in its local market first. So, develop your backyard first; that is where the gold is.

Freight costs may prevent one company from competing effectively in another market. The cost of shipping a product into a new market makes the company's product too expensive to be competitive. The company can, however, expand into the new market by setting up sales and production facilities or by purchasing a company in the market. Often, the buyer will prefer to acquire. When it acquires, it wants a company with a strong market presence in its own local market as well as other markets.

Supplier location also influences a sale. Sellers whose suppliers are very close probably can keep inventory levels low and costs down while still meeting just-in-time delivery requirements of customers. Obviously this is attractive to a buyer.

Raw materials are scarce in many industries, and these scarcities influence the profitability of many companies in that industry. Nearness to source of raw materials is a major factor in some industries and can have a material influence on the value of a company.

Inventory

The seller, in an attempt to shelter his income from the IRS, will have done some accounting tricks with his inventory. If he is a manufacturer, he will have expensed off thousands, perhaps hundreds of thousands, of dollars of inventory.

Generally, either LIFO (last-in, first-out) or FIFO (first-in, first-out) accounting rules are used in valuing inventories. LIFO accounting results in reduced profits when prices are rising and therefore less tax paid.

The difference between stated book value of inventory and its real market value is the place where buyers can find **hidden values** of assets. A buyer finds hidden values very attractive because of the leverage potential these assets provide.

If you are a seller, you should sell and get rid of slow-moving, obsolete, or outdated inventory. Begin by doing an aging analysis of inventory. First, break inventory down into four age categories: less than 6 months, 6 months to 1 year, 1 year to 18 months, and finally, inventory older than 18 months. Generally, the older the inventory, the less value it has. Your best strategy is to get rid of it.

Capitalized Assets

Understanding, the true earning potential of a company requires knowledge of its accounting practices, especially those regarding capital expenses, marketing, inventory, and research and development costs. Some companies' profits are inflated because of expenses that were capitalized than written off on current earnings.

When you figure out the price of a company based on earnings, the quality of those earnings becomes extremely important. Buyers prefer conservative depreciation policies because of what they do to earnings. A seller, therefore, should point out that his use of accelerated depreciation, while reducing his tax, was conservative and kept earnings down. The buyer will feel comfortable with this approach, so be sure to stress your conservative accounting policies when they apply.

Products Research and Development

The seller will need to satisfy a buyer's interest in the development of new products. The true earning power of a company may be overstated if the seller hasn't been allocating enough resources to product development. Maintaining a competitive position requires new products. How is your company researching and developing new products? How much are you expending in this area? What are the company policies regarding research and development or new product development?

Do the new products come from internal or external sources? Are there licensing agreements? How many new products have been developed over the past five years due to research and development? What percentage of sales do these products account for? What about profits from these new products?

Any company that is dependent on technology will be under great pressure to meet or beat competitors' products. The right research and development effort will significantly add value to a company.

Backlog

Your buyer's key concern is whether a backlog is profitable. A buyer who sees a big backlog with sales that are not very profitable will be wary. Backlogs represent costs and revenues. When backlogs are increasing, it could be because the company is buying business through low-ball pricing tactics. What are the backlog trends? Backlogs that are profitable and growing are a very attractive enticement to a buyer.

Warranties

Part of the purchase agreement will be devoted to warranties. The buyer will not want to assume hidden or undisclosed future claims against the company once he acquires the company. There may be product returns, product liability claims, wrongful discharge suits, income tax claims, an IRS audit, environmental claims, and so on.

The seller will be asked to guarantee for a specific period any claims made against the seller before the company was sold. After that time, the buyer is responsible. Usually, the seller is asked to place in escrow funds to cover those claims made by the buyer under the seller's warranties.

Any disclosed liabilities, such as a lawsuit, can be handled in a similar fashion. Often it is difficult to know the outcome of a suit. The seller and buyer might agree to a dollar amount. The seller will be responsible for everything under the agreed amount and the buyer responsible for the amount over the agreed amount. For example, the seller might agree to pay any lawsuit that is settled after the deal is closed that is over 3 percent of the purchase price with a cap of 25 percent. Lawsuits are red flags and can adversely affect what a buyer will pay for a business.

Pension Fund Liabilities

The pension fund is a true obligation of the seller. Some companies haven't set aside enough monies each year to meet their pension fund commitments. When this is the case, the buyer must make up the fund shortages after he buys the company.

A buyer will examine this area very carefully. When there is a large deficiency in the pension fund reserves, the deal won't go through unless the seller adjusts the price.

Balance Sheet

Sellers are advised to have a strong balance sheet. The stronger the balance sheet, the greater the value for their company. Let's examine a few key areas of a balance sheet that are green lights as well as buyer bewares signs.

First, let's discuss positive signs. A growing and high net worth is a sign of a healthy company. A healthy company has plenty of hard, fixed assets such as equipment, machinery, vehicles, real estate, and so on and is making enough money to finance capital improvements. Most of the liabilities are current bills, and long-term debt is negligible.

Earnings (retained earnings) show up as cash or accounts receivable. Inventories are mostly raw materials or finished goods and not work in progress. The current ratio is better than industry standards. Long-term debt is assumable without personal guarantees when the business is sold. This is an excellent buy signal for a buyer. It makes his corpuscles expand.

Other positive signs a buyer likes are accrued liabilities for taxes, sales tax, unused vacation and sick leave, and small pension plan payments that have remained steady over the past two or three years. There also are no off-balance-sheet liabilities or contingent liabilities such as product liability suits.

These positive signs tell a buyer that this is a good company to buy. Of course, this assumes a perfect world. Now let's explore some balance sheet signs that say "buyers be wary."

The first such signs are a negative or declining net worth. The company is losing money, a very bad sign. A buyer is wary when he sees vehicles and equipment that are mostly leased rather than purchased. This is a sign that a company may be having cash flow problems. A company like this also is difficult to finance because a cash flow lender will scrutinize those future income streams, and if they aren't predictable, the lender won't help finance the deal.

When an owner of a company takes too much cash out of the business, retained earnings (profits) will not show up on the balance sheet. Buyers like to see retained earnings that have been growing on the balance sheet. They will use industry averages as their guide.

Inventory that is old, obsolete, slow moving, or mostly work in progress is a negative sign to a buyer. It tells him to watch out and be careful. Another negative sign is long-term debt and mortgages that result in debt-to-equity ratios that are much higher than industry averages.

When a buyer sees accrued liabilities that are growing or are very high by industry standards, it's a warning that the business is having working capital problems. The business may be using tax money for working capital. This is a shaky business that astute buyers avoid.

A seller whose company currently has more bad signs than good should not sell his company. He should focus on straightening out the balance sheet of the company. Once he turns the negative balance sheet problems to pluses and puts the company on the market, buyers' eyes will light up. They will say, "Here is a deal we can't pass up." Consequently, the seller will receive good value for his business. When the balance sheet is loaded with negative signs, it spells trouble for the buyer. Then you can expect only bargain hunters who want to purchase for bargain basement prices.

Income Statement

The major difference between a public company and a privately owned company is profit. A public company tries to maximize profit. The higher the profit, the higher the price/earnings ratio, and the more the stock of the company sells for. Public companies try to manage their corporations in a way that maximizes the market price of their stock. The owner of a privately held company has a different objective. He is attempting to minimize profit so he pays the least possible tax.

A buyer is concerned about the income stream. How reliable, how predictable, and of what quality are those earnings? To find out what the company is earning, he must recast (reconstruct) those earnings. He needs additional knowledge beyond that shown on the income statement. A seller is going to have to show the buyer what his perks are. The buyer will want to know about salaries, especially excess salaries for the owner and his family.

It is not unusual to find a business owner putting a couple of kids through college and carrying them on the payroll. If the seller is real, he will provide this information. When a buyer recasts the income statement to reflect what it will look like after it is purchased, excess salaries will go to the bottom line. That increases profitability and, therefore, enhances value for the seller.

A buyer will ask about automobiles. Automobiles are perfectly legitimate expenses, but the buyer is looking to see if he can save money and add to the bottom line.

He'll also carefully scrutinize a company airplane as well as excessive entertainment and travel costs. The buyer isn't nosy; he just wants to be able to evaluate properly the earnings of a company so that he can figure out what to pay for it.

A seller is well advised to help a buyer learn about those hidden perks because it will add to the profits of the company and increase its value.

Depreciation is an area of the income statement that a buyer will examine closely. Normally, a seller's depreciation will be very aggressive, resulting in excessive depreciation that reduces earnings. The buyer needs to know how the seller arrived at depreciation. Depreciation reduces income, but it is added back to income to determine cash flow.

A buyer will scrutinize any off-balance-sheet liabilities such as rental equipment contracts. Excessive rental equipment charges may suggest an opportunity to cut expenses by buying a new piece of equipment. It may also show neglected maintenance and repair.

Your buyer will carefully examine gross margins. A company with gross margins that are static or growing is a positive signal to the buyer. It may mean better purchasing of raw materials, productivity increases, or price increases. The buyer will compare gross margins with industry averages. Better than average margins are a positive sign to the buyer. Obviously, gross margins below industry norms are a negative sign and may show competitive pressure that results in a reduced selling price.

Since the principal business of a company is sales, the selling corporation should understand how, why, and where its sales have come from and can project future sales for the company. The more the buyers are comfortable with sales histories and forecasts, the more likely they will buy your company and pay you a fair price. You'll need to prepare a five-year sales forecast with month-to-month sales for the first year, quarterly sales for the second and third year, and annual sales for the final two years. The more believable and the better your sales, marketing, and new product introductions, the more sellers will pay. Carefully document sales figures and show industry growth as well. Market research is the key here.

Looking for trends, a buyer will scrutinize your professional fees and service expenses. He knows an owner of a private company hates to pay professional fees and normally would expect to see these quite low. However, a sudden increase in this category would be a red flag. It may mean a lot more legal costs because of product liability claims among other reasons. The seller should be forthright about this and not try to cover this up. It is in an area like this, in the due diligence stage, where you can lose the trust of the buyer and the deal. The buyer will wonder, "What else hasn't been fully revealed? Is this owner honest? Can we trust him?"

Insurance is becoming very expensive to carry. Does the company carry adequate umbrella business insurance? Coverage is needed for product liability, environmental damage, hazardous waste, and worker's compensation. Is there officer and director liability insurance? Is the company adequately protected? A seller should have his business insurance agent thoroughly review and make recommendations in writing. Even if the company needs more insurance, a buyer will respect a seller and trust him when this is shown to him. The buyer will just subtract the extra cost from his recast income statement. No harm done.

A buyer will be alert for deferred maintenance and repair costs. How much will it cost to bring the leaky roof up to standard? What about fire and safety hazards? Does the building meet local fire code? A smart seller will have a schedule of maintenance and repairs and will have that available for inspection. He'll have accrued money for capital expenditures such as that new roof or equipment.

A buyer will examine the lease(s) to the facilities the company uses. Generally, the seller owns the building in his name as an individual and his company leases it from him. The owner uses the depreciation from the building to keep his personal taxable income down. In other words, the building is a tax shelter. In such a case, the buyer will be concerned that the rental or lease agreement is paying only the fair market value.

When the owner is making principal and interest payments on the building, rents will be high to cover the principal and interest payments. The buyer will want to know the difference because all this will be reflected in structuring the deal.

Where the lessor is not the owner, the buyer will be concerned about the terms of the lease, especially when it expires; this is also true for any personal guarantees or restore-to-original condition clauses. When a buyer sees a lease with very low lease payments, he knows that the lease might be old and soon to expire. Again, a seller needs to explain and document fully for the buyer his concerns in this area. When the seller cooperates and works with the buyer, the more likely both sides' needs will be satisfied and a successful deal transacted.

Bad debts and returns will be compared with industry averages. Businesses with bad debt allowances higher than, say, 3 percent usually are buying customers by extending credit to high-risk customers. Buyers rightly will see this as a negative factor. When bad debt has been climbing rapidly over the past three years, it usually means that the entrepreneur has been extending credit to high-risk or fringe customers. Subsequently, it has come back to haunt him. Miscellaneous and bad debt should be low. When it isn't, a buyer will see risk and discount the selling price.

SUMMARY

In this chapter, we've discussed many issues and concerns of buyers and sellers that add value or detract it from a business. The seller can look at those areas of weakness and try to improve on the ones he can. He can explain his strengths, knowing it will add value to his company. It is extremely important that you see your company's strengths and weaknesses through the eyes of your buyer. It's then possible to shore up some weaknesses before you sell the company. It allows you to show the buyer an action plan of how you'll correct the remaining weaknesses.

A buyer will not be afraid of risk or weaknesses in a company since *he knows how to manage those weaknesses*. It is up to the seller or his representative to show the buyer how to manage those risks. In doing so, the acquiring company can see the selling company management team in a positive light. Remember, buyers like to see strong, smart managers.

CHAPTER

4

HOW MUCH IS IT WORTH?

How to Determine the Maximum Value and Make the Buyer Pay for It

The standard measure for finding out the value of a company is the same as that for any exchange of property. Value is decided by what a willing seller and a willing buyer negotiate and agree on when both parties are informed of the pertinent facts and neither is under time pressures.

The best way for a seller to maximize value is to base the worth of the company on the future and not the historical earnings. Consequently, sellers should generally try to value the business based on its future earnings than only historical. Valuations for selling a company are less restrictive than in a stricter legal sense such as litigation or tax purposes. *Here historical earnings and assets are major determinants of value.*

I would highly recommend that a business owner obtain outside professional help to find out the value of his business. Valuations are quite complicated, and many factors come into play. An outside valuation document goes a long way toward convincing a buyer that a fair price has been established. It makes it much more difficult for the buyer to undercut the price when a creditable valuation is done by a respected firm independent of the seller. It falls into the same category as audited financial statements.

A buyer places much greater credence in the numbers and valuation and feels there is less risk involved.

My experience, however, has been that most business owners do not seek outside help to establish value. Generally, owners have an idea of what they want for their business and do not see the merit in paying someone to do an independent valuation. This is especially so with owners of smaller companies.

I'll use two true cases to make my point. Bill and his family own a company that they want to sell. The company is very profitable, but it is heavily in debt. Because of the debt, Bill can't grow the company. Earnings and sales have been erratic except the past two years when they have stabilized. The bank has been squeezing Bill and making his life miserable. He spends a great deal of his life trying to keep the bankers happy, and they have put several very restrictive covenants on him. He has not been taking much money out of the business and his salary is quite low. Bill has decided it is best to cash out and decides that the value of his company is $10 million. He chooses the purchase price based on the price/earnings ratio of public companies in his industry that at the time were at record highs.

Bill will not have his company appraised because he doesn't want to pay for a valuation or take the time needed to do a good job. Besides he is quite certain what his business is worth. A Fortune 500 company offers him $5 million in cash for his company based on the historical reconstructed financial statements. He refuses the offer thinking he can do better elsewhere. Negotiations are friendly but come to a halt. The buyer claims he has many opportunities to buy companies and refuses to overpay for a company based on its historical earnings. Bill may have gotten the price that he wanted for his company had the valuation been based on a discounted future cash flow valuation. He refuses to spend the money and considerable time it takes to do this kind of valuation. A year has gone by and Bill has still not sold his company. Bill complains that his business is worth more than buyers are willing to pay. However, he has yet to have a formal valuation done or accept any valuation from experienced buyers who are in the market for a company like his. What is Bill's business really worth? Is he wrong or are the buyers wrong?

The second case involves Tom, who has a small service and repair company for sale. Tom took $90,000 out last year for himself and wants

$250,000 cash for the stock of his S corporation. Tom is an integral part of the business and spends six days a week making sure the business prospers. It is totally dependent on Tom and would collapse without his efforts. Tom's company has been in existence for five years. Is Tom's business really worth $250,000? Can he realistically expect someone to pay all cash for his business?

Chapter 3, Factors That Impact Value, showed clearly that there is no clear-cut formula or appraisal guaranteeing the correct value of a company. Value, like beauty, is subjective and more in the eyes of the beholder. Value is not something inherent in the thing being valued. That is what cost is. Value is an attitude. It's an attitude toward something in view of its estimated capacity to perform a service and make money. Is there any wonder then why valuing a business is more art than science? Is there any wonder why buyers, sellers, and their advisers become confused about valuing a business?

There are some generally recognized principles of valuation that we shall explore that will help you better judge the value of a company. Any person or company interested in acquiring Bill's or Tom's business has one common concern. What future economic benefits will they receive because of the acquisition? The benefits can include earnings, cash flows, dividends, or another form of return. *The value of a business is then based on the future economic benefits that the buyer will obtain because of the acquisition; this future economic benefit then is discounted back to a present value at some appropriate discount rate.* This is what capitalized earnings are all about. The theory sounds easy and is. In practice the theory is very difficult to carry out. No one has a crystal ball that enables one to forecast future earnings, cash flows, and dividends accurately a year into the future, let alone five or ten years.

It is even more difficult to get two parties to agree with the different economic and business assumptions made when forecasting earnings and cash flows. Because of the difficulty of forecasting into the future, modern-day valuation methods tend to focus on historical rather than projected data. This is particularly true for smaller businesses. Larger companies tend to base value on projected earnings.

When existing or potential litigation is present, courts want facts based on historical performance unless future changes suggest that the historical record is inadequate as a basis of current valuation. Courts do rely on future projections in cases of bankruptcy, antitrust, and lost business opportunities.

Businesspeople can and should use their knowledge and experience for taking calculated business risks. Risks are intrinsic in valuations based on forecasts of an uncertain future. That is why I believe that Bill made a mistake in the first example by not spending the money for a valuation—especially if the valuation was partly based on the future earnings and cash flows of his business. I believe this ultimately costs him 20 percent of his selling price. Now, that is a cool $1 million. Tom's business valuation in the second example should be based on the historical record of his company since so much of his business is dependent on his personal efforts. This would be true of most small service firms where the business is so dependent on one person, the seller.

EARNINGS AND CASH FLOW ARE KINGS

There is no universal answer concerning which benefit of ownership is most important to base valuations on. However, there is consensus within the business valuation community that earning power is the most critical and important variable affecting the value of a business. That includes operating companies such as manufacturers, wholesalers, and service firms. There are five financial variables of a business that can affect valuation.

1. Cash flow
2. Earnings
3. Dividends or dividend-paying ability
4. Gross income multipliers
5. Assets

Each of these areas is discussed in greater detail in the paragraphs that follow. Besides these five financial considerations there are other variables that can and will affect the value of a business. See Chapter 3 for a full discussion. Value may also be influenced by the following four variables:

1. Cost of capital or return on investment
2. Risk involved in future earnings
3. Marketability of company
4. Whether controlling or minority ownership

Cash Flow Versus Earnings

Cash flow can be defined in several different ways. The accounting definition is generally net earnings plus book charges such as depreciation and amortization. Capital expenditures and increases in working capital are also subtracted from future cash flows when a valuation is based on discounted future cash flow projections. An example is provided later in this chapter that shows discounted future cash flow valuations.

Cash flow is a better measure to value a company on than earnings when a capital-intensive company's machinery and equipment are obsolete or outdated and need replacement. The timing and extent of capital expenditures and depreciation can materially affect earnings. These effects are better seen in cash flow, since depreciation is incorporated into the cash flow measure.

Another area where cash flow is a better measure to use for valuation than earnings is when a company's primary assets are improved real estate that is leased or rented out. In inflationary times most real estate holds its value or appreciates, and the depreciation charged against earnings does not represent a decrease in the asset's value.

The most commonly used definition of earnings is net income in the accounting sense, that is, net income after all expenses including owners' compensation, depreciation, interest and taxes, but before any capital expenditures or principal payments on debt owed. Definitions vary and are easily misunderstood. The key point is to make sure everyone understands what definition of earnings is used and how it was arrived at. Can the earnings be measured accurately? Can earnings be measured in a way that both buyers and sellers will use in deciding market value? For instance, earnings before interest and taxes (EBIT) are a common financial measure that companies use to establish a range of value for a company. Some industries and companies sell for a range of value between three and seven times EBIT. Still others use earnings before interest, taxes, and depreciation (EBITD) as a way to quickly grasp the value of a company. Obviously, five times EBITD will provide a higher value than it will on EBIT. Much discussion and analysis will center on the quality of earnings and how EBIT is arrived at. How are depreciation charges assessed? How are inventory levels accounted for? Which expenses should have been capitalized than expensed? How are owners' compensation and perks accounted for? A whole range of considerations must be carefully considered to understand accurately what the real earnings of the company are and what the quality and consistency of it are. How predicable are the earnings?

Arguments abound on both sides about which is best to use to value a company. You have proponents of earnings who think that is the only financial variable that counts. Others advocate cash flow with just as much fervor. If I were going to buy a business, I would spend considerable time figuring out the future cash flow of my business. Can I make the debt payments? Would cash flow be available for capital expenditures and growth in working capital needs? Would enough cash be available to meet emergencies? Would sufficient cash be available to meet my worst case scenario if my forecasts were way off target? Obviously, all these considerations would come into play into what one person would pay for a company. Another buyer might be more optimistic and be willing to accept more risk and consequently would pay more for the company. Still another buyer might be better financed and can raise capital should something unforeseen come up. That is why I said at the outset of this chapter that value is in the eye of the beholder.

Dividends

Current business valuation practice recognizes the importance of the dividend-paying ability of a company, but the earning power of the company is considered more important. This is because dividend-paying capacity stems from the earning capacity of the company. Once the company is making money, it becomes a matter of choice whether the directors want to pay dividends or retain earnings. Privately owned companies generally are run in such way that taxes are reduced as much as possible. Dividend paying may or may not be a good tax move. Sometimes, however, the dividend capacity of a closely held company may be severely curtailed because of the companies voracious appetite for machinery and equipment or other purpose.

Some industries lend themselves to valuation based on a company's dividend-paying ability. Utilities come immediately to mind. Minority ownership of stock in a privately held company also comes to mind. The value of the stock is a direct function of the dividends paid out, since a minority holder of stock has no control over how dividends will be paid. A lack of dividend payments to minority interest does not necessarily detract from the value when the company is sold. This is because minority stockholders generally have the right to have their stock appraised when they are not satisfied with the offer received. Based on the valuation, minority shareholders are paid cash when the company is sold.

Gross Income Multipliers

Service businesses such as advertising, insurance, and other business services are often sold where value is based on revenues than entirely on earnings. The same applies to professional practices such as accounting, medical, and law. Even when companies aren't profitable and have little in the way of physical assets, value can be ascribed to them. Value is imputed based on some multiple of sales.

I recently helped sell a long-distance telephone company that was not profitable and had not been profitable for several years. The company that acquired it wanted the sales dollars, customers, sales force, and nothing else. It closed the seller's headquarters down after the sale because it could handle all the administrative and technical parts of the business through its own company. The buyer never looked seriously at the financials of the seller but was very interested in the accounts and profitability of the long-distance business customers. Purchase price came down to a debate over what multiple of monthly gross income would be paid. After much negotiation, it was decided that the seller would receive a multiple of four times monthly gross. This is a common practice in this industry where value is based on a multiple of monthly gross revenues. Industry multiples vary by industry. The seller was happy because he got a fair settlement and was glad to get rid of a loser. And the buyer was happy because he could shave much administrative and technical overhead off the acquired company. From the day he took over it was a money-making venture.

Generally, it is unusual for gross revenue to be the sole factor in deciding value even when heavy weight is accorded to it in the valuation. Two service companies might have the same revenues, but one could be twice as profitable and have better growth prospects for sales, earnings, cash flow, and asset base. This profitable company is worth a much higher valuation.

The number of units involved in a transaction is also a good predictor of value in some businesses. Experienced buyers of nursing homes, for example, know just about how many beds are needed for a profitable operation and what they can afford to pay for each bed. Buyers of apartment buildings know just about how much they will pay for each unit and how many they need for a successful operation.

Assets

A company's underlying assets are an important consideration in the value of a company. For example, one company could have all state-of-the-art equipment and not need additional capital purchases to continue to provide the company's income stream. Another may be just as profitable but have assets that are getting old or obsolete and need replacing. If the assets aren't replaced, the company will begin to lose customers because of quality and cost of product. Obviously, the first company is worth more than the second, although the earnings are similar.

A share of common stock in a company does not represent a share in the ownership of the assets of the business. A share of stock represents a claim on the income derived from the assets of the company whose management runs the company. Of course, if liquidation is included in the offering, then asset values assume a major role in the valuation. Assets of most operating companies are considered as having a supporting role, similar to supporting actors in a movie. They are not the star attraction. *Assets provide the means for continuing earning power. They also provide some protection against a slowdown in the future earnings of the company.*

Some businesses' only value is in the assets of their business. For example, many businesses such as motels, have value mainly because of the underlying value of the land and buildings. As I write this chapter, the owner of a company that has been quite profitable over the years wants me to represent him in the sale of his company. The company happens to be in the scrap metal business and has been a very profitable operation for years. The owner is in his eighties and wants to sell because none of his family is interested in taking over from him. His business is worth $500,000. The underlying assets, namely, land, are very valuable, so the business will be sold for about $1 million. His land is near a growing office warehouse district and close to the central part of the city. His land is far more valuable than his business. As a result the business will be sold to a developer who will operate the business for a time until the construction building situation turns around. Here, assets are very important.

Another type of business in which assets are a determining factor in the value of a business is in the construction industry. Repair and construction companies such as a black top company can be readily started simply by buying and assembling the assets rather than buying an existing business. Repair and construction companies that are involved in government bidding jobs fall into this category. The assets play a major role in establishing the value for the company.

Risk and Cost of Capital

Business valuations are influenced by two major factors: the first is the size or amount of the expected future cash flows or earnings; the second is the risk that is associated with these returns. How chancy or unpredictable is the expected earnings or cash flows? Risk in this sense is the degree of certainty or doubtfulness of attaining the expected future cash flows or earnings from the business. When future earnings are predictable, risk is reduced and minimized. As a result, the present value of the future earnings is higher. Conversely, when future earnings are unpredictable, the risk is increased and the present value of those future earnings is decreased.

A buyer can estimate the element of risk in two ways. First, he can adjust the expected earnings or cash flow stream of the business to reflect the doubtfulness or unpredictability of those earnings. The second way risk can be treated is by using an increased discount rate in valuing the anticipated future income stream. The consequence of both actions is to reduce the value of the business. For these reasons it is important that the seller do everything possible to take the element of uncertainty or risk out of forecasting the future earnings of the business. Obviously, the past historical earnings performance of the company has a lot to do with the way the future earnings are seen.

A common definition used to describe the cost of capital is as follows: *cost of capital is the rate of return available in the marketplace on invest-ments comparable both in terms of risk and other investment characteristics, such as marketability.* Cost of capital or return on investment is an impor-tant determinant of business value. Cost of capital depends on the market and is outside the control of a business owner. Market conditions decide what a risk-free investment is and the amount of premium required for assuming various levels of risk. Again, a business owner can reduce the cost of capital by reducing the risk associated with the future earnings and by that increase the value of his company. The lower the buyers perceive the risk and the lower the cost of capital or return expected, the higher the value of the business.

The **rate of return** or return on investment is commonly stated as fol-lows: *the rate of return is equal to the ending price of an investment, minus the beginning price, and any cash flows received from holding that invest-ment, divided by the initial price.* For example, if Bill's manufacturing com-pany started the year at $5.00 per share, paid $0.50 in cash dividends dur-ing the year, and ended the year at $6.00 per share, the total rate of return for the year would be computed as follows:

$$R = \frac{\text{Ending price - beginning price + cash distributions}}{\text{Beginning price}}$$

$$R = \frac{\$6.00 - \$5.00 + \$0.50}{\$5.00}$$

$$R = \frac{\$1.50}{\$5.00}$$

R = 0.30, or 30 percent return on investment

It is possible to calculate the expected rate of return over any period when the stock's value or business value and cash flow are known. Investors use a formula like this to calculate their expected return on an investment, whether it's a new piece of equipment, business, or another investment. Expected rate of return and discount rate are the same.

You know that if you invest $1.00 at 6 percent interest, it will grow to $2.00 in 12.4 years. This is what compound interest is all about. This idea has been drilled into all of us. The corollary to this is that $2.00 paid out 12.4 years from now is worth only $1.00 today. That is what discounting future return to present-day value is all about. Discounting as it applies to valuing a business based on its future earnings stream is discussed later in this chapter.

Marketability

Business owners often compare their company with a similar public company. They feel this is a fair way to value their company. The assumption is that the privately held companies' stock should be valued the same as the public company. Even when all major valuation factors are the same, the owner of stock in a public company can instantly turn his stock in for cash. The owner of stock in a privately held company cannot. His is an investment that is not very liquid.

Ready marketability adds value, and lack of marketability detracts and diminishes the value of the stock. Markets pay a premium for liquidity and extract a discount when liquidity is not present. When two investments are identical in valuation criteria, except that one is liquid and one not so liquid, the market will assign a considerable premium to the one that can be instantly converted to cash. When a shareholder of a public company feels that the fortunes of his company are going in the wrong direction, he can sell and cash out. An owner of a privately owned company can sell his interest, but it may take a long time. By the time a buyer is found, the fortunes of the privately owned company might be in desperate condition and its value significantly reduced.

There is considerable evidence suggesting that the discount for a company lacking public company marketability should be about 35 to 50 percent. Privately owned companies often have agreements between partners with restrictive covenants. These covenants can include mandatory buy-sell agreements, first rights of refusal, requirements of consent to sell, pooling agreements, and voting trusts. All impact the salability of a company and therefore reduce its value when compared to ownership in a public company. It is for these reasons that *valuation comparisons between public and private companies are very difficult and seldom used.*

Control

Control is a very important variable affecting value. Buyers generally want controlling interest in a company. If one person owns 49 percent and another owns 51 percent, the 49 percent holder has little or no positive control. He can't even block certain actions of the 51 percent holder. With control go many rights, for example, the right to elect directors and appoint management as well as the right to set management compensation and perks and the right to make acquisitions, liquidate assets, award contracts, and declare dividends and determine their amount.

Control is a problem only when the parties wishing to sell their interest are not in agreement. Statutes affecting the rights of controlling and minority stockholders vary by state. In about half the states, a simple majority can approve major actions such as sale, merger, liquidation, and recapitalization of the company. Some states require a two-thirds or greater majority to approve such actions. A minority of just one-third has the power to block such actions. When control is lacking, any value attributable to control must be reduced.

Valuation can be broken down into two areas: valuations based on historical earnings and valuations based on future earnings. The remaining sections of this chapter discuss these two important valuation principles. First, I'll address the various historical earnings approaches to valuation.

VALUATIONS BASED ON HISTORICAL EARNINGS

Because of the difficulty of making creditable sales and earnings projections, most smaller transactions are based on the historical earnings of the company being sold. Of course, the buyer is looking to the future and is basing his best estimate of the future earnings on the past earnings of the company. Practically all the valuations using historical data can be divided into six main methods:

1. Capitalization of earnings or cash flow
2. Capitalization of dividends
3. Debt-paying ability
4. Asset value approaches
5. Combination of earnings and assets—excess earnings method
6. Industry rules of thumb

Each of these methods is based on getting an adequate measure of the historical earnings or cash flows. Which do you use? The most recent year? A three-year average? A five-year average? What happens when past earnings have been erratic?

In measuring earnings, certain adjustments are needed to accurately reflect the historical earnings of the company. For example, companies that want to show a good bottom line will capitalize items that fall into a gray area. Also, companies that want to minimize taxes will elect to expense items rather than capitalize whenever possible. There may be certain extraordinary or nonrecurring items that would tend to distort the company's current and future earning power. Items such as gains or losses on the sale of assets, proceeds from the settlement of a lawsuit, and insurance proceeds from property and casualty items are examples. Excess owner compensation and perks are other items that must be considered when making an assessment of the company's earning power as viewed from the buyer's perspective. See the chapter on recasting for a full discussion on this subject.

The most commonly selected historical periods for evaluation of earning capacity are the past five years. The general idea is that five-year results go far enough back to show some type of continuum, but not so far that past results are not about today's conditions or operations. When the underlying assumption of the five-year record does not apply, then a shorter period might be considered more appropriate. For example, if the company made some major changes in its operations in the past three years, then three years might be more appropriate.

There are three general ways to figure out the company's past earnings: simple **arithmetic mean** or average of the earnings, **weighted earnings**, and the **trend line method**. Each is most appropriate for certain circumstances. We'll work with one set of earnings as an example and apply the three methods to these earnings to see which method is most appropriate under certain circumstances.

The simple arithmetic mean is most appropriate to apply to the earnings history when there is no pattern to the earnings. That is, some years earnings go up and some years earnings go down from those of the previous year. To find the arithmetic mean, add up the five past-year earnings and divide by 5 as follows:

$$\$11.40 = \frac{\$10 + \$11 + \$11 + \$12 + \$13}{5}$$

The second method is also a simple and useful technique and is called weighted earnings. If the previous five-year earnings are being used, the most recent year is assigned a weighing of 5/15 of the total weight, the next most recent year 4/15, and so on until you get back to the earliest year, which is given a weight of 1/15. The weighted average would look like the following example:

$$
\begin{array}{rcccr}
\$10 & \times & 1 & = & \$10 \\
11 & \times & 2 & = & 22 \\
11 & \times & 3 & = & 33 \\
12 & \times & 4 & = & 48 \\
\underline{13} & \times & \underline{5} & = & \underline{65} \\
\text{Total} & & 15 & = & \$178 \\
\end{array}
$$

$$\$11.87 = \frac{\$187}{15}$$

When the company's past earnings trend is expected to continue, a trend line analysis of those earnings is appropriate. There is a formula that professional appraisers use based on regression coefficients. Don't let a few mathematical formulas frighten you from using this method because it is a good one and is easy to use, as the following example shows. The formula for calculating trends is as follows:

$y = a + bx$

where

$a = \Sigma y - b(\Sigma X) \div N$

$b = N(\Sigma XY) - (\Sigma X)(\Sigma Y) \div N(\Sigma X^2) - (\Sigma X)^2$

X_i = the ith year and weighting is accorded the ith year

Y_i = earnings in ith year

N = number of years or observations

Σ = sum of variables X_i, Y_i, and X_iY_i

To solve the formula using earnings for the five-year period, a format as follows is helpful:

X	Y	X^2	XY	(N = Years or observations)
1	10	1	10	
2	11	4	22	
3	11	9	33	
4	12	16	48	
5	13	25	65	

$\Sigma X = 15 \quad \Sigma Y = 57 \quad \Sigma X^2 = 55 \quad \Sigma XY = 178$

Solving the equation when $Y = a + bX$ indicates the following:

$b = [N(\Sigma XY) - (\Sigma X)(\Sigma Y] \div [N(\Sigma X^2) - (\Sigma X)^2]$

$b = [5(178) - (15)(57)] \div [5(55) - (15^2)]$

$\quad = [890 - 855] \div [275 - 255]$

$\quad = 35 \div 50$

$\quad = \mathbf{.70}$

$a = [\Sigma Y - b(\Sigma X)] \div N$

$\quad = [57 - .70(15)] \div 5$

$\quad = [57 - 10.50] \div 5$

$$= 46.50 \div 5$$
$$= \mathbf{9.30}$$

Substituting a(9.30) and b(0.70) in the formula Y = a + bX yields the following:

$$Y = 9.30 + .70(X)$$

To calculate the trend line for the earnings of the company in years 5 and 6 substitute years for X in the formula as follows:

Y = 9.30 + .70(5)	Y = 9.30 + .70(6)
Y = 9.30 + 3.5	Y = 9.30 + 4.2
Y = **12.80**	Y = **13.50**

What the trend line does is predict the best earnings trend for the past five years and for the next year too. The trend line could be used to forecast several additional future years, but the farther out you go, the less reliable the method is. Forecasted earnings for year 6 are $13.50. The trend line for year 5 is **$12.80**. In this example it is the number used to compare with the arithmetic mean and weighted average.

A summary of the three methods to arrive at the historical earnings of the company is as follows:

Arithmetic mean	$11.40
Weighted average	$11.87
Trend line	$12.80

The trend line gives the highest value for historical earnings of the three methods just discussed. The fifth year earnings in the example was $13. Both the arithmetic mean and weighted average produce a value less than the trend line approach. In this example the trend line is probably the best method to arrive at what the historical earnings of the company were.

A good case could also be made that year 6 with a value of $13.50 is the number that should be used. As this example has shown, when the earnings are stable, both the weighted average and trend line compute higher historical earnings for the company than a simple average. However, neither method produced an earnings figure as high as the last and most recent year of historical earnings. The trend line in this example computes the highest value of the three methods.

Few companies have as stable of an earnings history as that given in the example. When the earnings pattern is erratic and not stable, both the weighted average and trend line method are less reliable than a simple average to figure out the earning power of the company. It is best to use more than one method to arrive at earning power for a company. It is also best to try several historical periods.

Capitalization of Earnings or Cash Flows

To capitalize means to convert defined earnings or cash flow into value by dividing or multiplying the income stream by some factor called a **capitalization rate**. This means applying one divisor or multiplier to one earnings figure to arrive at value. What is needed are two figures. The first is a clearly defined measure of the company's earning power. The second is a divisor or multiplier. Thus the method is straightforward and simple to use. Figuring out a defined earnings figure whether earnings or cash flow is not so easy as we have already seen from our earlier discussions in this chapter. The income stream to be capitalized can come either before or after any items such as interest, depreciation, taxes, owner's compensation and perks, and so on. The income can be the latest years, a straight or weighted average of the last several years, a trend line value, or future income. Again, the key to the capitalization method is that the income or cash flow figure must be clearly defined. And the cap rate must be appropriate for the income stream used.

The capitalization rate depends on two key variables: relative degree of risk associated with the earnings and the expected growth of those earnings. The best guidance on what cap rate is appropriate for a given income stream is found by what other investors are willing to pay for a comparable earnings stream. What are the current rates in a given industry?

When a buyer wants a 20 percent rate of return for his investments, that means that he will divide the earnings by 0.20 or multiply the earnings by 5. Let's say your business has a defined historical income stream of $100,000. A cap rate of 0.20 would produce a value for the business of $500,000: $100,000/0.20 equals $500,000. Another way is to take five times the earnings. An investor who wants a payback of his investment in five years would use a capitalization rate of 0.20 or 20 percent.

Many businesses are priced based on the capitalization method. The problem associated with this method is clearly identifying the income and deciding the multiplier or divisor of the income stream. Investors often refer to a business as worth five times EBIT or five times EBITD. What is meant by these terms and how were they arrived at? EBIT, as we already know, is earnings before interest and taxes; EBITD is earnings before interest, taxes, and depreciation. Clearly defining these terms and knowing how they were derived is what this method is all about. *Capitalization does not consider the future earnings of the company or the supporting assets.*

The capitalization rate depends on many factors, including the nature of the business and industry, the stability and predictability of the earnings, and the risks involved. The riskier the business, the higher the return rate needed. The higher the rate of return needed, the less the business is valued. Buyers and sellers will negotiate long and hard over how a cap rate is determined.

Ibbotson Associates publishes capitalization rate and discount rate statistics. Its annual publication provides statistics on the economy as a whole and within specific equity returns. It is a most important tool for establishing both discount rates and capitalization rates. Its annual year book is entitled *SBBI, Stocks, Bonds, Bills and Inflation 199X Yearbook.* This source helps to reduce the debate over the correct cap rate or discount rate that should be used. Ibbotson is recognized as the industry leader in this regard.

Capitalization of Dividends

Dividends are a direct function of the earning and cash flow power of a company. Therefore, generally capitalization of dividends is not valued separately from the earnings. As a practical matter, most buyers aren't interested in the seller's dividend-paying abilities.

Internal Revenue Service Revenue Ruling 59-60 says that dividends or dividend-paying ability should be a consideration when a business is valuated for federal estate or gift tax purposes. Dividends are also factors in court cases involving dissenting shareholder appraisal rights. In valuing a minority interest, actual dividends paid out are more important than is dividend-paying capacity. The reason is minority stockholders usually can't force the company to pay dividends when it doesn't want to even if the company has the capacity.

Debt-Paying Ability

Most small business buyers use the debt-paying ability of the business to find out what they can afford to pay for a business. The business's ability to pay off the acquisition debt is the main consideration, not the capitalization rate. Most small-business owners must finance part of the sale of the business themselves if they want to sell their company. It is estimated that 80 percent of owners of small businesses finance part of the transaction. Generally, buyers will only want to put 25–35 percent on the down payment. They expect the seller to carry the balance owed. Because the buyer has limited resources, he'll not want to put all of his money into the deal if he can help it. Naturally, the seller wants all cash or a lot more down than what the buyer wants to put down.

Often small businesses are bought because the buyer is looking for a job, not a business. The buyer has been laid off from his job or can't find the kind of work he wants, so he goes business searching.

Generally, a small business valued under supportable debt method will be valued about one to four times pretax, preinterest earnings. Buyers want out from under the debt in four to five years. Depending on the business, risk involved, and the buyer, the payoff period can run as high as six or seven years and as low as three years. If the business is valued at more than four times earnings, the business usually can't support the debt. *A valuation of this kind definitely limits the amount of money that an owner can expect for his business.*

Let's revisit Tom's business. Tom, as you will recall, has a small service and repair company for sale. His historical cash flow is $90,000 a year based on the average of the last three years. The cash flow is *before* owner's compensation or perks.

Inexperienced buyers often pay too much for a business because they buy it based on the owner's take, here $90,000. They are buying a job as well as the business when they do this. Let's see what I mean.

Assume that reasonable competitive pay for a manager of a business like this is $35,000. That leaves a net before tax of $55,000 after you subtract $35,000 from the $90,000. Do you buy the business based on an income of $90,000 or $55,000? Many buyers needlessly spend an additional $100,000 in this situation because they buy the job and the business. Consequently, they are burdened with a business that has them strapped for cash so badly they can't take any money out for a salary.

Let's see what the transaction looks like under both scenarios, one where reasonable owner's salary is factored out of the earnings and one where it isn't.

	AL	JOE
Cash flow before owner's salary and perks	$ 90,000	$ 90,000
Owner's salary	35,000	0
Cash flow after owner's salary	$ 55,000	$ 90,000
Business value @ 4 times cash flow		
after owner's salary	220,000	360,000
Down payment	75,000	125,000
Balance owed @ 8% for 4-year		
amortization schedule	145,000	235,000
Annual interest and debt payment	37,000	60,000
Cash flow before owner's salary	90,000	90,000
Less: Owner's salary	(35,000)	(35,000)
Less: Interest and debt payment	(37,000)	(60,000)
Equals: Owner's net before taxes	$ 18,000	($ 5,000)
Owner's return on investment	24%	—

A reasonable purchase price for this business is $220,000. Al gave Tom $75,000 for a down payment and promised to make annual principal and interest payments of $37,000 to Tom for four years. Al learned that the business was risky and decided he needed a return on his investment (ROI) of 24 percent. He will get 24 percent ROI provided the companies earnings remain where they are. Because there is a definite risk that the earnings could go down, Al is rightly entitled to a 24 percent return on the money he put into the business. Since he will be working hard to repay Tom, Tom should not expect Al to pay for his job.

Joe, on the other hand, got carried away. Joe got excited and let his emotions run away. Tom convinced him that the business was worth three times his cash flow before owner's compensation, and Joe paid that amount. Joe has a real problem. He has a $5,000 negative cash flow. His options are to take a smaller salary or convince Tom that the loan terms should be extended to seven years, which would reduce his debt payments. Under the seven-year scenario, Joe's debt payment would be reduced to $34,473 annually, an amount that is closer to Al's debt payment. He now has a little room in which to maneuver in case the business should take a downturn. The deal would then be possible. Terms often drive the deal. When a seller is willing to be flexible on terms, it often is possible for him to obtain a higher purchase price for his business.

Tom's business is worth around $220,000, but it is possible to go as high as $360,000 if debt payments are strung out. Valuation is in the eye of the beholder. Some buyers will take more risk than others. Others want a higher return.

The business may be worth a lot less than what Al paid for it if the business is too dependent on Tom. On the other hand, Joe may have gotten a bargain if the company has great growth prospects. How well did Joe and Al understand Tom's business? Did Joe see something that Al didn't? All these factors can come into play and influence the amount that Tom receives for his business. As a result, *most small businesses are valuated based on the debt-paying ability of the business.*

Asset Approaches to Value

Unless liquidation of assets is a reasonable prospect, the assets' value has more to do with the ability to generate earnings. The values of the assets are not separate from the company's value based on its earning power. A strong asset base contributes value that strengthens a company's ability to survive downturns in earnings or even losses. Therefore, asset approaches to value carry more weight with holding companies than with manufacturing, distribution, and service companies, although highly liquid assets add value to a deal because of their very liquidity.

Book Value and Adjusted Book Value. The book value approach consists of the book value of assets, net of depreciation, amortization, and liabilities presented on the current balance sheet. This approach is not commonly used to determine fair market value. The reason is that it does not consider the earning power of the business. It also does not consider any intangible asset value other than that previously purchased by the business and reflected on the current balance sheet. *Its primary use is in an accounting setting, not as a valuation method.*

Values stated on the balance sheet represent the historical cost of an item, not the fair market value. Even when book values are adjusted to reflect their current value, the weakness for valuation is still there because intangible value and earnings are not reflected. When all the assets of the company are adjusted to reflect the tangible fair market values, the equity of the company is also adjusted to reflect the new status of the assets. Adjusted book value can be used as the minimum benchmark price of the business. It should be mentioned, however, that *some companies are not worth the fair market value of their tangible assets. The earnings or lack of earnings of the company does not support the costs of the assets.*

When it is necessary to adjust operating plant and equipment values of an operating business to arrive at value, **depreciated replacement cost value** is the method most often used. This means the present cost of replacing equipment and their useful lives must be estimated. **Depreciated replacement cost** is the current replacement cost reduced by the percentage of useful life over which the existing facilities already have been in service and any obsolescence inherent in the equipment or facilities.

Book value is available for almost all businesses. It is a value that has been arrived at by some generally accepted accounting principles (GAAP). Each asset or liability number that is a component of book value shown on the financial statements represents a specific set of assets or obligations that can be identified in the company's books. Therefore, book value usually is a convenient starting point for an asset approach to value.

Liquidation Value of Assets. This approach figures out the value of a business as if all the assets were sold quickly and piecemeal and all liabilities were paid off with the asset proceeds. Another way of describing liquidation value is it is what you would receive for the assets if they were sold at an auction, less any liabilities. Liquidation value is the amount that asset-based lenders use to decide how much to lend against assets. This method for finding out value is used for lending value. When liquidation value is computed for a business, the value derived usually is the floor or lowest value a company or business is worth.

Liquidation value is the opposite of going-concern value. It usually is either **orderly liquidation** or **forced liquidation.** Orderly liquidation means that the assets are sold over a reasonable period to try to get the best available price for each asset. Forced liquidation means the assets are sold as quickly as possible usually all at once at an auction.

The Excess Earnings Method—A Combination of Earnings and Assets

The **excess earnings method** is a widely used valuation method for pricing small businesses and professional practices. In 1968, the Internal Revenue Service restated the method with the publication of Revenue Ruling 68-609, which is still in effect today. The IRS calls it the ARM 34 method. Both the IRS and taxpayers have used this method widely. Its popularity stems from its ease of use and simplicity. However, the method has been used incorrectly, and false conclusions have been reached. The IRS advises in Revenue Ruling 68–609, "The 'formula' approach may be used in determining the fair market value of intangible assets of a business only if there is not a better basis available for making the determination." The ruling goes on to state, "The 'formula' should not be used if there is better evidence available from which the value of intangibles can be determined. If the assets of a going business are sold on the basis of a rate of capitalization that can be substantiated as being realistic."

The ruling defines the "formula" approach as follows: "A percentage return on the average annual value of the tangible assets used in a business is determined, using a period of years (preferably not less than five) immediately prior to the valuation date. The amount of the percentage return on tangible assets, thus determined, is deducted from the average earnings of the business for such period, and the remainder, if any, is considered to be the amount of the average annual earnings from the intangible assets of the business for the period. This amount (considered as the average annual earnings from intangibles), capitalized at a percentage rate of, say, 15 to 20 percent, is the value of the intangible assets of the business determined under the 'formula' approach."

Revenue Ruling 68–609 goes on to state, "The percentage of return on the average annual value of the intangible assets used should be in the percentage prevailing in the industry involved at the date of valuation, or (when the industry percentage is not available) a percentage of 8 to 10 percent may be used. The 8 percent rates of return and the 15 percent rate of capitalization are applied to tangibles and intangibles respectively of businesses with a small risk factor and stable and regular earnings; the 10 percent rate of return and 20 percent rate of capitalization are applied to businesses in which the hazards of business are relatively high."

The ruling also makes this point: "The past earnings to which the formula is applied should fairly reflect the probable future earnings. Ordinarily, the period should not be less than five years, and abnormal years, whether above or below the average, should be eliminated. If the business is a sole proprietorship or partnership, there should be deducted from the earnings of the business a reasonable amount for services performed by the owner or partners engaged in the business."

It is important to understand that the IRS does not require that this method be used to value a company that is for sale. This ruling applies to those situations where estate and gift taxes come into play, and then only if another valuation method is not more appropriate.

The excess earnings valuation method is based on return on assets and the income produced by the company. When you invest in an asset, you expect a return on it based on the risk involved. Any return more than the expected return is excess earnings.

This method is easy to use when valuing a company. It also gives an accurate range of values from which buyer and seller can negotiate to arrive at a purchase price.

The balance sheet prepared according to general accounting practices values the company assets based on their original cost. Now that the company is being sold, the original cost is irrelevant, and only the current fair market value is important. If the fair market value differs from the value shown on the balance sheet, an adjustment will be made.

Fair market value of assets is not defined as liquidation value, replacement value, or insurable value. An asset's fair market value is the value for a similar item. It must be of similar age, in the same condition, and have the same utility. Fair market value is the amount someone would pay for an asset if he located, purchased, and installed a similar item.

The fair market value of accounts receivables and inventory is also evaluated. Receivables that aren't collectible are written off. Obsolete inventory is sold or subtracted from inventory values. Obsolete equipment should be sold or disposed of since the buyer won't pay for this. In essence, if it is included in the sale, the buyer will get this free of charge.

You need to determine operating and nonoperating assets. Nonoperating assets are those that are not needed for the business to function. When nonoperating assets are included in the sale, be careful. Make sure those nonoperating assets enhance the price paid. When the buyer pays for only the operating value of the company and nonoperating assets are included, the buyer is getting those nonoperating assets for nothing. Since the seller receives no value for them, he should exclude them from the sale. These are the adjustments made in the balance sheet. For a complete discussion on how to recast or adjust your income and balance sheet, see Chapter 9 on recasting.

You also should adjust the liability side of the balance sheet. Generally, it is best to remove debt from the balance sheet, although it can be included. Removing debt from the balance sheet is an advantage when a standard presentation will be prepared for different qualified buyers. Some buyers will have a large amount of cash and won't want to assume your debt; others will have their own sources for securing debt; still others will want to assume as much debt as they can. When debt is removed, the presentation will have appeal to a wider group of buyers. Of course, this isn't always possible. The discounted future cash flow method discussed next removes all debt and uses this approach too.

The debt-free presentation is simple and easy to comprehend. Several different acquisition debt scenarios are possible under the debt-free situation.

The income statement also needs to be adjusted (see Chapter 9 on recasting). Excessive salaries and perks for the owner and his family need to be figured out and added to the pretax income. Remember, a privately owned company is operated to minimize taxes. Now, however, you must present your company in a way that maximizes profit. Excess earnings beyond what the assets are worth will create additional value for your company.

Depreciation should be added back to income when plant and equipment have been purchased, but are not currently in need of replacement. Nonrecurring expenses or one-time expenses should be adjusted on the income statement. These are items like vandalism or fire damage amounts that aren't covered by insurance. Naturally, the buyer dislikes these adjustments and will claim they aren't valid. In actuality, he will recognize your knowledge and ante up if he wants your company.

Nonoperating expenses and income are eliminated. These items include the cash value of life insurance, investments, real estate, and so on. Interest expense is added back to the net income as a part of the capital structure of the company, not the operations. The new company owner will have his own interest expenses and capital structure.

Recasting the income and balance sheet to reflect current value isn't the complete answer to the value of the company, but it is the place to start. You have to know the net current assets and the company's net long-term assets to find its tangible net worth at current market value. A realistic purchase price for a company begins here.

The buyer will pay dollar for dollar for tangible net assets of the business based on the asset's current fair market value. The buyer will also pay a multiple of the earnings of the company. Earnings will be defined as the company's adjusted normalized pretax income.

A key disadvantage to using the balance sheet approach alone is that it does not accurately portray the value of the business. Value of the asset's earning power is not reflected. There are only two real values of an asset: one is as collateral in securing financing; the other is the profit or earnings those assets will generate. This is why you have to consider both the asset value and earning potential of those assets. For example, assume that Company A and Company B have the same earnings but that Company A has twice the asset value. Which company should be valued more?

The most common earnings approach is the price/earnings ratio. It is used to evaluate a public company's worth. *It is not applicable to valuing privately held companies, however.* Remember, private and public companies have entirely different management objectives: public companies want to maximize earnings to drive their stock values up, whereas private companies want to minimize earnings to reduce the taxes for the company owners.

A good approach to find out value for a privately held company is the excess earnings method. Excess earnings are a very simple idea. When an investment is made, a return is expected. Excess earnings are above what would be expected from an investment of a similar risk level.

This approach begins with the rescheduled income statement after you've made all the expense adjustments. Once you've prepared the adjustments and the income statement, you have a company's adjusted pretax income. This adjustment should be done for the last couple of year's so that you get a normalized earnings figure that I discussed earlier in the chapter. This figure is the source for the calculation of excess earnings.

Let's see how the excess earnings method works with an example. The accompanying income statement (Table 4.1) and balance sheet (Table 4.2) represent a manufacturing company with sales of $15,750,000. Both the income statement and balance sheet have been adjusted. It must be emphasized that the buyer will want to see detailed documentation of the adjustments made. Be sure you use reasonable adjustments and document them.

TABLE 4.1

Seller's Income Statement Before and After Adjustments (in 000s), December 31, 199X

Total sales	$15,750
Cost of goods sold	11,250
Gross margin	$ 4,500
Operating expenses	
General and administrative	1,800
Depreciation	300
Other operating expenses	1,050
Total operating expenses	$ 3,150
Net operating income	**$ 1,350**

Interest expense	<u>90</u>
Pretax income	<u>$ 1,260</u>

Adjustments

Owner-related items[1]	$	587
Nonrecurring items[2]		90
Nonoperating items[3]		70
New organization[4]		<u>0</u>
Total	$	747
Adjusted pretax profit		**$ 2,007**

Notes to Income Statement

1. Owner-related items

a. Owner's salary and bonus	$300
Fair market salary	<u>(150)</u>
	$150
b. Eliminate owners' excess perks including travel, car, entertainment, and insurance	50
c. Eliminate owner pension expense	30
d. The seller owns another company that buys raw materials, stores them and delivers them to the seller's company at a $200,000 profit	200
e. The owner receives a commission of 1 percent on company sales paid to his marketing company	<u>157</u>
Total	<u>$587</u>

[1]Accounts receivable reserves are increased $50,000 to cover bad debts. Adjusted receivables represent the net realizable value.

[2]Inventory is adjusted downward because $88,000 of inventory is considered obsolete and not salable.

[3]Land, plant, and equipment are adjusted to reflect their fair market value as determined by appraisal or agreed-to value by buyer and seller.

[4]This represents a nonoperating asset that should be sold or removed from sale. It is a real estate investment and is vacant land.

2. Nonrecurring items
a. Eliminate nonrecurring bad
   debts related to the bankruptcy
   of one customer $35
b. Eliminate the one-time expense
   of installing and replacing
   a telephone and voice mail system   40
c. Vandalism losses not reimbursed
   by insurance   15

                        Total $90

3. Nonoperating items
a. Eliminate the following
   nonoperating items
b. Interest expense $90
c. Gain on the sale of fixed assets   (20)

                        Total $70

4. New organization
A. At this point the land and plant are a part of the corporation. The
   owner wants to sell the land and building with the company.
   No adjustment needed.

Table 4.2

Seller's Adjusted Balance Sheet (in 000s), December 31, 199X

	Book	Adjustment	Recast
Assets			
Current assets			
Cash	$ 675	$ —	$ 675
Accounts receivable	1,800	(50)[1]	1,750
Inventory	1,688	(88)[2]	1,600
Other current assets	112	—	112

[1]Accounts receivable reserves are increased $50,000 to cover bad debts. Adjusted receivables represent the net realizable value.

[2]Inventory is adjusted downward because $88,000 of inventory is considered obsolete and not salable.

Total current assets	$4,275	$(138)	$4,137
Fixed assets			
Land	900	$1,000^3$	1,900
Plant and equipment	4,500	$1,000^3$	5,500
Total fixed asset, cost	5,400	2,000	7,400
Accumulated depreciation	(1,800)	1,800	0
Total fixed assets, net	3,600	3,800	7,400
Total other assets	819	$(819)^4$	40
Total assets	$8,694	$2,843	$11,537

Liabilities and Equity

Current liabilities			
Notes payable	$ 225	$ $(225)^5$	$ 0
Accounts payable	788	—	788
Current portion of long-term debt	337	$(337)^6$	0
Accrued expenses	675	$(200)^7$	475
Contingent liability—			
Lawsuit	810	$(810)^8$	0
Interest payable	90	(90)	0
Total current liabilities	2,925	(1,662)	1,263
Total long-term liabilities	$1,575	$$(1,575)^6$	$ 0
Total liabilities	4,500	(3,237)	1,263
Total shareholder's equity	$4,194	$6,080	$10,274
Total liabilities and equity	$8,694	$2,843	$11,537

[3]Land, plant, and equipment are adjusted to reflect their fair market value as determined by appraisal or agreed-to value by buyer and seller.

[4]This represents a nonoperating asset that should be sold or removed from sale. It is a real estate investment and is vacant land.

[5]Short-term borrowing is paid off at closing.

[6]Long-term debt is paid off at closing.

[7]Accumulated vacation and sick leave pay earned by employees that have not been paid, unpaid sales commissions earned by company's salespersons, and portion of annual property taxes that should be charged to this years that haven't been billed yet.

[8]This is a lawsuit in which the company believes its maximum liability is $810,000. Therefore, this is a one-time liability that will be settled and paid by seller at closing.

The only return on a business is the profit of that business. By calculating excess earnings you can see the true return of that investment.

Begin by examining the important adjusted pretax net profit figure from the bottom of the recast income statement. The quality of these earnings is key to the value of the business. Our example shows only a one-year income statement. When completing yours, do a recast on at least the last three years of your income statement. Then use average earnings or whatever method is appropriate for your earnings history. Include only the most recent year and most current month for the balance sheet.

Often buyers will look at the last three to five years and make an average of those years. This, of course, may be appropriate if earnings and sales have been erratic. However, if sales and earnings have been increasing steadily, then the last year's numbers are most appropriate or a weighted average or trend line. Should the buyer insist on the last three years as an average when sales and earnings have been up, then the seller should insist on using a three-year forecast. Generally, both sides accept the last year as an appropriate beginning in this instance.

Now, go back to the recast balance sheet. On the recast balance sheet take the current assets and subtract the current liabilities to arrive at your company's net current assets. Our example's net current assets are $2,874,000. Next, take your total fixed assets and subtract total long-term liabilities. This equals the net long-term assets, which is $7,400,000 in our example. You add the net current assets and net long-term assets, and you have an adjusted net worth of $10,274,000. The seller will receive dollar for dollar the value of the adjusted net worth assets. In the example, the seller would receive $10,274,000 as the fair market value of the adjusted net worth. Page 77 has a summary of these calculations.

The adjusted net worth is the company's tangible net worth. It excluded intangible net worth such as goodwill, customers, patents, trademarks, and trained employees. This is a company's added value above the tangible net worth.

What kind of return should a buyer expect from the tangible net worth of his company? There is risk involved in buying a business. The risk is much greater than with U.S. Treasury bonds, a safe investment. Because of the risk, the buyer should expect a return higher than a safe investment. If a conservative investment is returning 8 percent, then a return of 12 percent would compensate the buyer for the added risk. The risk level of buying current assets is higher than of buying a government bond, but not as high as buying the long-term assets. Since government bonds are returning about 8 percent, the expected return on current net assets should be 150 percent of a government bond, or 12 percent. Net long-term assets should be 188 percent of a bond or 15 percent.

A true business investment should provide two kinds of return: namely, (1) an investment's return on assets such as machinery, equipment, fixtures, vehicles, inventory, receivables, and, if its included, cash and (2) a payback above and beyond the return on the assets themselves—this is the excess earnings part.

Excess earnings are really a stream of profits above and beyond the return you expect from an investment in assets alone. Technically, it is termed goodwill. The problem in deciding a fair price for the business is how to set a value on that stream of profits. The solution must address the issue of how reliable or risky the continuation of the profits from the sales to those customers will be in the future.

If the present customers didn't buy from the business beyond one year and if no new customers could be found the first year, then the value of the excess earnings over the return on assets would be one. If the income stream dried up at the end of one year, then the stream's value can be no more than one times a year's excess earnings. This would be a highly risky business since it would require that you recover your investment in excess earnings in one year, which is a 100 percent return. If you stretched the customer life to two years (twice excess earnings), it would represent a 50 percent annual return. A return like this is what you might expect in a high-risk venture capital speculation. Fifty percent returns are speculative, not investment, returns.

The process of multiplying the expected return by the numbers of years in which you expect to recapture your investment is called **capitalization**. You are turning a flow of profits into a fixed value of capital. When you multiply the earnings by the number of years, the multiplier is called a **cap rate**. Investments in privately owned companies that aren't liquid commonly call for a return of 20–25 percent on the excess earnings. In other words, the investment is paid off in four or five years. Here the earnings stream or quality of earnings is stable enough to recover the investment in

four or five years. Where returns of 33 percent are required, a business may
be too risky to purchase. This calls for a payback of investment in three
years. A return of 33 percent could be expected for companies that have
been in business for a short time. High returns of 33 percent would also
apply to those companies whose sales and earnings have been erratic and
unpredictable.

The price/earnings ratio is not the same and is useful only for publicly held
companies. The capitalized value of the seller's excess earnings is needed.

Let use Table 4.3 to examine recast income and balance sheets and see
what results when the excess earnings model is used.

Table 4.3

Excess Earnings Example
(all figures are taken from the adjusted balance sheet and income statement)

Adjusted pretax profit	$2,007,000
Adjusted total current assets	4,137,000
Less: Adjusted total current liabilities	1,263,000
Equals: Net current assets (working capital)	$2,874,000
12% Return on net current assets	344,880
Adjusted total fixed assets	7,400,000
Less: Adjusted total long-term liabilities	0
Equals: Net long-term assets	$7,400,000
15% Return on net long-term assets	1,110,000
Excess earnings[1]	552,120
Net current assets	2,874,000
Plus: Net long-term assets	7,400,000
Equals: Adjusted net worth or book value	10,274,000

[1]Excess earnings equals adjusted pretax profit less 12 percent returns on net current assets
and 15 percent returns on net long-term assets.

The adjusted pretax profit of $2,007,000 is selected from the adjusted
income statement. From this figure we will subtract the return expected on

net current and net long-term assets; the result is excess earnings or earnings above what a reasonable return on assets would produce.

Excess earnings are $552,120. When you add net current assets and net long-term assets, you have an adjusted book value or net worth of $10,274,000. The buyer will then pay $10,274,000 for the net worth.

The purchase price range is summarized in Table 4.4.

Table 4.4

How to Decide a Purchase Price Range with the
Excess Earnings Valuation Method

	25% Return Cap Rate	20% Return Cap Rate	16.7% Return Cap Rate
Excess earnings	$552,120	$552,120	$552,120
Times: Cap rate (in years)	× 4	× 5	× 6
Equals:	$2,208,480	$2,760,600	$3,312,720
Add: Adjusted book value	$10,274,000	$10,274,000	$10,274,000
Purchase price range (rounded)	$12,482,000	$13,035,000	$13,587,000
Purchase price (rounded to nearest hundred thousand)	$12,500,000	$13,000,000	$13,600,000

The purchase price should be somewhere in the $12,500,000 to $13,600,000 range. Since there are excess earnings, this business is providing a return on investment beyond the return in the assets of the business.

When you value a business, return on investment is the best method to use. The excess earnings method bases its value on the return on assets beyond what a fair return on the business should be. Two important keys to this calculation are the determination of the return rates used on tangible assets and the capitalization rate used for excess earnings. A difference of one or two percentage points in the cap rate can result in a major change in value.

Deciding the true economic earnings of the business is another difficulty with the excess earnings method. This is why earnings must be based on a recast income statement to arrive at the true earning power of the company.

Common Errors Associated with the Excess Earnings Method. This method has both its followers and detractors. It is denounced by many professional valuators as not being appropriate for any valuation. Because of its widespread use and acceptance by so many people, let's examine in more detail several errors that are commonly made in its use. These errors can render the value arrived at with this method as useless.

1. The rates of return that are applied to tangibles and intangibles are arbitrary. Bad guesses or bad estimates can be worse than no valuation at all. The rates suggested by the IRS in its ruling should not be used. The rate should be that prevailing at the time for a given industry. Time- and industry-specific rates are important variables in the determination of appropriate rates. Using capitalization rates that are too low or too high inevitably result in either a gross overvaluation or a gross undervaluation of the business.

2. Failure to allow for the owner's salary is a major omission especially for smaller businesses. A reasonable allowance for the replacement salary and perks of a manager should be factored into the earnings of the company. Not subtracting from earnings a reasonable allowance grossly overstates the value of a business. However, from the seller's position it is good strategy to insist that valuation be based on his total earnings and not after a reasonable allowance for a new person's salary to replace him.

3. The parties fail to use a realistic basis for deciding past earnings. Good valuation methodology requires that an average of the past several years be used so that earnings are normalized. Weighted average and trend analysis are both appropriate methods for establishing a fair basis to decide an earnings figure to base the capitalization and return rate on. Sellers could benefit by insisting that the most recent year is most appropriate, especially when it has been a good one compared to previous years. This strategy, while not good valuation methodology, is good for the seller because it inflates the purchase price.

4. Often buyers insist that the business be purchased based on what the financial records say the earnings are. This, of course, means the business will be valued based on depressed earnings. This is not fair to the seller. The seller should insist on having the income statement recast to more accurately reflect the real earnings of the company.

5. If this method fails to prove positive excess earnings, some people conclude that the company has no goodwill and is worth only its tangible net asset value. However, good valuation analysis might conclude that the business is worth less than the computed tangible net asset value. A smart seller will insist that the floor for his company be the tangible net asset value. This will prevent someone from arguing the case for a value less than tangible net asset value.

Rules of Thumb

Every seller is aware of industry averages or rules of thumb. But what is an average company? Every seller believes his company is above average. What is an above-average company?

For example, assume that Company A and Company B have similar sales, products, and distribution methods but that A is twice as profitable. Company A also has a proprietary product, a leadership position in a fragmented, growth industry, and an outstanding future in terms of sales and earnings. Do industry averages or rules of thumb apply to Company A?

Company B has commodity-type products, is not a leader in its market, and has a new competitor ready to attack it. The industry is consolidating and shrinking. Margins are falling and its future is unpredictable. Is Company B average? There are many factors that need to be considered when valuing a business. Factors such as tax considerations, terms of the deal, and legal issues are a few. Despite these considerations, rules of thumb are used every day to establish a purchase price for a company. The problem is the price can be unrealistically high or low. The result is the seller doesn't get enough money for his business or the price is so high that a buyer can't be found and the business doesn't sell. One well-known company in the Midwest estimates that it can't sell 25 percent of the companies it represents because the businesses are priced beyond what buyers will pay.

Despite this caution, companies are sold regularly based on some sort of rule of thumb. Rules of thumb have been developed by trade associations and business brokers. When rules of thumb are used to value a business, the rule of thumb is generally used mainly with small businesses and service-type companies. There are, however, many exceptions. Sometimes the rule of thumb is more highly relied on than any other method of valuation. For example, one company I know sold its beauty salons on a piecemeal basis. Each salon was valued at 40 percent of its gross revenues. This worked out to be three times pretax operating income for each salon. Earlier I mentioned that long-distance telephone companies were selling for four to eight times gross monthly incomes. Each of these ratios was based on an industry average rule of thumb.

If you are interested in knowing more about rules-of-thumb valuation techniques, there is a good book out on the subject. It's called the *Handbook of Small Business Valuation Formulas,* Second Edition, by Desmond and Marcello, Valuation Press, Marina del Ray, CA 90292. This book is available in many libraries, or it can be ordered directly from the publisher. It gives hundreds of examples of businesses that can be valued by the rules-of-thumb valuation method.

The capitalization of gross revenues approach is applied most frequently to service industries such as insurance agencies, professional practices, advertising agencies, and mortuaries. Capitalization of gross revenues can be considered a shortcut to a capitalization of earnings approach. The assumption is that so much revenue should produce so much earnings in a given industry. For certain industries, it may be much easier to derive an appropriate multiplier of gross revenues than adjust the income statement to arrive at the earning power of the company. Gross multiplier industry averages make a good checkpoint to test the valuation one has arrived at based on the capitalization of earnings or cash flow approach. When the two methods of arriving at value are in harmony with each other, your valuation probably is accurate for that company in that industry.

Corporate buyers of service businesses often can eliminate many discretionary expenses and improve earnings through tried and proven management methods and thus increase earnings. They accomplish this by centralizing purchasing, accounting, and administrative functions. They eliminate overlapping expenses and provide economies of scale. Therefore, the buyer may know the value of a given level of gross revenues despite the earnings that an independent business may or may not have. As a result, he can base the value of the business on a multiple of the gross revenue. This was the case with the example I used to describe the acquisition of the long-distance telephone company. The buyer had a good idea what the gross revenues would produce in earnings despite what the previous owner's financial records showed. The main consideration the buyer had was the *predictability* of the future revenues and the quality of the customer base.

Service companies sold on the justification of gross revenue multipliers do have a foundation on the company earnings on which to place value. For example, assume that an advertising agency is producing $1,000,000 of annual revenues and earns an average of 10 percent on its sales. If buyers of ad agencies insisted on a 20 percent return on investment, then buyers would be willing to pay 0.10/0.20 = 0.50, or 50 percent of annual gross revenues. A company with 10 percent returns on sales of $1,000,000 yields $100,000 of earnings. If the capitalization rate is 20 percent, the company would be worth $500,000 ($100,000/0.20 = $500,000). The $500,000 is equal to 50 percent of sales or six months of gross revenue. The gross revenue multiplier then is 0.50, or 50 percent of annual sales.

There are two good reference sources of information for earnings based on return on sales. You can find out what the industry average for return on sales is by referring to these references. If the average earnings on sales divided by a satisfactory capitalization rate comes out close to the gross revenue multiplier, then the multiplier is probably accurate. The reference sources to consult for this information are *Annual Statement Studies* by Robert Morris Associates. This annual publication is a compilation of ratio and other operating statistics for more than 350 different industries and is available from Robert Morris Associates, 1 Liberty Place, 1650 Market Street, Suite 1300, Philadelphia, PA 19103. Another good source for operating statistics and ratios is *Industriscope* by Media General Financial Services. This monthly publication documents operating and performance data for over 250 industries and 5,000 common stocks. Contact Media General Financial Services, P.O. Box C-32333, Richmond, VA 23293.

Another good source of reference material to aid in the valuation of your company is *Mergerstat Review* by Merrill Lynch. This annual publication reveals merger and acquisition activity for the past year. Data include both public and private companies with transactions of $500,000 or more. Contact Merrill Lynch, Mergerstat Review Department, 854 East Algonquin Road, Schaumburg, IL 60173.

Gross revenue multipliers aren't the only industry rules of thumb used. Quite often a multiple of some unit of volume or capacity is used. Examples would include nursing homes at so much a bed. Service stations and fuel distributors at so much fuel sold per month at so much per gallon and apartment buildings at so much per unit. The idea is that volume or units can be translated into revenue and earnings.

Discounted Future Cash Flow Method

The discounted cash flow method is based on present value. This theory advocates a company is worth the present value of its anticipated future cash flows over a typical period of, say, five years to ten years. Once the future cash flows are figured out, you multiply the cash flows by an appropriate discount rate and find the present value of each cash flow. The **discount rate** is a rate of return used to convert a series of future cash flows into present value. You then total the present value of the flows and arrive at the company's value. (Discount rate value tables are available in the business section of any library.)

This approach is time consuming and does not give an accurate picture of value, since you are dealing with cash flow, not pretax profit. However, a positive aspect of the method is that it is based on future earnings (cash flow).

Net present value is based on the proverbial bird in the hand. A dollar is worth more today than a dollar five years from now. Further, having the dollar today is less risky than waiting five years for it. Inflation trends need to be considered. Net present value also addresses what you could earn if you invested the money at a safe return.

There are three basic factors to consider when finding out the value of a dollar today versus five years from now:

1. Prevailing interest rates
2. Consumer Price Index
3. Risk

Discounted future cash flows require the recasting of both the balance sheet and income statement. You begin by recasting the balance sheet and income statement and adjust all the asset values to present fair market value. Then subtract the bad debts from the receivables, dispose of obsolete inventory, and clean up the notes receivable. Fixed assets are given their replacement value. Real, tangible net worth of the company at current market prices is then calculated. (Refer to Chapter 9 on recasting for a more detailed discussion of the topic.) For discounted cash flow methodology to be effective, you must closely examine all facets of the quality of present and future earnings.

The discounted cash flows (DCF) method state that the value of a company can be estimated today by forecasting the company's future financial performance and by identifying and evaluating the cash flow. A discount rate determines the net present value of future cash flows. This value is the market value of the company. Accordingly, DCF views a company strictly as a cash generator. The more cash flow generated, the more valuable the company.

The method considers the initial return on a buyer's investment and the seller's future profitability in cash flow over time. Also considered is the value of the company's cash flows after the agreed-upon time, typically five years, but it could be ten years.

Many factors must be considered:

1. What period will be used to estimate cash flows? Five years? Seven years? Ten years?
2. What is the residual value of the seller's company at the end of the forecast period? Usually, a period of time is used until the comfort level of the buyer disappears.
3. What discount rate will be used? When the selling company's risk is judged to be the same as the buyer's general risk, the appropriate rate for discounting the seller's cash flow stream is the buyer's cost of capital. A discount rate can vary depending on the riskiness of the venture.

Forecasting cash flow over time is risky at best. Forecasts of sales, sales growth, gross margins, net working capital increases, and capital expenditures all need to be estimated.

The discounted cash flow method requires six steps to find out value:

1. Develop a debt-free forecast of the selling company's financial performance and condition for five or more years.
2. Identify the surplus cash (cash flow) negative or positive that is forecasted for each year.
3. Estimate the value of the company at the end of the forecast period. This is often called the "terminal value" of the company.
4. Estimate the discount rate that will be used based on the seller's risk-adjusted cost of debt and equity.
5. Discount the forecasted cash flows and the terminal value amount by the discount rate.
6. Subtract today's long-term and short-term borrowing of the seller.

Begin by finding out cash flow. **Surplus cash flows** are sales less operating expenses and other nonoperating, noncash expenses, such as the amortization of goodwill, which equals earnings before interest and taxes. Subtract income taxes from EBIT, and you have debt-free earnings after taxes. Now add depreciation and subtract capital expenditures and increases in working capital. The result is cash flow that can be used to pay interest and principal payments on any acquisition debt or interest on short-term borrowing. An example of forecasted cash flows over a five-year period is presented in Table 4.5.

Table 4.5

Year-by-Year Forecasted Cash Flows (in 000s)

	Years				
	1	2	3	4	5
Sales	$15,000	$16,000	$17,000	$19,000	$21,000
Earnings (before taxes and interest) (EBIT)[1]	1,000	1,050	1,100	1,250	1,400

[1]Represents operating profit of company.

Income taxes on EBIT[2]	(400)	(420)	(440)	(500)	(560)
Debt-free earnings after taxes[3]	600	630	660	750	840
Add: Depreciation[4]	200	200	200	300	300
Less: Capital Expenditures[5]	(300)	(300)	(300)	(400)	(400)
Less: Increase in working capital[4,6]	(150)	(150)	(150)	(200)	(200)
Cash flow[7]	350	380	410	450	540

[2]Represents income tax based on EBIT even if company has interest expenses.

[3]Represents after-tax profits before debt service.

[4]Obtain from statement of changes in financial position.

[5]Same as footnote 4.

[6]Represents additional cash needed to grow business, such as receivables and inventory net of current payables and accruals.

[7]Surplus cash available for principal and interest payments on debt. This is the figure used to figure out value in the discounted cash flow method.

Surplus cash (cash flow) is at the bottom of Table 4.5. To avoid wide fluctuations in value caused by historical borrowing, cash flows are calculated as if the company were debt free throughout the forecast period. Future cash flow, therefore, excludes the cost of debt financing. This figure can be used to decide if there is enough cash flow to cover debt payments. Incidentally, those who use the supportable debt method to arrive at value use these same calculations.

Tables 4.6 and 4.7 give a summary of the discounted future cash flow method using future cash flows and discounting them to today's value. The discount rate is a weighted average based on the cost of capital (debt and equity) to the selling company. For our purposes, two discount rates are used: a 12 percent rate and a 20 percent rate. The higher the discount rate is, the less the purchase price; the lower the discount rate, the higher the purchase price. Study both tables carefully to see the impact the discount rate has on value.

Besides cash flows, it is necessary to figure out the value of the company five years from now (residual value). This residual value is then discounted to present-day values. Several methods are used to arrive at residual value, the most common of which is known as the perpetuity assumption.

The perpetuity method assumes that the operating cash flow in the last forecasted period (fifth year in the tables) will remain constant forever. It is based on the idea that competitors will enter the business and drive down the returns of the seller's company until the value of the company cannot be increased by more investment in the company.

Table 4.6

Summary of Discounted Cash Flow Method Assuming a 20 Percent Discount Rate (in 000s)

Year	Cash Flow	Discount Factor	Present Value[1]	Cumulative Present Value
1	$ 350	0.833	$292	$ 292
2	380	0.694	264	556
3	410	0.579	237	793
4	450	0.482	217	1,010
5	540	0.402	217	1,227
Residual value[2]	2,700	0.402	1,085	2,312[3]
Less: Present value of debt assumed				(700)
Add: Assets not required by operations				100
Value of seller's company				**1,712**

[1]Present value is obtained by multiplying the present-day discount factor by cash flow.

[2]Residual value is perpetuity value obtained by taking cash flow of the fifth year and dividing by the discount rate: $540,000/0.20 = $2,700,000.

[3]The cumulative residual value represents the value of the company's total equity (both debt and equity).

Another method to arrive at value is to use a multiple of EBIT. Price/earnings and a multiple of book can be used as well to arrive at the residual value.

Table 4.7

Summary of Discounted Cash Flow Method Assuming a 12 Percent
Discount Rate (in 000s)

	Cash Flow	Discount Factor	Present Value[1]	Cumulative Present Value
1	$ 350	0.893	$ 313	$ 313
2	380	0.797	303	616
3	410	0.712	292	908
4	450	0.636	286	1,194
5	540	0.567	306	1,500
Residual value[2]	4,500	0.567	2,552	4,052[3]
Less: Present value of debt assumed				(700)
Add: Assets not required by operations				100
Value of seller's company				**3,452**

[1]Present value is obtained by multiplying the present-day discount factor by cash flow.

[2]Residual value is perpetuity value obtained by taking cash flow of the fifth year and dividing by the discount rate: $540,000/0.12 = $4,500,000.

[3]The cumulative residual value represents the value of the company's total equity (both debt and equity).

The examples presented in Tables 4.6 and 4.7 use the perpetuity method. But it would be wise to test several methods of arriving at residual value because terminal value often accounts for more than half the purchase price. Use caution and reserve in figuring out terminal value, the value placed on the company five to ten years into the future and then discounted to a present value.

The market value of the seller's company's total capital (debt and equity) is the sum of the net present values of the cash flows and the terminal value. Since most companies have some debt, it is necessary to subtract it to arrive at the present value to the owners. Debtholders have a stake in the value of the company and must be paid off in theory before the sellers are paid.

Nonoperating assets are not included in the discounted cash flow valuation method. DCF values only the operating entity. Accordingly, nonoperating assets such as marketable securities, unused land, unused buildings, plant, and machinery should be valued separately and added to the DCF business value. Nonoperating liabilities should be subtracted from the DCF liabilities.

Tables 4.6 and 4.7 show the value of the seller's company at a 12 percent and a 20 percent discount rate. The 12 percent rate suggests a value of $3,452,000, a 20 percent discount rate suggests a value of $1,712,000. The lower discount rate (12 percent) would result in $1,740,000 more to the seller than the higher discount rate of 20 percent. A seller wants the lowest possible discount rate and the buyer wants the highest.

The present-day value for the residual value of the 12 percent discount rate is $2,552,000. Under the 20 percent discount rate, it's $1,085,000, and that is a difference of $1,467,000 for pricing the present-day company value five years into the future.

It is easy to see why this method places an importance on determining the discount rate. A change from a 20 percent to a 12 percent rate results in the seller receiving $1,740,000 more for his company. Both buyer and seller will need to negotiate intensively to arrive at a mutually acceptable number.

Discounted cash flow method is complex, time consuming, and difficult to use. Because of the many variables involved, DCF values vary widely. Forecasting sales accurately over one year is difficult enough without taking cash flow into consideration and then forecasting five years into the future.

Residual terminal values are often 50 percent or more of the selling price. Residual value must be decided five or more years into the future, and that is a difficult task at best. Capital expenditures have to be predicted, and a discount rate has to be agreed upon. Forecasting, three, five, or more years into the future are perilous at best.

A buyer who uses DCF to arrive at value must understand that there is no room for value creation. DCF should be thought of as the maximum you would pay for a company. DCF should establish the upper limit of the purchase price.

For the seller, this valuation method results in the highest purchase price for his company. The seller's dilemma is if his sales forecast is too aggressive, he risks losing his credibility with the buyer. Being too conservative can also be lethal. In this instance, the buyer may conclude the company has less potential than anticipated and not purchase it. The buyer's lender may balk as well.

Why do companies persist in using DCF? DCF forces the buyer to translate future benefits from a business into hard dollars. It forces a buyer to think about the future and understand all aspects of the business. He must know where sales will come from and what future capital expenditures will be needed. He must know how profitable the company could become under the new owner's management and many other important factors.

In many merger situations involving larger companies, the discounted future cash flow method is the most valid and accurate approach available for valuing a company. Large corporations are accustomed to using the discount method outlined. Any acquisition—whether paid in cash, stock, or debt—is an investment that represents payment today for a future stream of income. Thus the same discounting techniques used historically in evaluating equipment purchases, plant additions, marketing programs, and other capital investment outlays are applicable in acquiring and valuing a company.

For the seller, a good, sound, discounted future cash flow analysis can easily make a difference of 20–25 percent in the price a company sells for compared to valuations based only on historical earnings. If the company sells for $5 million, that could amount to a million dollars or more. It is hard work doing the forecasts and understanding the model. Are you prepared to leave 20 percent or more of the purchase price in the buyer's hands simply because you didn't want to do the work necessary to present your company properly?

SUMMARY OF VALUATION METHODS

Placing a value on a business is not an exact science, subject to a precise formula. Valuation can, however, be based on relevant facts, elements of common sense, informed judgment, and reasonableness. Sound valuation requires that one gather the pertinent facts, analyze those facts, and arrive at value. Two competent valuators can arrive at different values based on different assumptions or methodology.

Revenue Ruling 59-60 is regarded as one of the most accepted guidelines to be used to arrive at value. Many courts have held that Revenue Ruling 59-60 is a valid basis for deciding the valuation of a closely held business. The ruling lists the following eight factors that must be considered:

1. "The nature of the business and the history of the enterprise from its inception."
2. "The economic outlook in general and the condition and outlook of the specific industry in particular."
3. "The book value of the stock and the financial condition of the business." It is a mystery why the ruling discusses book value when book value is rarely equal to fair market value.
4. "The earnings capacity of the entity." Earnings are the most important criterions of value. The narrative of the ruling in Section 5(a) states: "In general, the appraiser will accord primary consideration to earnings when valuing stock of companies that sell products or services."
5. "The dividend-paying capacity of the entity." This usually does not apply to private companies. Courts realize the tax cost an owner incurs when earnings are taken out as dividends and not other forms of tax-deductible payments.
6. "Whether or not the enterprise has goodwill or other intangible value." *Blacks Law Dictionary* (p. 625) defines goodwill as "the ability of a

business to generate income in excess of a normal rate on assets due to superior managerial skills, market position, new product technology, and so on."

7.   "Sales of the stock and the size of the block of stock to be valued." The best indicators of value are arm's-length transactions. Where those transactions are available, and they seldom are, the information could be used in reaching conclusions as to value.

8.   "The market price of stocks of corporations engaged in the same or similar line of business having their stocks actively traded on a free and open market, either on an exchange or over the counter." This is commonly known as comparable method when the value of a company is decided. One of the major problems with this method is finding comparable companies. The U.S. Tax Court in a 1967 decision described the closely held company as follows: "A publicly traded stock and a privately traded stock are not . . . the same animals, distinguished only by the size, frequency, or color of its spots. The essential nature of the beast is different."

When everything is said about valuation, company's values are figured out by earning power and/or prospective liquidation of assets. The values attributable to those two factors are found out by market forces.

There is perhaps no business decision more important than the price at which to sell a company. Summarized next are the key principles outlined in this chapter concerning valuation:

1. The value of a business is directly related to the expected future earnings its owner receives. The future earnings are then discounted back to a present value for the length of time the economic benefit is expected to be received.

2. The market decides the appropriate discount rate for figuring out market value. This rate depends on risk compared to other similar investments.

3. It is difficult to forecast accurately and reliably future earnings. It is also hard to come to an agreement on an appropriate discount rate. Therefore, most smaller companies and businesses are valued on the current and historical earnings than projected or forecasted earnings. Measures

of historical economic benefits include cash flow, earnings, dividends, gross revenues, dividends, and asset values. The ability to pay off debt based on the earnings of the company is an important valuation consideration for smaller companies. Benefits accruing to the owner include earnings from operations, earnings from investments, liquidation of assets, and sale of business.

4. The value of a share of stock may be worth more than or less than than the value of the company's underlying net asset value. This is because a stockholder has no direct claim on the corporation's assets, only its income, unless the company's assets are liquidated.

5. Because privately owned companies lack the liquidity and marketability of a public company, the value of shares of stock is worth considerably less for a privately held company than a public company.

6. Several valuation methods should be used to derive value when historical earnings are used as a basis of value. Rules of thumb, capitalization rate, excess earnings, and the debt-paying ability all can be compared to arrive at fair market value.

7. Careful examination of historical earnings will require that the income statement be recast to reflect more accurately the earnings of a company. An average of the last several years can be use to decide the earnings. Weighted value and trend lines can also help figure out the earnings value.

8. Capitalization rates should reflect what the current rate is for the particular industry the company is engaged in.

If doing the calculations by hand and understanding all the nuances of valuation are more than you can bear, there is a solution. The solution is ValuSource. ValuSource is a software company that specializes in valuation software for the professional appraiser, CPA, business broker, intermediary, financial adviser, attorney, and anyone who want to use computers to do valuations. ValuSource has several different kinds of software ranging from informal valuations to highly sophisticated formal valuation systems for IRS compliance and litigation support. ValuSource can be reached at ValuSource, 5405 Morehouse Drive, Suite 230, San Diego, CA 92121, 1-800-825-8763.

5

SELLING STOCK OR ASSETS

The Pros and Cons of a Tax-Free or Taxable Sale

As a seller you need to understand the advantages and disadvantages of selling assets compared with selling stock. Each method of property transfer has advantages and disadvantages, and buyer and seller needs differ in each transaction. Do you want the transfer of your company's stock or assets to be taxable or nontaxable? In a nontaxable transfer, you pay no federal income tax. C corporation and S corporation tax reporting affects the transfer of your business from a tax viewpoint as well.

Let's evaluate the taxable and nontaxable transfers and how both affect the seller and buyer in both asset and stock transfers. S corporation transfers are treated in a separate section at the end of this chapter. If you own an S corporation, turn to the end of this chapter.

TAXABLE EXCHANGES

There are two types of taxable transfers for C corporations: a sale of business assets and a sale of shares of stock.

The buyer will prefer an asset sale to a stock sale. When you sell assets, the buyer avoids the assumption of hidden liabilities, such as product liability claims. An asset sale also allows the buyer to allocate the sales price to the various assets and to increase the tax basis of the assets purchased. The resulting increased depreciation charges reduce income and taxes.

Let's say the selling company is a manufacturer and one of its assets is a lathe with an original tax basis of $20,000 that has been depreciated to $10,000. The fair market value (FMV) is $20,000. In a stock purchase, the buyer would take a carry-over tax basis of $10,000 in the lathe—the same basis as before the sale. However, in an asset purchase, the buyer begins with a tax basis of $20,000. In this example, the buyer has twice the depreciation potential; thus he shelters his company's income and reduces his income tax liability for his new company.

An asset sale greatly reduces the liability exposure of off- balance-sheet items. An example could be employees who haven't used all their vacation and sick leave because the seller doesn't have a use-it-or-lose-it policy. A buyer knows that all these employees have to do is holler, "I haven't used it, and I want to be paid for it." He could be on the hook for substantial sums of money. The buyer also knows there could be potential litigation over worker injury claims that haven't been filed yet. The same could exist for product liability claims, product warranties, and pension funds that have not been funded.

Sellers of stock in a C corporation pay only a single capital gain tax on the difference between the proceeds received for those shares and the tax basis of those shares.

In a stock acquisition, the buyers deal directly with the shareholders. After the buyer or buyer's board has approved the purchase, a stock purchase agreement is executed. This is the simplest and easiest way for a seller of a C corporation to transfer ownership.

The sale of assets for a C corporation causes double taxation for the seller: once, at the corporation level and, again, when he distributes the proceeds of the assets sale to the shareholders after he liquidates his corporation. A corporation pays tax on the excess of the of its assets over its tax bases. The corporate shareholders pay capital gain tax on the difference between the proceeds paid to them after the company is liquidated and their tax bases in the stock.

It is possible for a C corporation to retain a shell corporation and not liquidate. In this case, the shareholder would not pay a tax. However, a personal holding company tax could apply, and the proceeds could be subjected to an additional tax on undistributed personal holding company income. This personal holding company tax can be avoided by paying out all after-tax income in dividends. Many IRS rules apply. Sellers should proceed cautiously and obtain expert tax advice.

The seller's and buyer's boards of directors hold separate meetings to authorize the sale of assets. They then execute a sales agreement, subject to approval by the selling company's shareholders. Those who disagree with the transaction may be given appraisal rights that require valuation of their shares. State laws vary with respect to shareholder rights.

If the parties agree to the terms of the asset transfer, the seller will issue a bill of sale at the closing in exchange for the purchase price. When the seller liquidates his corporation, he will distribute assets to the shareholder in exchange for the shareholder stock.

The bulk sales act requires that several days pass before an asset-based sale can be closed. This is intended to protect the unsecured creditor whose rights are protected by this law.

The seller and buyer must resolve tax problems and off-balance-sheet liabilities. The buyer may have to pay a higher price in an asset sale to cover the additional taxes the seller will be required to pay. The liability issue in a stock sale can be resolved if the seller places part of the purchase price in escrow. The buyer can look to this escrow for redress if unknown liabilities come up after the sale that existed before the close of the deal. Chapter 14, on legal issues, suggests several ways to deal with this problem.

A buyer may want a stock sale than an asset sale for many good business reasons besides taxes and liabilities. Perhaps your company has certain valuable contracts, franchises, leases, or licensing agreements that cannot be assigned to the buyer or cannot be assigned on favorable terms. Your corporation may have an excellent credit rating that the buyer wants and that can usually be gotten only through a stock transfer.

TAX-FREE EXCHANGES

So far we have concerned ourselves with transactions that are taxable to the seller. Can you accomplish a tax-free exchange of assets or stock? Absolutely! There are two keys to making this happen:

First, you must be willing to accept the buyer's stock or securities as consideration in the transaction. Not more than 20 percent of the purchase price can be cash. The other 80 percent must be stock or securities. And, second, you must find a willing buyer whose stock you are willing to accept as payment on the purchase price

Under Section 368 of the Internal Revenue Code, seven types of reorganizations qualify as nontaxable exchanges. Whatever the form of reorganization, the stock or securities received by the seller must be the stock or securities of a party to the transaction. There must be a bona fide business purpose, which means it cannot be done for the sole purpose of tax savings. In addition, there must be a continuity of the shareholder's interest through membership in the acquiring corporation. The business must continue as it has in the past. Should you fail to meet the statute requirements, the IRS will deny the tax-free status of the deal.

The three most common types of nontaxable exchanges or reorganizations are Type A, Type B, and Type C.

A Section 368(1)(A) reorganization involves a merger or consolidation. A **merger** is a union of two or more corporations in which one corporation retains its corporate existence and absorbs the other. **Consolidation** is the formation of a new corporation to replace two or more constituent corporations that subsequently lose their corporate existence. In essence, a consolidation creates a new corporation.

The Type A statutory merger is the most flexible form of acquisition from the standpoint of consideration. Generally, at least 50 percent or more of the seller's stock must be exchanged with the acquiring company. The balance of the consideration can be in cash, notes, securities, or other types of consideration.

A Section 368(a)(1)(B) reorganization requires the acquisition of the stock of the selling corporation by a second corporation in exchange solely for all or part of its voting stock. The buying corporation must have control of the selling corporation; control means at least 80 percent of the combined voting power of the stock and at least 80 percent of the total numbers of shares of all other classes of stock.

For example, if a public corporation exchanges its voting stock for control of a private corporation, this qualifies as a Type B reorganization, and the private corporation will become a subsidiary of the public corporation. A Type B reorganization is easy to accomplish if the selling corporation is closely held. It's more difficult to accomplish if the shares are widely held. Since the selling corporation continues to exist, shareholder meetings are unnecessary, and dissenting shareholders generally have no right to have the business appraised.

A Type C reorganization under IRS Code 368(a)(1)(C) allows an **asset-only sale** by the selling corporation. The buying company must get substantially all the assets of the seller in exchange for the voting stock of the buying company. When a public company acquires a private company's assets, this transaction qualifies as a Type C reorganization. The public company acquires only those assets it wishes to assume and is not liable for unknown or contingent claims since it has met the state's bulk sales act requirements. Generally, the buyer needs to acquire at least 90 percent of the fair market vale (FMV) of the seller's net assets and at least 70 percent of the FMV of the gross assets. No more than 20 percent of the purchase price can be cash or other property because 80 percent of the assets obtained must be paid for with the buyer's voting stock. The buying corporation may assume the liabilities of the selling corporation. However, the amount of assumed liabilities counts against the 20 percent rule so that, as a practical matter, when liabilities are assumed, no other consideration than stock will be permitted.

In the three reorganizations described, there is no federal income tax liability to the selling company. The seller may have to pay sales taxes, deed taxes, and other types of taxes, however. Selling stockholders generally cannot immediately sell their stock without jeopardizing the tax-free status of the deal for the other selling stockholders who do not want to sell their stock. In other words, the IRS will disallow the tax-free exchange if some shareholders immediately sell their stock.

Tax-free sales apply to qualifying consideration. Qualifying consideration refers to the stock of the buyer. Long-term debt instruments of the buyer also qualify for a tax-free exchange. Cash, property, and other consideration will be taxed.

The tax theory behind a tax-free exchange is that a taxpayer has simply converted an investment in one corporation to an investment in another corporation. Consequently, no taxable event is deemed to have occurred; taxes are deferred and will be paid when any gain or loss results from the sale of the stock later. The seller of the company pays tax only when he sells the stock the buyer gave him for the deal.

One of the issues a seller must consider when taking shares of stock in a transaction is that stock prices can go up or down dramatically. The seller's fortunes become tied to the market value of the acquiring company. Further, the shares of stock may not be registered with the Securities and Exchange Commission, and thus the seller can't sell his stock for two years. A lot can happen in two years to the value of that stock.

S CORPORATIONS

When the seller has an S corporation and is selling his company as either a stock or an asset sale, there is just one tax at the shareholder level. When selling, an S corporation has more flexibility with respect to stock or asset sales than does a C corporation. Here, the double tax doesn't exist on an asset sale, making it easier to meet the needs of both buyer and seller. The seller has a major advantage with an S corporation because of this flexibility.

Before the passage of the Tax Reform Act of 1986, gain on appreciated property distributed by an S corporation was not recognized at the corporate level. Taxes to the shareholder were based on the FMV of the assets minus the tax bases in the shareholder's stock. This was simple and straightforward for an S corporation.

The rules are different today in the liquidation of an S corporation. However, the tax results are about the same. When an S corporation sells assets now, the shareholders of the corporation receive a pass-through of the gain equal to the increase in the basis of the stock. When the sales proceeds are distributed to the shareholders, the gain or loss to the shareholder is figured out by comparing the value of the property received to the adjusted basis in the stock. The basis increase allows the shareholders to receive a tax-free distribution equal to the increase in basis.

A stock sale has similar results because the shareholders recognize gain by comparing the value of the cash received for the stock to the adjusted basis of the shares.

If you're thinking of selling your company and it's established as a C corporation, you should consider the effect of converting to an S corporation. This may allow you to minimize the tax effect of future appreciation of your assets by putting a cap on the gains. There are rules you must follow. The effect is to reduce your taxes at sale time by eliminating the double tax on the growth of your assets after the S corporation election.

Appraisals of assets must be in place the first day of the S corporation year.

The S corporation makes it easier to meet the needs of a buyer and seller in a taxable transaction. It prevents the seller from being hit with the double tax that he'd pay if he were selling a C corporation. Therefore, in this example, an asset sale is more likely to meet the needs of the buyer.

The following is a summary of the key considerations involved in a sale of assets or stock or a merger. Both the buyer's and seller's perspective are summarized. Each type of transaction is viewed according to the requirements of tax, accounting, shareholders' and dissenters' rights, and state and federal securities registration.

A brief discussion of each of the four basic issues involved in a transaction follows. Each type of transaction is summarized. Three tax-free transactions are summarized as well as taxable asset and stock sales.

THE FOUR BASIC TRANSACTION ISSUES

There are four basic issues involved in the acquisition of one corporation by another: (1) the tax treatment, (2) the financial accounting treatment, (3) states laws relating to shareholders' rights, and (4) federal and state securities registration requirements. Each is described briefly in the paragraphs that follow.

1. The Tax Treatment of the Sale

The seller's concern will be whether the consideration received will be taxable, how much the tax will be, and when the tax must be paid. Mergers are most useful if the stock of the surviving corporation used as consideration is readily marketable and if the shareholders of the merged corporation intend to continue their ownership interest. When these two conditions exist, a merger is an excellent strategy for the seller to defer tax indefinitely.

In a merger, selling company shareholders surrender their stock in the merged company and receive stock of the surviving entity. This is a tax-free exchange. Shareholders of the merged entity are taxed when they sell shares of the surviving company. The issuance of shares by the surviving company is not a taxable transaction either. Mergers that comply with the regulations contained in Section 368 of the IRS Tax Code are tax free.

To comply with Section 368, a business must have a valid purpose. This is easy to establish when the transaction isn't done just for tax reasons. The merged company must also continue the historic business of the selling company or merged entity. Former shareholders of the selling corporation must also continue to hold their stock in the surviving corporation for sometime. Tax-free status will be denied if the shares are sold immediately after the merger is completed. All other kinds of deals, in which stock is not the major consideration, will be taxed and have various tax ramifications.

The buyer's primary concerns will be the assets. Will the assets have their tax basis adjusted to current fair market value, or will those assets have a carry-over basis from the seller?

When the selling corporation has a net operating loss, the buyer will be concerned about whether the net operating losses will go with the acquisition. When the losses carry over, the buyer will want to know the extent to which he can use those net operating losses against the income of the selling company and the income of the buying company.

2. The Financial Accounting Treatment of the Transaction

The buyer, particularly a public company, will be concerned with whether the transaction will be accounted for as a purchase or as a pooling of interest. The pooling-of-interest method permits the existing book value of the assets to be carried over to the buyer. Buyers prefer the pooling method because recognition of goodwill can be avoided.

There are several criteria that must be met for pooling-of-interest accounting to be in effect. One important criterion is that consideration for the acquisition must be solely common stock with voting rights identical to those of the majority of the outstanding voting common stock of the acquiring company. The consideration must be issued in exchange for substantially all the voting common stock of the selling company. The voting stock must be 90 percent or more. Some flexibility is given to cash for dissenting shareholders and fractional shares. But no cash or other nonqualifying stock is permitted.

The purchase method accounting applies to asset purchases or where the preceding criteria are not met. Purchase accounting methods require that all the assets be recorded at their fair market value. Consideration in excess of the asset's fair market value is assigned to goodwill following the residual allocation of assets method. The increased values assigned to the purchased assets generally result in increased depreciation or amortization reported in the financial statements. Goodwill is not amortized for tax purposes when stock is sold but is amortized over 15- years when the assets are sold. This new 15-year amortization of goodwill is a new tax provision under the Revenue Reconciliation Act of 1993. See Chapter 13 for a complete discussion of this issue. A stock purchase under purchase accounting is treated the same as asset purchase.

3. State Law Considerations

Both buyer and seller want to know whether the transaction will require that shareholders vote on the proposed sale. Both buyer and seller also want to know whether shareholders who do not approve the transaction can exercise dissenters' rights or can otherwise block the sale. Generally, dissenters' rights require that the company be formally appraised under court supervision and, further, that the dissenters receive their pro rata share in cash based on the appraisal, not the actual selling price.

4. Federal/State Securities Law Applications

Both parties to the transaction will want to know whether there is a required filing of a registration statement with the Securities and Exchange Commission or with the securities departments of the various states involved. Generally, the selling company's shareholders will be exempt from the registration requirement of the Securities Act of 1933. The transfer of stock by the selling shareholders to the acquiring company will not be a distribution of securities, and the shareholders of the selling company will not be issuers, dealers, or underwriters for the purposes of the 1933 act. The buyer will normally be a sophisticated investor with access to relevant information and one who is not considered to require the protection of the registration requirements of the 1933 act.

The transaction will not be considered a public offering under Section 4(2) of the Securities Act of 1933. Similarly, where a small group of shareholders exists in the selling company, the proposed swap of securities may qualify under a private or small offering exemptions or as an intrastate offering.

Because the shareholders of a privately held company are likely to end up with unregistered securities, the seller may want the buyer to include language in the acquisition agreement that provides that the stock is registered.

Issuance of securities concerning a sale may trigger registration or other filing requirements under the securities laws of a particular state as well. For example, in Minnesota corporations may avoid registering securities when the shareholders are required to vote on the transaction. Such transactions include a merger of the selling company with the buyer and an exchange of shares between corporations. The commissioner of securities must be notified and furnished with general information within ten days or less when stock is issued by the acquiring company.

SUMMARY OF TAXABLE ASSET SALE, TAXABLE ASSET PURCHASE, TAXABLE STOCK SALE, AND TAXABLE STOCK PURCHASE

Taxable Asset Sale Summary

Advantages to Seller

1. S corporation pays a single tax with no tax at corporation level. Gain flows through to individual shareholders. When the shareholders pay tax on this gain, it increases their bases in their shares. In subsequent liquidation, the shareholders can use this increased basis to offset any corporate distributions, thus resulting in only a single tax. S corporation election must be before 1987 or since incorporation.
2. Seller maintains corporate existence.

3. Seller maintains ownership of nontransferable assets or rights such as license, patent, franchise, and so on.

4. Seller maintains corporate name.

5. A seller's net operating losses can shelter gain from sale of assets.

6. An S corporation can receive the benefits of deferred taxes under the installment sale method when the buyer gives the S corporation qualifying notes. Code Section 453A applies. There should not be a problem when the S corporation does *not* liquidate until after installment notes have been satisfied. Careful planning is required where S corporation plans liquidation immediately after selling. Unless careful planning occurs, Code Section 453B(h) will be major tax trap for the unwary under installment sales provisions of the code.

7. Certain types of assets do not qualify for installment sale tax treatment, and gains are treated as ordinary income with taxes due in the year of the sale. However, a seller must be aware of this tax situation, especially in an installment sale when front-end money could be insufficient to meet tax owed in the year of the sale. Among the assets not qualifying for an installment-sale tax treatment is gain on inventory, personal property sold in the normal course of business on the installment plan, real property held for sale to customers, and so on. Depreciation recapture must be reported as ordinary income in the year of the sale as well. Thus, if you have used more depreciation than straight line and have significant depreciation recapture, a large tax bill could await you in the year of the sale although you won't receive payment for several years.

8. Shareholder approval is required and dissenters' rights are available to selling shareholders.

Disadvantages to Seller

1. C corporation pays a double tax. The gain on the sale of assets is paid at the corporate level. When the C corporation liquidates, the shareholders have a gain if the proceeds received in liquidation exceed their basis in their shares.

2. The sale of assets generates various kinds of gains or loss to the seller based on the classification of each asset as ordinary income or capital gain.

3. The lender's consent is required for the buyer to assume the seller's debt.

4. Seller may not be able to transfer unwanted, disclosed, undisclosed, or unknown off-balance-sheet liabilities such as product liabilities that occurred before the sale.

5. The transaction may be costly and complex when many assets and liabilities are transferred. Title to each asset must be transferred and recorded.

6. The sale of business assets that are tangible personal assets such as machinery and equipment may be subject to a sales tax. For example, Minnesota instituted a 6.5 percent sales tax in 1991 but reversed itself and withdrew the sales tax in June 1992.

7. Gain on depreciable property assets (capital assets) held for more than one year will result in capital gain taxes. The gain can be deferred through installment sales or deferred payments. Taxes are paid when payment is received from the buyer. Recapture of depreciation over straight line, however, will be treated as ordinary income. Taxes will need to be paid in the year of the sale no matter when the income is received.

8. Depreciation recapture, LIFO (last-in, first-out) inventory recapture, gain on the sale of inventory, and accounts receivable are treated as ordinary income. Further, they will be taxed in the year of the sale no matter when income is received.

9. The seller must pay interest on part of the deferred taxes when the seller receives $5 million or more in deferred installment notes.

10. The seller cannot pledge as security for a loan any notes received in an installment sale that has a value more than $150,000. Should the seller pledge as security any notes received from the buyer, the IRS will disallow the deferred payments and make all deferred payments immediately taxable.

11. There is essentially no restriction on the type of consideration that can be used in this transaction. Stock is permissible. However, the use of

stock that is not marketable will cause the transaction to be taxable on the receipt of stock although it does not generate any cash to pay the tax.

12. Bulk sale transfer laws must be complied with in those states having such laws.

Taxable Asset Purchase Summary

Advantages to Buyer

1. Allows a buyer to step up the basis in the assets to purchase price. A buyer depreciates or expenses the assets and realizes full tax advantages on a higher basis in assets. This allows buyers the advantage of expensing or depreciating assets at their fair market value than at the seller's basis. When the purchase price exceeds the fair market value of the assets, the excess must be treated as goodwill. Goodwill is now amoritizable over 15 years as a result of the tax law changes made in the Revenue Reconciliation Act of 1993. See Chapter 13 for a more detailed discussion.

2. The buyer can assume no liabilities, or he can assume specified and scheduled liabilities. In essence, the buyer can select liabilities. Some liabilities follow the assets, however. For example,

   a. Recorded liens follow purchased assets. This includes security interest properly perfected, state and federal tax liens, judgment liens, and mechanics' liens.

   b. The buyer takes over the experience rating of the seller for determining unemployment compensation. Usually, this rating is lower than ratings assigned to a new employer. This condition usually applies only when the buyer acquires all or nearly all the assets. The liability for unpaid unemployment contributions is also acquired. This varies by state.

   c. The buyer may be liable for environmental cleanup costs with respect to purchased or leased real estate. This varies by state.

d. The buyer will be required to recognize and bargain with the union when the buyer retains a majority of the seller's union employees. However, the buyer is not required to accept the before-sale collective bargaining agreement.

e. Successor liability may apply in some states under which the buyer of assets who continues an active business may have responsibilities for seller obligations.

f. Bulk sales transfer laws may also apply. Obligations in favor of a seller's creditors could follow purchased assets unless proper notice is given.

3. Employee benefit plans may be maintained or canceled.

4. The buyer is not bound by any accounting method used by the seller.

5. The buyer's shareholders do not need to approve the acquisition.

6. Since it is unlikely that any stock will be involved in a taxable asset purchase, neither federal nor state securities registration will be required. Form S-4 for federal registration is available should any part of the consideration be stock. State registration generally will not apply when stock is issued because the selling shareholders have been required to approve the sale of the assets.

Disadvantages to Buyer

1. Net operating losses can't be used by the buyer.

2. A seller's business contractual relationship may not be assignable to the buyer. This could include nontransferable rights or assets such as franchises, patents, licenses, and so on. Contract rights and obligations are generally assignable unless the contracts specify otherwise. Generally, important agreements prohibit assignment, and the buyer must secure the consent of the other party.

3. There is no carry-over of a seller corporation's tax attributes such as tax basis of assets, earnings and profits, operating and capital loss carry-forwards, accounting methods, installment reporting, or previous sales and employee benefit plan contributions.

4. Transferring many assets may be more costly and complex than a stock sale, for each asset's title must be transferred and recorded. State sales taxes may apply also. A sales tax generally makes stock deals more attractive than asset transactions because there is no sales tax on the sale of stock.

5. An asset sale could cause the buyer to lose the right to use the corporation's name.

6. Purchase price must be allocated to the assets purchased using the residual allocation method. Any excess of the purchase price over the asset's fair market value must be allocated to goodwill. Goodwill is amortizable for tax purposes over a 15-year period.

7. A buyer may be responsible for product liability claims regarding products manufactured or sold by the seller. Normally, the buyer is not responsible for these claims. Many states are moving in the direction of making buyers in asset sales liable.

8. For accounting purposes, taxable purchase of assets will be treated as a purchase for accounting purposes.

Taxable Stock Sale Summary

Advantages to Seller

1. There is only a single tax to a seller whether an S or a C corporation; there is not a tax to the corporation. Tax is paid at the shareholder level to the extent that proceeds from the sale exceed the basis in the stock. Capital gain taxes apply, for stock is considered a capital asset.

2. All disclosed, not disclosed, unknown, and contingent liabilities can be transferred to the buyer, subject to any covenants of indemnity made to the buyer.

3. Stock sale provides capital gain or loss so that there is no need to determine gain or loss by asset type. Ordinary income gains are usually avoided.

4. Installment sales or other tax deferral methods are possible because stock is treated as a capital asset. Capital gain taxes can be deferred, and the tax can be paid as installment payments are received.

5. There is no sales tax imposed on the sale of stock because it does not involve the transfer of tangible personal property. However, some states do impose a documentary tax stamp on such transfers. Florida is an example.

6. Installment treatment is available on the sale of corporation stock when notes are given by buyer. Buyer notes can't be publicly traded. IRS Code Section 453A, as amended by the 1988 act, imposes an interest charge on the seller's deferred tax liability when buyer notes exceed $5 million. Buyer notes over $150,000 cannot be pledged as security for a loan by the seller. Should this occur, the notes would be immediately taxable.

Disadvantages to Seller

1. Ownership of nontransferable rights or assets such as license, patent, or franchise is lost.

2. The buyer generally will not agree to assume liabilities to employees because the seller's employee health and benefit plans may be self-insured. If the buyer adopts a health and benefit plan less generous than the seller's, employees are entitled to make a Consolidated Omnibus Budget Reconciliation Act (COBRA) election. This COBRA election would allow a seller's employees to maintain coverage under a plan for 18 months. Although employees pay premiums, the premiums may not cover the seller's self-insurance risk.

3. Under current environmental laws, the seller will be liable indefinitely for any environmental problems caused by the seller at any of his facilities. After the sale, it may be difficult to determine whether the buyer increases environmental problems and hazards. Therefore, a seller should have an environmental audit done for his own benefit. This will record the environmental condition of the facilities or property when sold and prevent increased exposure because of what the buyer does after the sale.

Taxable Stock Purchase Summary

Advantages to Buyer

1. The buyer's tax basis in the seller's stock is stepped up to the purchase price. However, there is no step-up in asset basis. This isn't as good as when assets are stepped up. However, when the stock is sold, less tax will be paid on the shares because of the stepped-up basis. This would be important should part of the stock be sold soon after the acquisition.

2. All seller tax attributes carry over to the buyer, that is, tax basis of assets, earnings, operating and capital loss carry-forwards, accounting periods, installment reporting on previous sales, and employee benefit plan contributions.

3. Stock purchase generally avoids restrictions imposed on sales of assets in loan agreements.

4. There are no changes in corporate liability, unemployment, or worker's compensation ratings.

5. Nontransferable rights or assets such as license, a franchise, patent, and so on can be retained by buyer.

6. Stock transfers avoid any sales tax on assets.

7. Right to use corporate name is preserved.

8. Section 338 of the Internal Revenue Code allows a corporate buyer (not an individual) to file a 338 election that allows the assets to be stepped up to a new basis equal to the purchase price paid for the company. This means that a stock purchase is treated as an asset sale for tax purposes. The buyer pays the taxes due. Because the taxes can be substantial, the buyer will ask the seller for a reduction in selling price during the negotiations. For this reason, the seller wants a stipulation in the purchase agreement that prevents a 338 election. A buyer may want a 338 election when net operating losses can be used to offset the gain from the deemed sale of assets caused by the election. Appraisals are required under a 338 election.

9. There is no requirement for allocation of purchase price since the assets of the selling corporation are not the subject of the transaction.

10. The net operating losses survive and go with the buyer since there is no change in the legal entity. A corporation that has generated net operating losses can carry forward those losses in future years to offset its taxable income. When a corporation is acquired, the tax attributes normally continue and include net operating losses. The losses are subject to Section 382 and 384 of the IRS Code and limit the amount of the loss available each year. For example, when the buyer pays $5 million for stock of a company that has $1 million of net operating loss carryforwards, and the long-term tax-exempt rate on government securities is 6 percent, then $300,000 of the $1 million loss (or 6 percent of the selling price) is available to offset earnings each year until used up. Thus a buyer won't pay a premium for net operating losses.

11. Stock transfers are generally treated as a purchase for accounting treatment.

12. Shareholder approval varies by state. Under Minnesota law, when the buyer deals directly with individual shareholders, approval is not required. However, when a plan of exchange approach is used, shareholder approval is required. Dissenters' rights are available under the plan of exchange approach. When the buyer deals directly with individual shareholders, dissenters' rights are limited to the right to retain their stock in the selling company and remain minority shareholders.

13. Normally, a taxable acquisition of stock does not involve the issuance of stock by the acquiring corporation. When no stock is issued, neither state nor federal registration requirements are an issue. However, if stock is a part of the consideration, then Form S-4 is available for federal registration.

Disadvantages to Buyer

1. The buyer acquires the corporation's assets and liabilities including revealed, not revealed, unknown, and contingent. The buyer is not individually liable for the corporation's liabilities. Liabilities may be limited by requiring detailed representations and warranties from the

seller and an indemnification clause in the purchase agreement. Should the seller breach any of the representations and warranties, the buyer may sue for damages. The buyer may also have an offset against damage from undisclosed liabilities by having part of the purchase price placed in escrow to cover unknown liabilities.

2. Assets do not receive a step-up basis. Assets retain and carry over the basis and tax attributes of the acquired company. When assets have been fully depreciated, no additional depreciation is available after the deal is closed. Appreciated assets also retain the presale basis. When these assets are sold later, the buyer must pay tax on the gain.

3. Stock transfers generally result in the continuation of employee benefit plans.

4. Minority shareholders of the selling corporation who oppose the sale of stock may demand an appraisal of the company. Further, they may receive cash payments for their share of the appraised value.

5. Many contracts provide that change in control of a contracting party is an assignment. Thus certain contracts may require approval from the holder just like with an asset sale.

Summary of Three Tax-Free Transactions

In a typical tax-free sale, the shareholders of the selling corporation receive stock of the buying corporation. And they do not recognize any taxable gain or loss until the stock is sold. The exception to the rule is when consideration other than stock is received, such as cash, notes, or other property. This is consideration that is not qualified and will be taxed. The sellers receive stock in the acquiring corporation through a merger or through direct exchange of stock for stock or stock for assets. The tax-free transaction just described is a desirable transaction for seller shareholders who want to defer tax on the gain in their stock and when their shareholders wish to become shareholders in the acquiring company.

The main disadvantage for the sellers of a tax-free transaction is that they will hold the stock of the acquiring corporation and will not have cashed out.

The main advantage to the buying company is that it can use stock as the consideration and not cash. The buyer's main concern will be dilution of stock. As with a stock purchase, the surviving entity of a merger becomes party to all contracts, leases, and other agreements by law. A major caveat is that a change in control can constitute an assignment and require the other party to the agreement to approve the assignment. A merger is treated the same as a stock purchase with respect to the assets. The assets of the merged new company retain the seller's old company's tax attributes and their basis. If these assets already have been fully depreciated, then no additional depreciation will be available to the surviving company.

The surviving company assumes all contractual rights of the selling company. It also assumes all liabilities of the selling company, which becomes part of the new merged corporation.

There are three main types of mergers involving tax-free exchanges. There are several variations of each, but those discussed in the upcoming paragraphs are the major ones. A summary of the key requirements for each is discussed. The summary is not detailed or complete, so you will need to discuss with your legal and accounting advisers the advantages and disadvantages of each transfer of ownership method. However, if you understand the brief explanation given for each requirement, you will have the knowledge needed to ask good questions of your advisers. Of course, this enables you to make the best decision possible.

Type A Merger or Consolidation Summary

Section 368(a)(1)(A)

A merger involves a union of two or more corporations in which one retains its corporate existence and absorbs the other; a consolidation results in the formation of a new corporation to replace two or more constituent corporations that subsequently lose their corporate existence.

Type A Seller's Perspective

1. This is a tax-free transaction for all stock received in the deal. The consideration taxed would be any cash, notes, or property other than stock.

2. This is the most flexible of the tax-free merger plans because up to 50 percent of the consideration received in the transaction can be types of payment other than stock. Of course, consideration that is not stock would be taxable income to the seller.

3. Stock received from the buyer can be in common or preferred stock and need not be voting stock. An important rule is that at least 50 percent of the selling corporation's stock must be exchanged with the buying corporation. The 50 percent rule is applied on an aggregate basis and not on a shareholder-to-shareholder basis.

4. Shareholder approval may be required. Minnesota requires shareholder approval of the selling corporation.

5. The merger may trigger the exercise of dissenters' rights by the shareholders of the selling corporation. Dissenting shareholders may have the right to have the company formally appraised and receive cash based on the appraisal at the time the deal is closed. Generally, when selling shareholders have a right to vote on the merger, dissenting shareholders are entitled to their rights under the law.

6. Federal securities registration is available, and the S-4 procedure may be used. The Form S-4 requires less comprehensive information than the general registration forms (e.g., Form S-1). Registration may be required in the state as well. Registration requirements are not required in Minnesota with this form of a merger.

Type A Buyer's Perspective

1. There is no adjustment to the tax basis of the assets for the buyer. The buyer takes a carry-over basis in the assets from the seller.

2. Net operating losses of the seller survive the closing and pass to the buyer. Net operating losses are limited to the extent of Sections 382 and 384 of the Code.

3. Pooling-of-interest accounting applies and can be used by the acquiring corporation only when 90 percent of the selling corporation's stock is purchased and exchanged for voting common stock of the acquiring corporation.

4. Acquiring company shareholders may have to approve the transaction. Minnesota, for example, requires shareholder approval when there is a 20 percent increase in the amount of voting and participating stock of the acquirer outstanding.

5. Dissenters' rights generally will be triggered when shareholders of the acquiring company are required to vote on the merger.

6. The more simplified federal registration Form S-4 is available. When the selling company is merged into a subsidiary of the acquiring corporation, the results and requirements are similar for both the seller and the buyer. The acquiring company shareholders generally aren't required to approve this type of transaction, and therefore dissenters' rights won't be available. When the selling company is merged into a subsidiary of the buying company, the merger is called a triangular merger.

Type B Stock-for-Stock Exchange Summary

Section 368(a)(1)(B)

The selling corporation becomes a subsidiary of the acquiring corporation. Type B is the most restrictive of the tax-free acquisition techniques in terms of permissible consideration. The only permissible consideration is stock.

Type B Seller's Perspective

1. Seller shareholders exchange their stock with the acquiring corporation.

2. This is a tax-free exchange for selling shareholders.

3. The selling corporation continues to exist and shareholder meetings are not necessary.

4. Consideration that is not stock will not be permitted and only voting stock of the buying corporation may be used. If any nonqualifying consideration is issued, the entire transaction will be treated as a taxable stock sale.

5. The acquiring company must control 80 percent of the total number of shares of each class of stock of the selling corporation. Type B reorganization can go forward even if some shareholders decline to participate in the exchange of stock. This is provided the buyer can purchase 80 percent of the stock of the selling company.

6. Selling shareholders can't sell their shares of the acquiring corporation too soon after the deal is closed or the IRS will take away the tax-free status of the deal.

7. Dissenters' right is a right to retain their stock, not to have the appraised fair market value of the stock paid to them in cash. This rule may apply when the seller negotiates directly with the individual selling shareholders. States vary on the procedure, but this is an example of how Minnesota handles dissenter rights when the selling shareholders deal directly with the buyer.

8. The buyer can elect to proceed with a plan of exchange in some states. Under this form the stock exchange would have to be submitted to shareholders for approval similar to that of a merger or sale of assets. By using this approach, the buyer can purchase 100 percent of the stock as long as a majority of the shareholders approve the transaction. Dissenting shareholders have the right to have their stock appraised and cashed out for the appraisal value. The tax-free nature of the deal can still be preserved for the nondissenting shareholders. The selling corporation buys back the dissenters' stock, and the deal goes forward as a tax-free transaction.

Type B Buyer's Perspective

1. The tax basis of a seller's assets will be carried over. A buyer will also take a carry-over basis in the seller's stock.

2. Any net operating loss carry-overs of a selling corporation will remain with the transaction following the acquisition of the stock. It will be subject to the annual limitation amount under Sections 382 and 384 of the code.

3. There is no change in the legal status of the selling company.

4. Pooling-of-interest accounting treatment will probably be available in this transaction. Pooling-of-interest accounting will not be available if voting preferred stock is used to purchase the selling company. Preferred stock is permissible for the tax-free transaction but will not allow pooling-of-interest accounting.

5. The federal securities simplified registration is available with Form S-4.

6. State registration may be required. Minnesota allows the buyer to deal directly with the individual selling shareholders. He can also file a plan of exchange approach and have the deal submitted for approval to the selling shareholders. Depending on the method used, shareholder and dissenter rights vary.

Type C Assets-for-Stock Summary

Section 368(a)(1)(C)

Type C Seller's Perspective

1. When the buying corporation purchases substantially all the assets of the selling corporation by transferring its common stock, this qualifies as a Type C reorganization. The acquiring corporation assumes only those liabilities it wishes to claim. It is not liable for unknown or contingent claims if it has met the state's bulk sales act requirements. Substantially all the assets means about 90 percent of the fair market value of the net assets of the seller and at least 70 percent of the fair market value of the gross assets.

2. This is a tax-free transaction to the shareholders of the selling company since no nonqualifying consideration such as cash or notes will be issued. Unless the liabilities are small, it will not be possible to use any consideration but voting stock of the acquiring company.

3. Cash, notes, or other property received in the transaction can't exceed 20 percent of the total purchase price because 80 percent of the consideration must be in voting stock. As a practical rule, when liabilities are assumed, no other consideration will be allowed.

4. Selling shareholders generally must approve the transaction.

5. Dissenters' rights generally are available under this transaction since dissenters must approve the sale.

6. State securities registration may be required. When shareholders do not approve the sale, registration may be required.

7. Federal securities registration is available under the simplified S-4 Form registration procedures.

Type C Buyer's Perspective

1. There is no adjustment to the tax basis of the assets of the selling corporation purchased by the buyer.

2. Any net operating losses of selling company will carry over to the acquiring corporation subject to the limitation of Code Sections 382 and 384.

3. Pooling-of-interest accounting may apply since only stock is used to make the transaction. Type C, for tax purposes, allows the use of voting preferred stock as the acquisition consideration. However, when preferred stock is used as consideration, pooling-of-interest accounting is not available. This is because pooling of interest requires that the acquisition must be done in exchange for voting stock of the buyer.

4. The general rule is that the only consideration permitted is voting stock of the buyer. This can be voting common or preferred.

5. Generally, the acquiring company shareholder approval is not required nor do dissenters' rights apply.

6. The simplified federal securities registration procedures with Form S-4 are available. State registration exemptions may apply.

CHAPTER
6
THE IRS IS SMILING

How to Keep the Chips and Stiff Arm the IRS

Your partner in the sale or merger of your company is the tax man. He wants his share of the proceeds from the sale. Not only does the tax man have a keen interest, but your buyer has a keen interest in taxes also.

Your principal goal of tax planning should be to minimize the amount of taxes you pay and by that maximize the amount you put in your pocket. Devising the tax strategy for the sale or merger entails reducing your taxes and providing tax benefits to the buyer at little or no tax cost to you. It is wise to have a tax strategy before you talk price, terms, or anything else with a buyer. Generally, both buyer and seller will try to structure the deal to minimize the aggregate tax costs and allocate the tax burden between them through an adjustment in price. This is why tax planning is so important and why taxes will play a major role in how you structure the deal.

You need to understand several important tax questions to avoid major tax problems when you sell your company.

1. How can you avoid double taxation when you are a C corporation?
2. How much of the purchase price will be long-term capital gain and how much will be considered ordinary income?

3. Can you defer tax obligations by taking part of the purchase price in deferred payments?
4. Can a tax-free sale be accomplished?

AVOIDING DOUBLE TAXATION

If you are a corporation and are filing taxes as a subchapter S corporation, you won't pay a double tax. Double tax occurs when you are a C corporation. The C corporation pays a tax and then the stockholder pays a tax on the distribution of the proceeds of the sale. Any income or property received by a C corporation is taxable to the corporation. When the corporation makes a distribution of property or pays dividends, taxes are paid twice—once by the corporation and once by the shareholder.

You can avoid double taxation if your business is incorporated as a C corporation by selling the stock of the corporation rather than the assets. The sale of stock qualifies as a sale of capital assets by the shareholder and thus is subject to capital gain at the shareholder level. Because the corporation receives no income, there is no tax at the corporation level. Double taxation is avoided. The new owner of the company inherits the liabilities of the company.

The buyer will want just the opposite. He won't want your liabilities, and he will want a higher basis in the assets. The buyer, therefore, will want to purchase the assets of the company and not the stock. By getting a higher basis in the assets, the buyer reduces his income taxes to his new company. The question of an asset versus a stock sale generally results in much negotiation, and sometimes it prevents you from structuring a deal. (See Chapter 5 for a full discussion on the advantages and disadvantages of asset and stock sale transactions.) You can work out a compromise, however, where part of the purchase price is allocated to the common stock and part to a noncompete covenant (see Chapters 12 and 13 for ideas on how to structure deals).

CAPITAL GAINS AND ORDINARY INCOME

Ordinary income and capital gains were treated about the same prior to the Revenue Reconciliation Act of 1993. Whether income received was ordinary income or capital gain, the tax rates were about the same. Consequently, the seller didn't care much how a deal was structured from a tax standpoint when it came to receiving ordinary income or capital gains income. The 1993 tax law changed this situation considerably. A preference is now given to capital gain over ordinary income. You'll pay less tax when you receive capital gain income than when you receive ordinary income. The maximum capital gain rate remained at 28 percent after the 1993 tax law changes. However, the individual tax rates changed considerably, especially for those in the upper income brackets. Pre-1993 maximum tax rates for marrieds filing jointly was 31 percent. After the 1993 tax law, the top rate is 39.6 percent for taxable incomes in excess of $250,000. The taxable income brackets for marrieds filing jointly are:

Up to $36,900	15%
$36,900 to $89,150	28%
$89,150 to $140,000	31%
$140,000 to $250,000	36%
Over $250,000	39.6%

The tax brackets for singles is much worse because the top rates kick in much sooner.

Up to $22,100	15%
$22,100 to $53,500	28%
$53,500 to $115,000	31%
$115,000 to $250,000	36%
Over $250,000	39.6%

One other tax high income earners must be aware of is the alternative minimum tax (AMT) that kicks in if you do too good a job of holding down your regular tax. AMT was a flat 24 percent under pre-1993 tax law. Now it's 26 percent on the first $175,000 of income and 28 percent on higher incomes. Generally these rates apply only to those taxpayers who have substantial itemized deductions.

Tax planning is more important than ever because of the disparity between capital gains and regular tax. The law keeps 28 percent as the top rate for long-term capital gains, the profits from assets owned more than one year; that means the IRS can claim just $280 of a $1,000 profit from a stock sale, while it can take $396 from income that is treated as ordinary income when you are at the top rate. That is a whopping 29 percent less tax for income that is long-term capital gain. So you can see when you sell your business it is going to be very important to know which items will be treated as ordinary income or long-term capital gains. Obviously, selling the stock of your company will result in the best tax strategy for you when you are in the upper income bracket because the income will be taxed as capital gain. Deferring taxes through installment sales and taking stock from the acquiring company will take on increasing importance as a tax strategy.

The tax rate schedules for C corporation taxable incomes are as follows:

Up to $50,000	15%
$50,000 to $75,000	25%
$75,000 to $100,000	34%
$100,000 to $335,000	39%
$335,000 to $10,000,000	34%
$10,000,000 to $15,000,000	35%
$15,000,000 to $18,333,333	38%
Over $18,333,333	35%

The Alternative Minimum Tax (AMT) for corporations is 20 percent. The top corporate tax rate for capital gains is 35 percent. In addition, a corporation may not offset capital losses against ordinary income. Capital losses may be used to offset capital gains only. Any excess capital loss is subject to carry-back and carry-over provisions.

Personal services corporations are subject to a flat 35 percent. This high tax forces the income out of the corporation and is reported on individual income tax returns. Dentists, doctors, and lawyers are typical examples of people who have personal service corporations.

The above tax information is presented so it will alert you of the need to plan your tax moves carefully when you divest a company. It also should serve as a reminder of the need for good tax advice. Remember also that tax laws change regularly so be sure to get updated tax advice.

An Example of Double Taxation

Assume that a C corporation has a combined state and federal income tax rate of 40 percent. Assume also that an individual has the same tax rate of 40 percent. If the corporation earns $1,000, it will pay $400 in state and federal taxes and retain $600. If the corporation's $600 is then distributed to the shareholders, they will pay tax of 40 percent on the $600 or $240. As a result the shareholder retains only $360 of the initial $1,000 earnings. The net result is a punitive tax rate of 64 percent on the earnings of the corporation.

Do the Tax Benefits to the Buyer in an Asset Sale Exceed the Tax Costs of a C Corporation and Its Shareholders?

Generally, the answer is no. The tax benefits to the buyer arising from a step-up amount in the assets are realized over time through depreciation and interest deductions. The immediate cost to the seller is greater than the present value tax benefits to the purchaser. Stock acquisitions are the rule rather than the exception. When the buyer insists on an asset transaction, the seller will want a higher purchase price. A higher purchase price creates further tax liability to the seller and additional financing needs to the buyer.

There is one circumstance where the selling corporation can gain a tax benefit from an asset sale. A corporation with net operating losses or capital losses that are carried forward can be used to offset or shelter the gain realized on the assets sold.

HOW DEFERRED PAYMENTS REDUCE THE TAX BITE

The easiest and simplest way to reduce the seller's tax obligation is to postpone the recognition of gain. This may be accomplished in a tax-free or partially tax-free acquisition or via the installment sale method.

Suppose the seller (S) wants to sell his stock to a buyer (B) for $1,000 and the basis in the stock of S is $0. S agrees to accept $800 in cash and $200 in B's stock. This transaction qualifies as a partially tax-free transaction. S will not pay tax on the $200 gain on the receipt of B's stock. S will be taxed when S sells the stock. Similarly, if S accepts $800 in cash and a $200 debenture, S will not recognize a gain until the principal of the debenture is paid.

The deferral of the tax payment on the receipt of the stock or debenture permits S to reinvest $200 of the consideration undiminished by taxes.

An installment sale occurs when at least one payment is made to the seller after the close of the taxable year in which the sale occurs. An **installment sale** is a sale or exchange for a promissory note or other debt instrument of the buyer.

In an asset sale, all forms of gain normally taxable as ordinary income, are considered ordinary income and are taxed in the year the asset is sold. This rule applies, for example, to the sale of receivables, and inventory. If you receive payments over several years for those assets, you'll pay tax as if you had received full payment in the year of the sale. This is a potential mine field for an unaware seller. Your down payment could be inadequate to cover this tax liability.

The sale of capital assets or stock is a different matter. Deferred payments will result in deferred taxes. A capital asset sold for a promissory note results in the gain on the sale pro rata whenever principal payments on the note are received or when the installment note is paid in full. For example, if you sell a capital asset for $1,000 and the basis is $600, then you have a $400 gain. The gain is 40 percent of the purchase price. Whenever a payment is received under the installment method, then 40 percent of the payment will be treated as taxable gain and the other 60 percent will be treated as a nontaxable return of capital. Any excess depreciation over straight line must be recaptured and treated as ordinary income. This means it will be taxable in the year of the sale although you receive payment over the next several years.

You need to decide the type of income, whether ordinary or capital gain. The definition of ordinary income or capital gain is the same whether in an all-cash purchase or an installment purchase. There is one important exception, however: if part of the sale price is to be paid on an earnout contract or another form of contingency payment, and those purchase payments are made from the earnings of the company, those payments will be treated as ordinary income, not capital gain. In such a case you may have to pay tax on all future earnout earnings in the year the sale was closed. This is not good news. In addition, contingent payments without fixed minimum amounts will not be treated as part of the sale price of the company for tax purposes. Therefore, it will not be used to calculate installment sale income.

When deferred payments are made using seller financing with specific terms, then these fixed payments are regarded as part of the sale price and included in installment sale calculations.

One other caveat. You must charge the buyer an interest rate equal to the current federal rate, or the IRS will impute an interest rate on each payment. This will diminish the benefits of the installment sale by the amount of cash attributable to this interest income.

For example, assume you accept a $100,000, 6 percent, five-year note. Let's say the applicable federal rate (AFR) is 9 percent, compounded annually. The note for tax purposes will be treated as a note with 9 percent interest and a principal amount of $88,331. As a result, the seller will have less capital gain but more interest income over the next five years. Check with the IRS so you know what the rate is before doing any negotiations.

TAX-FREE SALES

Be sure to read Chapter 5, which deals with the sale of assets or stock, because you can do a tax-free exchange and owe no taxes. Chapter 14 has some excellent financing strategies that can significantly reduce the tax bite as well.

Tax laws are complex, and Congress is forever changing them. I hope I've alerted you to some tax pitfalls and issues and the importance of having a deal-doing tax adviser and accountant.

7

PREPARING THE COMPANY FOR SALE

Eight Great Moves to Make Before Selling

What does every buyer want to see in a business? Buyers want to see a well-run, well-managed company with employees who are productive, motivated, and happy. You'll want to do everything you can to achieve this ideal. You'll sell your company faster and for more money when you do.

You'll need to examine some areas before you put your company up for sale. Review each of these and see how you stack up. Make improvements where you can.

You'll need to be sure you are on top of

1. First impressions. They are lasting.
2. Management reports and documentation you'll need.
3. Retention of key employees.
4. Resolving contingent liabilities.
5. A list of inventory, equipment, and other assets.
6. Your contracts. Are they assumable?
7. Your reputation. Is it sterling?
8. Financial statements. They're a buyer's best friend.

FIRST IMPRESSIONS ARE LASTING

We all know the importance of first impressions. When we go to see our banker or a customer, we know how important it is to dress and act properly. The same is true of your company, its employees, and your physical facilities and outside grounds.

Nothing speaks louder than when your buyer drives into your parking lot to inspect your plant and notices it's in poor repair and that the shrubs haven't been trimmed. He notes the debris in the parking lot and that parking space is limited and cramped. When he approaches your building, he sees two employees smoking outside. He sees them butt the cigarettes out on the sidewalk. As he enters the building, he notes the reception area is cluttered and dirty. The receptionist is busy on the telephone and makes him wait without acknowledging his presence. He notes that she is abrupt when she tells him you are on the telephone and that he'll have to wait.

While he is waiting, he sees four people standing in line to use the copy machine. The buyer notices the copy machine is down and that the employees stand around waiting for someone to fix it. He pays close attention to their dress, their demeanor, and their attitude. The lighting is satisfactory, but the office doesn't seem cheerful or well lit. He notices, also, that the carpet is worn and dirty.

Your potential buyer has spent only 3 minutes at your business, but he has learned a lot already. You should do everything to fix up, paint, and add lights wherever you can. Transform your plant into a bright, airy, cheery place. Repair holes in the parking lot. Trim the shrubs and don't forget the rest rooms, lockers, and employee cafeteria. Make them clean, attractive, and odorless. Whatever you spend on painting, cleaning, and brightening up will be returned fivefold: it says you believe in maintenance and have taken good care of the plant; it is not much different from selling a house.

Don't forget the employees. Dowdy, dirty employees tell a potential buyer that your employees are losers. When you can, have dress-up days as well as dress-down days. When bright uniforms are appropriate, use them. Instill pride in your organization.

Imagine the difference when a buyer drives up to your plant and notices that it is well-maintained, attractive, bright, and cheery. Imagine his reaction when he goes into your well-lighted and freshly painted plant and sees well-dressed employees enjoying their work. He sees a winning company that he wants to own.

MANAGEMENT REPORTS AND DOCUMENTATION

Nothing impresses a suitor more than a company that is well run and well managed. When you sell to a larger company, you will be dealing with managers who are MBAs and are accustomed to financial analysis, business plans, budgets, long-range plans, and various financial controls. These buyers are impressed with a management book that contains the various reports each manager receives. Buyers feel more comfortable when they know that decisions are based on accurate, timely information.

Your management book should contain financial statements, sales reports, budget documents, backlogs, production reports, customer analysis, employee policies, operations manuals, and so on. A book with your various day-to-day and longer-term management reports helps the buyer because he knows this information will be available to him after the sale. He'll see what controls are in place and how well organized the company is. He'll also know what improvements he'll want to make. It tells him that management is on the ball here.

Entrepreneurs generally dislike paperwork and resist having organizational charts, employee policy manuals, and job descriptions. They tend to feel this is a waste of time and money. However, an outside buyer doesn't. He feels that it's a sign of a well-run, well-managed company.

Having your financial records audited is worth the cost when it comes time to sell. Most buyers are highly skeptical of financial statements prepared internally. Certified audited statements will be scrutinized far less than internally prepared records. An audit adds credibility to your records, it says you are well managed, and it enables the buyer to obtain outside financing more easily. Audited statements reduce the risk to a buyer. Whenever possible, you'll always want to reduce risk because a buyer will pay more when he sees less risk.

RETENTION OF KEY EMPLOYEES

Many company owners want to sell their business and then hang around just long enough to ensure a smooth transition. Let's say you want to be involved with the business for only six months after the sale. Who is going to run the company when you are gone? Who can run it?

Many buyers do not want to be involved in the day-to-day operations of your company. They'll want someone who is experienced and can run your company, someone who is with your company now. Therefore, you should be preparing, developing, and grooming someone to step in and take over the reins from you. Nothing turns off a would-be buyer faster than learning that the only strong management member of your company is you. So build your management's team now. Buyers like to see strong, capable management.

What should you do if no one on your current management team can run the show? You should anticipate that this could be a problem and be prepared to deal with it. Start by writing a CEO job description and run a blind ad in the classified section requesting resumes and salary requirements. When a buyer expresses a concern about your replacement, explain what you have done and offer the resumes as potential replacements for you.

Buyers will also want to retain those employees who are keys to the success of your company. Their worst fear is that the day they take over your company several key employees will jump ship. One way to alleviate this fear is to identify the key employees and have bonuses tied to a period during which they must remain with the company. Buyers will be comfortable with this idea. You and the buyer should agree on who should receive bonuses and the amount and period involved. A buyer may not always agree with your idea of who the key employees are. Disagreements arise over how long they should remain with the company, or the type and amount of incentive, they should receive. So be sure to develop this idea jointly with the buyer. Be sure to keep updated resumes and recent performance reviews on key employees.

RESOLVING CONTINGENT LIABILITIES

One big worry a buyer has is that contingent liabilities will become real liabilities once he has taken control of your business. Therefore, you should do everything possible to resolve any contingent liabilities before you put your company up for sale. Your buyer will have enough worries of his own and doesn't need to inherit your problems, so try to resolve as many as you can before you sell. The simpler and less complex the sale, the more likely you will get the deal done.

Be sure to resolve any unsettled IRS tax claims. Otherwise, the IRS can put a tax lien against your property at an inopportune time, and this could kill the deal. When an asset sale is contemplated, it could take months for you to get the IRS to settle and remove the lien. The same holds true for local and state tax matters.

Resolve all legal suits and disputes. Settle them before closing, or you'll have to adjust the selling price. A knowledgeable buyer will not gamble on losing cash in a suit of your doing. He'll be extremely conservative in assessing the potential damages and will demand a concession or adjustment to the selling price. You probably can negotiate a deal with your buyer that says something like: "If the suit and fees are less than $100,000, you owe me the difference. If it's more, I'll pay you." The problem with this is that the buyer has no incentive to negotiate and settle for less, so you can bet you won't get a rebate from the buyer.

Settle any pension fund claims and insurance claims. Insurance companies and pension trustees can drag their feet. A buyer knows this, so you'll be wise to resolve these before the close. Remember, you want this sale to be simple, easy, and worry-free for the buyer.

Negotiate and settle any customer and vendor disputes. Again, customer and vendor disputes usually just muddy up the water and make things more complicated than simple. Your goal is to prove that your company is managed well.

One area you cannot ignore is your union contract. Don't sell your company when the union contract is up in three months. A buyer will not want to buy your company when a union contract is about to expire or while it is being negotiated. When the union gets word that your company is for sale, they'll believe they can get a better deal from the new owner—and they are right. The new owner won't know enough about the history of your labor-management relations, and so he won't negotiate very hard. He won't dare risk a strike when he takes over. So, sell your company in the first year of the union contract, not the last year.

Count and List Inventory, Equipment, and Other Assets

Buyers want to know what they are getting for their money. Take a physical count of inventory and equipment. You might be surprised that there is a big difference between what your books show and what you have in the plant. The buyer wants to know the actual count. He'll want a list of inventory and equipment along with cost invoices and a physical count of equipment, inventory, and supplies. If you aren't in the habit of taking regular, physical inventory counts and reconciling the totals with your records, you better start now.

Are Your Contracts Assumable?

When you sell your company's assets, your buyer must renegotiate those contracts that are not assignable, including lease and debt instruments. When the buyer can't assume these contracts without substantial cost increases, he'll expect you to reduce the selling price to cover his increased costs.

It's usually easier and less complicated to sell your business when leases and debt instruments are assumable. Be sure you know which contracts are assumable. Are there any balloon payments and acceleration clauses? When you are negotiating contracts, try to make assumability a part of the contract. You'll be glad you did when you decide to sell your company, especially if you're contemplating an asset sale.

Is Your Reputation Sterling?

Selling your company is a lot easier when your reputation and your company's reputation are solid and above board. You can bet your shirt that a buyer will check out your character and the reputation of your company. The buyer will look into where you live, where you work, and the industry you are a part of. He'll ask questions. Buyers want to hear that you are honest and reliable and that your company sells quality products at a fair price and delivers them consistently on time.

Anything you do now to improve your reputation and your company will make selling much easier and will increase your profits from the sale.

Financial Statements Are A Buyer's Best Friends

The buyer will scrutinize, inspect, and analyze your financial statements more than anything else. He wants proof that your company is profitable. He also will want to know about the quality of its earnings; the buyer will want to know the financial condition of your company and how timely your financial statements are. Generally, he'll want to see monthly financial statements that are prepared as close to month end as possible.

The buyer will calculate and compare with industry averages, receivable collection ratios, and inventory turnover ratios. Try to meet industry averages or expect questions in this area.

Different financial information is important to different buyers. But you would be wise to consider the more important financial ratios and do what you can to bring these ratios up to industry averages. Remember, a buyer views very positively ratios that are above industry averages. What follows is a list of the more important financial ratios besides the receivable and inventory ratios we've already discussed.

Profitability Ratios

$$\text{Return on assets} = \frac{\text{Pretax, preinterest operating profit}}{\text{Total assets}}$$

$$\text{Return on equity} = \frac{\text{After-tax profit}}{\text{Stockholder's equity}}$$

1. A poor return on equity (ROE) can be improved by controlling expenses and keeping sales-to-assets ratios as high as possible.
2. Return on equity can be improved by keeping debt to equity ratios at optimum levels too.

Liquidity Measures

$$\text{Current ratio} = \frac{\text{Current assets}}{\text{Current liabilities}}$$

$$\text{Quick ratio} = \frac{\text{Current assets - inventory and prepaid expense}}{\text{Current liabilities}}$$

$$\text{Debt-to-equity ratio} = \frac{\text{Total liabilities}}{\text{Stockholder's equity}}$$

Besides the receivables, inventory, profitability, and liquidity measures, a sophisticated buyer analyzes many other areas on both your balance sheet and income statement. He'll be looking for trends such as unexplained sudden increases or decreases. He'll examine sales trends month by month, quarter by quarter, and year by year. He'll want to see profitability levels and gross margins for product lines and large customers.

This is why you should prepare a detailed analysis of your current financial situation and condition. Try to see it from the buyer's perspective. Because you have been suppressing profits, you'll want to recast your financials and clean them up so that they illustrate the true earning power of your company.

Get rid of obsolete inventory and equipment. The buyer won't pay for it. He'll get it free. He also won't want receivables more than 90 days old and those he can't collect in 90 days; he'll want an offset against the purchase price for these. Take those bad receivables and write them off, take them with you, or increase the pressure and collect them.

Remove from your company any personal items, such as notes receivable or notes payable, investments, and boats, airplanes, and cars. Also delete from your financials those nonoperating items that are personal and don't contribute to sales. Pay off any notes payable that are owed you. The buyer won't want this; he'll either consider a note payable to you as equity or will ignore it.

When you remove personal items from the financial statements, the buyer is assured that your business is a well-run, professionally managed, clean operation, not a company with hanky-panky, hard-to-figure-out, tricky accounting gimmicks. You'll also simplify your transaction. There won't be any confusion over what is company property and what is personal property.

Planning for the sale at least one year ahead is very desirable, if possible. Besides the suggestions I've already made, you can do early retirements, consolidate offices and departments, and toughen plow-back investments. You can also defer new start-ups or acquisitions and step-up profit incentives for key management.

CHAPTER
8

A BLOCKBUSTER
SELLING TOOL

A Selling Memorandum That Will Make Buyers Beat a Path to Your Door

When you sell your product or services, you have a sales sheet that shows the features, benefits, and specifications of each of your products. It is a four-color glossy that presents your company and product very positively. How much more difficult is your company to sell than a single product? A great deal. That is why you want to prepare a sales presentation prospectus that presents your company in an outstanding and positive light. It should answer many questions a buyer will be interested in and, therefore, save you many hours of answering the same questions repeatedly. This is especially true when your transaction involves more than one buyer or when several buyers take a close look and decide to pass.

When the buying company is out of your region, which often is the case, this selling tool can help interest the buyer in taking a serious look at your company. Without it, most won't look twice.

A well-packaged, tight, precise sales presentation prospectus will be a powerful selling tool when placed in the buyer's hands. Here is your chance to impress a buyer with your management knowledge and skill.

Most entrepreneurs, however, hate paperwork. Putting together a selling prospectus is a real pain and chore. They avoid doing it. They prefer to give the buyer their financials and product catalogs and say, "Here is my business. Make me an offer." *Because the buyer has inadequate information, he passes on the deal because he won't go to the effort to dig for information, or he hedges his bet and offers less.* A buyer needs all the financial, product, customer, industry, marketing, management, facilities, and equipment information possible before he can make an intelligent offer for your company. When it's not readily available, he won't dig for it. But if you do it right the first time, you'll be paid better in the end. Furthermore, your buyer's lawyer will require you to represent and warrant that the information you provide is true, accurate, and complete. Even more reason to have it in writing.

Someone else, such as your merger and acquisition intermediary, can draft the sales memorandum for your review and approval. You can tell the employees who provide the information or who write sections of the selling piece that you need the information for a business plan for a bank, a marketing plan, or for a management consultant. The detailed selling memorandum can present your company in a positive light and highlight opportunities and accomplishments.

Your company's selling memorandum does not need to comply with SEC regulations as would a public stock issue. Consequently, you can use it as a selling tool that points out the benefits of acquiring your company.

Hiding the truth can kill a deal. Nothing is worse than for a buyer to spend much time and money only to discover that you have hidden or distorted some important fact. When the buyer finds out, he won't trust you and will walk away from the deal. His attitude will be, "If he didn't tell me this, I wonder what else he isn't telling me. I don't trust him." You must be totally and completely honest and candid. By mentioning a problem and discussing a potential solution, you have gone a long way toward controlling the problem. Remember, *the buyer is not afraid of risk. The buyer is, however, afraid that he can't manage it.* Show him how the risk can be managed.

Your selling memorandum should be brief, compact, and written with an easy-to-read style. It should answer questions the buyer will ask. Use adjectives and superlatives that a great salesperson would use. Make it as lively and interesting as possible. Write as you would speak. Make the reader want to dive into the material. This isn't a bank loan application; it's a selling tool. Make the buyer drool over your company.

Toot your horn. If your company's management talents are outstanding, say so and support your statement with concrete examples. If you're the only one in the country who owns a new piece of state-of-the-art equipment, say so. When you have the best product, say why.

Remember that your buyer is more interested in the future of your company than in the past. Sure, you have had problems in the past, but look at the opportunities in the future. That is why you need to include a five-year plan. You've got the idea.

The outline that follows contains those areas of information a buyer will be interested in. Adapt, delete, and add to this list as you see the need. Remember the 80-20 rule; that is, be sure to cover the 20 percent of the information that accounts for 80 percent of the business. Don't lose the buyer with trivia.

Your selling tool includes ten important sections. A tool in the hands of the right person can build an empire. This is your turn to sell your empire and amass a fortune in the process. It will be the most important and biggest sale of your life. Do it right the first time.

The outline that follows is self-explanatory. Use it as a framework for writing and developing your selling tool. A discussion of each major area of the outline follows.

YOUR COMPANY'S PAST, PRESENT, AND FUTURE

I. The Kick-off

A. Begin with a hard hitting, two-page summary of the most important selling points you want the reader to know; be sure to pull the best from your industry section and put it up front.

II. Description of Company

A. Outline terms of ownership.

B. Give reason for sale.

C. Provide history of the company. Emphasize major changes in product lines or markets, additions or disposal of facilities, growth trends, and management or ownership changes.

D. Provide key highlights and general business description.

E. List key events that shaped product development.

F. Give sales history by product line.

G. Specify if you own your own supply and distribution system.

H. Describe your major strengths and weaknesses with respect to marketing, finance, production, distribution, management, purchasing, and technology.

I. Describe the company's key success factor, and enumerate why you are competitive in the market compared to your competition in terms of
   1. Price
   2. Technology
   3. Service
   4. Quality
   5. Delivery time
   6. Reputation
   7. Location

III. Offering Price and Terms

A. Specify what is for sale—assets, common stock, real estate.

B. Specify the asking price.

C. Specify the terms.

D. List the nonoperating assets that will be excluded.

E. Outline how you arrived at the price and terms.

F. List any special needs you have that should be met.

IV. Industry, Markets, Products, and Customers

A. Describe industry trends. What is happening? What changes are taking place?
   1. Discuss whether the industry is growing or dying in terms of numbers of companies, sales, and employees.
   2. List the states or regions that are leaders in terms of concentration of companies, sales, and employment.

3. Give the size of the industry as it relates to sales, employees, and number of companies.

4. Specify what percentage of the total market your area or niche has in terms of sales or employees.

5. List your major customers. Describe them.

   a. What is happening to their industries that they sell too?

   b. What trends are developing? See (A)(1).

   c. Devote one page for major customers and a half page for describing smaller customers.

   d. Describe your customer service and what you do to ensure customer satisfaction. How do you measure customer satisfaction?

B. Specify the ranges of products or services offered by the industry. What are the trends in terms of technology, new equipment, new products, and pricing?

C. Describe the major market segment of your industry and any special characteristics it has:

   1. What are your market share and your competitors' by product line?

   2. How big is the market? How fast is it growing?

   3. What are your channels of distribution?

   4. Who are your customers? Why do they buy from you? Do you have any customer with more than 5 percent of company sales?

   5. What markets are your customers in? How large are those markets?

   6. What are the trends in terms of pricing, ease of entry, foreign competition, technology, government regulations, and so on?

   7. Have any changes occurred in market demand?

D. List the trends and conditions outside the control of the industry that determine growth or decline in the industry.

E. Specify if the industry is cyclical or seasonal.

F. Define your industry life cycle in terms of embryonic, growth, mature, or aging.

G. Outline what makes your product or service different from your competition or unique.

   1. Describe your product lines and services offered.

   2. Is it proprietary?

3. Any patent protection?
4. Any trademarks?
5. Any copyrights?
6. Any royalties paid?
7. How are the prices established for your product?
8. Describe who sells and how your products are sold. Tell about your sales force.
9. How are new products developed and brought to market?
10. Are there any new product and marketing opportunities?
11. List the sales by product line for the past three years. Show your product line, the market size, market share, and growth rate of each market.

V. The Human Side of the Organization

A. Provide an organizational chart showing function, title, name, tenure, salary, and exempt or nonexempt status.

B. Describe key management in brief terms, emphasizing their performance, training, experience, longevity, and remuneration.

C. Describe your marketing and sales organization and its strengths.

D. Describe your manufacturing and engineering organizations and their strengths.

E. Describe the financial and administrative organization and its strengths.

F. Briefly describe the bargaining unit and labor relations.

G. Provide a three-year history of the numbers of full-time and part-time employees and outside independent contractors by major job title.

VI. Real Estate, Machinery, and Equipment

A. Briefly describe the plant or buildings, age, condition, physical dimensions, and locations.

1. Include in the appendix a drawing of the plant.
2. Include in your appendix any recent appraisal and list the book value and estimated fair market value. How was FMV determined?
3. Include in the appendix a location map and photo of plants and buildings.

B. Describe the machinery and equipment.

    1. List and describe the machinery and equipment's age, condition, book value, and fair market value.

    2. Attach any recent appraisals and place in the appendix.

    3. Where machinery and equipment lists are too many, limit the list to those pieces over a certain dollar value and lump and estimate miscellaneous items.

C. Show whether you lease or own assets.

D. Any real estate or equipment owned personally that is not on the company's balance sheet should be so designated and listed separately.

E. Provide colorful photos showing people working in the plant, key equipment, and an aerial view of the plant. Pictures sell.

VII. Geographic Description

A. Briefly describe the state and city using demographics and descriptions from the Chamber of Commerce and the state commerce department.

B. Include a map showing your company and plant locations.

VIII. Sell the Future—What Is Your Five-Year Plan?

A. List your five-year goals for the company.

B. Specify the strategies or tactics you will apply to achieve your goals.

C. Enumerate the important risks, assumptions, and problems that exist.

IX. The Financial Story

A. Provide three-year, audited or reviewed financial statements, with month-to-month and quarterly sales graphs for the past three years.

B. Provide three-year adjusted income and pretax cash flow statements and a one-year adjusted balance sheet.

    1. Give reasons why you made adjustments.

    2. Provide clear documentation of adjustments made.

    3. Specify if you have considered operating versus nonoperating assets.

C. Five-year pro forma financial statements. Listed assumptions are

    1. Tied to a five-year strategic plan.

2. Clearly defined and documented.
3. Expected local, regional, national, or international economic growth based on gross domestic product, interest rates, and inflation.
4. Expected industry growth based on solid third-party estimates.
5. Capital equipment needs.
6. Sales forecasts by product line and product mix.
7. Pricing and gross margin assumptions and rationale such as competitor impact on prices.
8. Labor increase assumptions.
9. Other assumptions can be based on historical averages such as inventory turns, number of days in accounts receivable, and so on.
10. Key ratio analysis compared to history and industry standards.
11. Assumptions should include a statement that the company will be run like a public company with emphasis on maximizing profits than minimizing them.

X. Appendix

A. Company financial statements

B. Product literature

C. Asset lists and appraisals

D. Maps and drawings

E. Photos

F. Resumes of key management

THE KICK-OFF

This section is your best chance to get the buyers' attention so they'll read your report. You must make them hungry enough that they will want to feast on the meat of your selling tool. This section will include very brief excerpts from the main body of your selling document. It should be the complete essence of the transaction and should contain the information that could be communicated in a three- to five-minute oral presentation. Remember, this is like the beginning of any book. If the reader's interest isn't whetted at the beginning, he won't make it to the end.

DESCRIPTION OF THE COMPANY

Here is where you cover the key points about the company including ownership (whether this is a C or an S corporation) and the reason(s) for selling. The reasons for selling are very important to the buyer, and you must satisfy this need by revealing your true reason here. If you are bored and want to retire, say so. If you are tired of the pressures of meeting a payroll, say so. Whatever your reason, it is okay.

Outline the key success factors of your company; it's an important segment. Be sure to include both your strengths and your weaknesses. For example, if your company is strong in sales, make that known by saying something like: "Our sales have averaged 15 percent compounded annual growth over the last three years. This is twice the industry average." If you have a proprietary product or are a leader in a market area, highlight this. A buyer will drool over a company that has a proprietary product and is a leader in its market.

If you feel you are undercapitalized for growth, say so. There are many buyers with cash who will see an opportunity in your weakness. If you are strong in production but weak in sales, stress that. A buyer sees your weaknesses as an opportunity. When you have had a product failure, say so and detail both what went wrong and how you are solving the problem.

Be brief when discussing the history of the business. Include important happenings, whether it is a new plant built because of a fire or a new product that sold like crazy.

Under the ownership section, be sure to list all the shareholders along with the number of shares and percentages each owns. If there are too many shareholders, then list those who own 5 percent or more of the stock. You can write this section. Use the outline and pick those areas that are most important to you. Sell the sizzle!

Briefly tell about your five-year strategic plan and how, for example, you expect annual growth rates of 10 percent. "The growth will come from existing customers and a new account sales program or sales force expansion. A revamped sales organization, and the introduction of two new product lines, will set our company on fire." Use a little enthusiasm. These predictions may not happen, but the possibilities are what dreams are made of. Your plan is just that—a plan with many assumptions and conditions that your company must meet for it to achieve your goals.

You and your merger and acquisition broker or consultant now have this buyer 50 percent sold. That is one benefit of using a merger and acquisition consultant/broker. He'll screen out the tire kickers and competitors so that only the qualified buyers will have access to this proprietary sales tool.

OFFERING PRICE AND TERMS

You might say something like this:

"This is a restricted private offering for the negotiated sale of certain common stock owned by Ohio Five Star Corporation of Columbus, Ohio. All inquiries concerning this offering should be directed to Robert Bergeth, International Mergers and Acquisitions, exclusive agent to the seller."

"All common shares of the company are offered for a sale price of $10 million cash at closing. This must be a stock sale as no offers for all or part of the assets will be considered. Current and projected earnings support this price. After January 1, 199X, this offer will be withdrawn."

You don't need to say any more about price and terms. You have just completed the first round of negotiations and easily won the round. You have set the pace of negotiations by taking a stand on a stock sale and termination date. You have left a little wiggling room for negotiation on price and terms. You have him on the ropes. He must try to figure out how much you are willing to give away in terms and how firm you are on price. You have boxed him into the corner, and it's only round 1. You are winning the fight.

INDUSTRY, MARKETS, PRODUCTS, AND CUSTOMERS

Market research is the key to selling your company for the most profit. What is the future potential of your company? Can you clearly document this future?

The buyer is interested in the future of your company. That is how he'll be paid. A bad past is okay. A bad future isn't. The buyer won't be paid on what your company did in the past, so sell the future of your industry, your markets, product, and customers. The better job you do here, the more excited your buyer will be about your company and the more he'll be inclined to pay for it.

Begin by identifying the size and growth of your industry and the industries your key customers sell too. Sometimes information isn't readily available. But there are ways to estimate the growth and size of your market and industry. Use third parties to cite growth and size because it is much stronger and more credible than if you say it. Provide documentation in the footnotes.

Try using competitor credit reports. You can quickly build and prove the industry average by listing the competitor's name, revenue, and profits. By knowing what percentage of the competitor's revenue is profit for each of the past years, you have a way to find out average growth of those profits. For example, review Table 8.1:

TABLE 8.1
Industry Average Growth

Year	Revenue	Profit	Profit %
199X	$10,000,000	$800,000	8%
199X	$11,000,000	$990,000	9%
199X	$12,000,000	$1,200,000	10%

You can see the average profits have been growing by 1 percent each year. Sales have been growing by 10 percent annually. Buyers like to see the revenues and profits of others who are in the same business they are thinking of entering. They think, "If others can do it, so can I." Try to break down the markets you sell and do it for your competitors. Try to find an industry source, analyst report, or publication that quantifies the size and growth and outlook for the industry. For example, consider the data in Table 8.2:

TABLE 8.2
Size, Growth, and Outlook for Market Segments

	Market Size	Industry Annual Growth	Market Share by Self (S) and Competitor (C)			
			S	C1	C2	C3
Financial Services	10,000	10%	60%	20%	10%	10%
Printing	15,000	7%	25%	25%	40%	10%
Publishing	50,000	5%	15%	10%	50%	25%

A reader can quickly see that you are number one with 60 percent of the market share in financial services. Financial services are growing at 10 percent a year, and you and your competitors are selling $10 million a year to that market. Identify your sources in the footnote. There is no question about your strength in this market.

The buyer wants to know your largest markets, their size, who your competitors are, and their share of the market. How do you reach or sell these markets? What are your plans to hold those markets? Let's see how you might do it.

Financial Services Market. You might begin your report on the market section by describing your largest market. For example,

"Financial services are our number one market in size with combined sales of $10 million. We sell $6 million to this segment and control 60 percent of the market. We are a market leader selling three times the product to this segment than our nearest competitor. The market is growing at 10 percent a year and will continue to expand at that rate for the next five years (name source). Sales to that industry should equal $16 million by 199X. If we hold our market share, our share will be $9.7 million."

"There are 37 major customers in this market. We sell 20 of these customers 50 percent or more of their purchases of similar products in a given year. None of these customers accounts for more than 5 percent of the company's sales. Each has been with us for three years or more, and 10 of them have been our customers for more than 15 years. Our gross margins are above industry averages."

"Because shipping costs are high, it is very difficult for a new competitor to enter our market. While the market is mature, we see a continued need for years for our product."

"Our number one competitor is Company X located in Dallas. Its sales are $25 million. Its product pricing levels are about the same as ours, but we believe we can produce our products for less than X can. We are nonunion and it is union. In the past five years X had one strike lasting a month. We know our morale is higher because three of its employees have come to work for us. We haven't lost a single employee to Company X. X is strong competition but not predatory."

"Because of the quality of our product and our outstanding service, we should continue to maintain our market share. Further, we have identified a new product need for this market that we will introduce by 199X. In addition, we are pulling one salesperson from our national accounts to beef up coverage of this market segment. Our goal is to dominate our local market and carefully expand our regional market."

"The members of our sales force are specialists in each market segment, such as financial services. Our salespeople are the best trained and most knowledgeable in our industry. We place great emphasis on this area. Sales turnover is below the industry average because we have a competitive compensation system and treat our sales force with respect. We listen to them. We want to know how they view our products and what customers say. Our product sales managers are responsible for all phases of the business and have both sales and profit responsibilities. Manager bonuses are tied to attaining profit quota levels. This will ensure that we continue to make profitable sales to these markets."

"Products are delivered to the door of the customer by our own trucks. While our products tend to be commodity-like, we break our backs on quality, delivery, and service. We are leaders because we work hard on this phase of the business. Because our service and quality are top notch, our margins remain at industry averages. We also avoid government contracts or customers who use mostly bid practices. We go after bid business in situations where a piece of equipment has a low backlog and then do so only during the slowest part of the year."

"Our suppliers are nearby; therefore, we seldom need to back-order products to our customers, although our inventories and raw materials are lower than industry averages. We have backup suppliers and try to maintain three vendors in all key areas."

You have the idea. If you've got it, flaunt it. Focus your industry story on your best markets where your strength is, where 80 percent of your products are sold. Where your markets are weak, explain why and outline a brief plan. If there are threats to the industry, say it—but tell how to manage the risk.

Focus on the big picture, those things that are really important. You can conclude this section by saying you have a detailed strategic growth plan for the next five years. You will share this with the buyer once his due diligence begins and he's signed a letter of intent.

You can see how important this is to a buyer from outside your market. Let's say your business is pretty much regional and confined to a five-state area. A buyer from outside your region could read this and become excited about buying your company and expanding his company through an acquisition. It could also be a supplier to your market who would understand the size, scope, and the role you play in it.

Keep the buyer focused on the future of your company. You want to sell the future, not the past. That is why the buyer is interested in your company and will pay you a premium for it.

THE HUMAN SIDE OF YOUR ORGANIZATION

You have discussed everything but the most important part of your organization: the people who make things happen. The buyer will analyze your management team very closely. He'll want to know that he is inheriting a strong team to work with. So, coach, you must sell that great team you've put together.

Don't ignore this section. Include each of the seven points in the outline. Yes, you don't have an organizational chart because you think it's a waste of time. It is not a waste of time, however, to the foreign buyer or the buyer far away. These buyers want to see it. You might as well prepare the chart now. The buyer knows his lenders must be persuaded that no personnel or human resource problem will prohibit or harm his chances for success.

The organizational chart gives a bird's-eye view. If you need to, use several pages to show the levels of management and salaried employees. You won't need a chart for hourly employees. Start with a box for each key manager who reports to the president. You must provide the key elements about each position, including function, title, name, tenure, salary, exempt or nonexempt status, and number of people reporting to that position. Here is an example for your sales or marketing head.

SALES
Vice President
Mary Smith
15 years—$75,000
(E) 8

For a floor supervisor it might look like this:

```
┌─────────────────────────────────┐
│        MANUFACTURING            │
│      Production Supervisor       │
│         Tom Anderson            │
│      22 years—$27,000           │
│            (E) 10               │
└─────────────────────────────────┘
```

Then list the number of people by job title in each department. You should profile your key managers, emphasizing their experience and tenure with the company along with their education and key accomplishments with your company. Who is the person who can run the company when you are gone? Build him up.

If you are a union shop, mention it but don't dwell on it. If labor relations have been good, say so and stop. There is no need to raise questions.

REAL ESTATE, MACHINERY, AND EQUIPMENT

You need to decide what the operating and nonoperating items will be and those you plan to keep personally, sell, or leave with the business. Place your lists and fair market values of them in the appendix. The fair market values let the buyer know you value the hard assets at more than what the books say. The fair market values say you know the score and he is going to have to pay for them. You will need to justify and document why you value these assets higher than book value. Good documentation will give your assets and you more credibility.

In a half page, summarize the data from the outline and make sure you highlight all the important points. The lists can go in the appendix along with any appraisals.

Do you have too many assets and don't want to list them all? If so, choose a dollar figure and report only those at or above this amount and estimate the remaining dollar amount.

GEOGRAPHIC DESCRIPTION

Out-of-state buyers may not be knowledgeable about your state and community. It is important that you present the buyer with current geographic and community information.

Your local Chamber of Commerce or local or state industrial or development commission publishes the information you need.

You also need to sell the buyer on the community and state in which your business or plant(s) is. Devote a half page to a full page to this information.

SELL THE FUTURE—WHAT IS YOUR FIVE-YEAR PLAN?

By now you know the buyer is more interested in the future than the past. That is why you must discuss the future. You want the buyer to pay for that future.

This section doesn't need to be long, nor is it necessary to give away any company secrets. You must list your five-year goals and support them with strategies and assumptions. Limit your discussion to three important goals.

Here is how it might go for one objective:

"Our company's sales will grow at a minimum rate of 10 percent compounded annually, resulting in sales of $25 million by 199X."

"To accomplish this objective we will employ the following tactics:

1. We will cut back our national sales efforts to focus on the East Coast. Consequently, two national account reps will be shifted to the East Coast and will be assigned to the financial services market, our fastest-growing market.

2. We will flank the market leader in uncontested areas by redirecting our telemarketing efforts into the areas where our sales reps aren't making calls.

3. We will change the focus of our advertising from women, ages 16–35. This market segment is growing at only 3 percent per year. Our new focus is women, ages 35–54, a market that is growing 12 percent annually.

4. We will retain more customers by improving customer service. We will print a toll-free telephone number on each product package so customer complaints can be handled quickly.

5. Our customer order turnaround will be improved by 20 percent. We will reduce our turnaround time by 6 days. The previous average of 30 days will be reduced to 24 days. We'll accomplish this through improved scheduling, shipping, and order processing.

6. We will conduct customer surveys annually rather than every two years. Top management will identify trends and major problems we need to resolve. We will hold focus groups for each product line.

7. We will upgrade product line B, making it the best in the industry. This will result in a quality image and higher profit margins.

8. We will reposition product line C to emphasize reliability and value.

9. We will replace all manufacturer reps by company sales reps in the financial services market segment. This is the fastest-growing segment in our company.

10. New business development will receive top attention by management. Monthly recognition and awards will be personally presented to the top salespeople in each division by top management."

You have the idea. Limit your discussion to three objectives and then list some strategies. Don't list anything you feel uncomfortable in revealing to a buyer. If you are planning to introduce new products, just say you have a strategic plan. You'll share the details with the buyer after he signs a letter of intent and is well on his way to signing a purchase agreement. Confidentiality is very important. Do not put anything in this report that could hurt you if it got into the wrong hands. Prepare the report with the idea your competitor is going to read it. You can have proprietary information available for the buyer after the letter of intent and purchase agreement have been signed and are close to the final closing date. This is the safest way to release proprietary information.

The Financial Story

Your buyer will scrutinize the financial section. It is a crucial section that must be thoroughly researched and professionally presented.

The financial section consists of the three following parts:

1. Historical financial statements for the previous three years, including income and balance sheets. Also, include the most recent cash flow statement.

2. Restated or recast three-year historical income statements and one-year restated balance sheets.

3. Five-year pro forma income, balance sheets, and cash flow statements tied to your five-year strategic plan.

Each of these sections should clearly document the underlying assumptions. The financial statement adjustments should be clearly identified so it is possible to see how the historical and adjusted financials compare and why any differences occurred.

Be sure to identify clearly how much money you have taken out of the company and how much money you plan to take out in the future. A genuinely interested buyer can obtain complete financial statements, both actual and forecast, later. Therefore, this section should focus on highlights of the past statistics. The forecasted five-year plan includes sales, operating profits, income taxes, and net profit. You'll need to itemize key balance sheet items such as receivables, inventory, and capital expenditures.

Your purpose in this section is to be truthful yet to whet the buyer's appetite without going into many pages of numbers and details. The due diligence phase is when the buyer can get a complete picture of your financials. There is no need for full details here.

Be absolutely certain, however, that you are truthful about historical events. When the buyer does his due diligence, he'll be working from your tax returns and audited financial statements.

APPENDIX

The appendix is the place to put all key samples of product literature, resumes of key management, and lists of assets and appraisals. It's also a good place to include several photos that tell the company's story. Nothing speaks better about your people, facilities, and operations than a good picture or two. Also, include maps and drawings of your plant's location in the community.

You could include detailed company financial statements here if you decide that is desirable. This is especially helpful when the expected buyer might be some distance away.

9

RECAST YOUR FINANCIALS

Show Your Company's Maximum Earnings

Public and privately owned companies are managed in entirely different ways. Public companies try to maximize earnings to increase the price/earnings ratio of their stock, and by that increase the value of the stock. Privately owned companies, on the other hand, try to keep profit levels to a minimum, and by that reduce the income tax bite as much as possible.

Private companies reduce their income tax liability in many different ways. As a result, the profits they report on their income statements do not reflect the true earning power of the company. Because value is at least partly a function of earnings, the greater the earnings, the greater the value of the company. It is, therefore, necessary to adjust or recast both the income and balance sheets. The idea is to show the company at its maximum earning power than its minimum.

Balance sheet assets are reported and valued at their original cost. Original cost is important for historical and tax purposes, but is meaningless for valuing a company at today's value. One example could be that land purchased ten years ago is worth twice as much today. The same can be said for other real estate, equipment, and plant. These values must reflect the fair market value today.

When both the income statement and balance sheet have been adjusted to their fair market values, you'll show your company's maximum earning performance. Adjust tangible assets only. When adjusting the financial statements, be sure to keep accurate, detailed records of those changes. The buyer will want to see those adjustments and the detail supporting them. He will want to know that the adjustments are fair and reasonable and that the changes aren't inflated, thus distorting the financial picture of the company.

DECIDE WHICH ARE OPERATING AND NONOPERATING BALANCE SHEET ASSETS AND LIABILITIES

Assets

An operating asset gives value to an operating company. An operating asset or liability is one that is an integral part of the normal day-to-day operations of a company. It contributes to the sales of your company. The most obvious items are cash, accounts receivables, inventory, and prepaid expenses. Nonoperating expenses are owned but are not a part of the day-to-day operations, such as investments, excess cash, cash value of life insurance, obsolete equipment, and old inventory. So are owner perks, such as a condominium, car, boat, airplane, and so on, as well as any accrued or prepaid income tax.

When selling your business, it is best to exclude all nonoperating assets and liabilities from the business. Generally, the buyer will not pay for these. The rule is if the asset or liability doesn't contribute to the sales of your company, it is nonoperating and should be excluded. If you decide to include nonoperating assets in the sale, make sure they add to the purchase price; otherwise, the buyer is getting those assets for nothing and you receive no value for them.

Let's examine some common balance sheet items and see which are operating and are nonoperating items.

Cash

Cash is usually stated at fair market value on the books, and you don't need to adjust unless excess cash exists. For example, if you normally have three weeks' cash on hand and you now have six weeks', you could remove three weeks' cash. Cash is a necessary operating asset, and some cash should remain with the company. Cash includes marketable securities and certificates of deposit.

Accounts and Notes Receivable

The value of accounts and notes receivable is the present value of the expected collections. Prepare an accounts receivable aging report. Discount or write off past-due accounts. Bad debts should reflect today's debts, and reserves should be increased or decreased accordingly. Some companies carry receivables on their books indefinitely, with little or no doubtful account allowance. This results in an overstatement of earnings and net asset value. On the other hand, an aggressive write-off policy that writes off receivables that are later collected understates the earnings and net asset values.

When the owner has borrowed money from the company, you should write off or forgive the loan. Sell notes from employees at a discount to a bank or finance company. These all are examples of nonoperating assets.

Inventory

Value inventories at current replacement cost. Sell obsolete, excess, and slow-moving inventory. The buyer won't pay for this. If you don't sell the excess, obsolete, or slow-moving inventory, then the value should reflect its value today and be discounted accordingly. Inventories are operating assets.

Prepaid Expenses and Other Assets

This category represents amounts paid in advance by a company for benefits or services to be received in the future. Common items are insurance payments, rent, commissions, and real estate taxes. Remove any nonoperating expenses.

Fixed Assets

Fixed assets are usually long-term operating assets used by a business over several years, such as machinery and equipment, trucks, forklifts, office furniture, computers, and so on. Fixed assets also include land and buildings. Eliminate nonoperating assets, such as land held for investment, from this category. All fixed assets should be adjusted to reflect their fair market value. This is an example of the hidden value a buyer will try to get without paying for it.

Other Assets

This is a collection of items, and some may not be operating assets. Officers' notes receivable, investments, and the cash value of life insurance are not. They are nonoperating assets.

Liabilities

Let's look at liabilities. Most accounts payable are operating expenses. So are accrued wages and accrued expenses, such as accumulated vacation and sick pay earned by employees that have not been paid. Unpaid sales commissions and portions of annual property taxes that should be charged to this year but haven't been billed yet. Accrued expenses are estimates, while payables are exact and have an invoice. All are examples of operating expenses.

Loans, debt, and other notes payable are gray areas. Debt is a capital structure decision and, therefore, nonoperating. However, buyers frequently assume the debt of the company, which is part of the purchase price.

You can successfully present the adjusted balance sheet to a buyer with or without the debt. This is because different buyers will be shown a standard presentation. You want to appeal to many buyers, not just a few. Some buyers will have lots of cash or will have their own sources of financing. These buyers may not want to assume any of the existing debt. Other buyers may want to assume as much debt as possible.

The debt-free presentation is simple and easy to comprehend. A buyer can look at a debt-free company and see several financing possibilities. When you present him with only one scenario, it may not meet his needs. A debt-free company is very appealing to a buyer because he can use part of the assets to finance the purchase price. A debt-free situation gives him more financing possibilities.

When you deduct debt, you'll deduct interest payments on the income statement side as well. When debt is left in the balance sheet and it is interest bearing, you must leave that portion of interest in as an expense on the income side also.

Whatever you do, keep verifiable, accurate, detailed records of the adjustments you make to your balance sheet. The buyer will insist on seeing these.

One of your first decisions should be to decide which assets and liabilities you will sell with the business and which you will not sell.

An owner of the company has several options with nonoperating assets. The seller can take possession by transfer of title, the items can be sold separately from the company, or the items can be included in the sale.

Once you have figured out which assets and liabilities are nonoperating, you adjust the remaining operating assets and liabilities to make sure they represent the current fair market value.

THE INCOME STATEMENT

Buyers will pay more for a company when long-term sales trends and profits are growing and predictable. Consequently, you need to show at least three years of adjusted income statements.

There are several methods of presenting income statements with adjustments. The best way is to show your standard income statement. Each adjustment is then presented along with a footnote that explains the adjustment.

Adjustments or recasting of the income statement can be classified in four areas:

1. Nonrecurring expenses
2. Owner-related personal and family perks and expenses
3. Nonoperating income and expenses
4. New owner organizational changes

Nonrecurring or Extraordinary Items

In analyzing a company's historical earnings as a guide to estimating the company's earnings base, reasonable efforts should be made to adjust the income statement to eliminate past items that misconstrue the company's current and future earning power. Both extraordinary gains and losses must be *unusual* in nature and *infrequent* in occurrence. Unusual in nature means the event or transaction should possess a high degree of abnormality and not be related to, or only incidentally related to, the ordinary and typical activities of the business. By infrequency in occurrence, it means that the item would not reasonably return in the future. Since the extraordinary designation is so restrictive, many items will not meet the strict definition for accounting purposes. However, many items may be regarded as nonrecurring. Some items that could be considered nonrecurring are

1. Gains or losses on the sale of assets. These gains or losses on assets are those assets not sold regularly as part of the operating income of the company.
2. Proceeds from the settlement of a lawsuit.
3. Insurance proceeds from a property or casualty claim. Life insurance proceeds on a key manager.
4. Effects of a strike.
5. Gains or losses from the sale of a segment of the business.

Personal and Family-Related Perks and Expenses

The owner of a company rightfully is entitled to take money out of the company in various forms. For example, it could be from rent above the current market rates that his company pays for the building he owns personally. It could also be for the salaries above fair market salaries for the seller and members of his family. It could also be the limousine and full-time driver available for himself and family, travel and entertainment excesses, automobile, insurance, and so on. Pension fund contributions are another area to which he may have made significant contributions.

Don't eliminate all expenses, just those that are more than what a company would have to pay someone else to manage your company. Good documentation is essential and will be required by the buyer.

Nonoperating Income and Expenses

The most common nonoperating item is income from investments. Income or expense adjustments could also occur with real estate and the cash value of life insurance.

New Owner Organizational Changes

A new owner of the company may reorganize the company. It might be a new corporation that has just purchased the assets of your company, for example. Frequently, the owner of real estate will want to sell the business but not the plant or building. The seller may need and want the depreciation from these assets to shelter ordinary income received from the sale of his company. Consequently, the buyer will lease the building from the seller at current market rates. The difference between current lease rates and costs associated with the plant in the income statement should be reflected in the adjusted income statement.

CAPITALIZATION VERSUS EXPENSING OF COSTS

Many items fall into a gray area that requires a judgment call to decide if an item should be expensed or capitalized. Companies that want to show good earnings will capitalize an item that falls into a gray area. Companies that want to reduce their income taxes will expense rather than capitalize an item whenever possible. One gray area is maintenance expenditures. An item could be written off in the year the work was done, or it could be capitalized. Certain leases are called capital leases and must be capitalized, and certain leases are operating leases and must be expensed. Often an argument can be made either way; that is, the lease can be expensed or capitalized.

METHOD OF DEPRECIATION

Depreciation can be either straight line or some form of accelerated depreciation. Straight line is the most conservative of the depreciation methods. A company that uses a conservative depreciation method will show greater earnings on its income statement. Conversely, accelerated depreciation or more aggressive depreciation will result in reduced income statement earnings. Because many buyers will base their valuation on the earnings of the company, any company with a lot of accelerated depreciation will be perceived as being less valuable than one whose earnings are based on more conservative depreciation practices. The method of depreciation should be explained and emphasized if it is to the seller's advantage.

INVENTORY ACCOUNTING METHODS

The method of accounting for inventory can affect the cost of goods sold and earnings. FIFO, or first-in, first-out, inventory accounting method assumes that the first unit of an inventory item purchased is the first unit sold. LIFO, or last-in, first-out, inventory accounting assumes that the last unit of inventory purchased is the first one sold. The difference between FIFO and LIFO shows up in the ending inventory on the balance sheet, affecting both the costs of goods sold and earnings. When prices are going up, LIFO inventory accounting results in lower earnings for the company than if FIFO is used. Since LIFO inventory accounting is acceptable for federal income tax purposes, many companies use LIFO rather than FIFO. When there have been significant inventory cost increases, a business that wants a higher valuation would be wise to use the FIFO method of accounting. Earnings will be greater, and as a result, the company has greater value, especially when valuation is based on earnings.

REVENUE AND EXPENSE TIMING

Many companies recognize revenue and expenses in different timing periods. For example, expenses could be deferred into the next fiscal year of the company. The result could be a significant increase in earnings. Billings could be recorded as revenues, but the actual collection of the receivable could be so far into the future that the receivable may never be collected. For example, when a company introduces a new product to the retail discount market, it is not unusual for that product not to sell through the stores. As a result, there could be huge returns of the product.

For these reasons, a wise buyer does not base the value of the company on the most recent one-year earnings history. He knows that the earnings can be manipulated. As a result, valuation will be based on the last three to five years of earnings. The buyer knows that it is much more difficult to manipulate the numbers based on the last several years than only one year. Sellers who try to fool the buyer by manipulating the most recent year's earnings in the hope of gaining a better price usually are only fooling themselves. Once a buyer figures out what has happened, he won't trust any of the seller's numbers, and the deal will be aborted.

SUMMARY

You have now identified the operating and nonoperating assets, liabilities, income, and expenses. You have decided which items you'll include in the sale and the ones you'll leave out. You have also established the fair market value of assets and adjusted the balance sheet and income statement.

Your current balance sheet is now irrelevant because the values now assigned are based on cost, not on current fair market value. When the fair market value is different from the value shown on the balance sheet, you need to make an adjustment.

Fair market value is not liquidation value, something that asset-based lenders base a loan on. It is not replacement value, nor is it salvage or insurable value. Fair market value is the value for a similar item, the amount someone would pay if he located, purchased, and installed a similar item. A similar item is one with similar age, similar utility, and similar condition.

Accounts receivables are decreased by the amount of uncollectible accounts or bad debt. Inventory is generally book value less any obsolete inventory. Inventory is based on the current value of inventory. Thus, if inventories have gone up in value, use the current value. If current prices are less, then use that value.

You've eliminated the nonoperating items and assets are now at fair market value. The adjusted balance sheet is complete and should be included in the selling documents.

While the all this sounds like work, begin by focusing on the major items and ignoring the smaller stuff. You may use only part of what we've discussed. When you use the excess earnings method of valuation, you and the buyer can agree to the value of assets. You can get a businessperson's appraisal of assets that will give a reasonably accurate assessment of the value of the assets. This appraisal can go in your selling document. If the buyer won't agree with the values you have assigned to the assets, the contract for sale can be written subject to an appraisal of the assets. Just remember, a buyer will be thinking of using those assets to help finance the deal. His lender will want an appraisal. That lender appraisal will be conservative, to please the lender. You don't want liquidation value; you want fair market value. The appraiser can do both.

The income statement and balance sheet presented in Tables 9.1 and 9.2 are examples of how one company might appear after the adjustments have been made.

TABLE 9.1

Seller's Income Statement Before and After Adjustments (in 000s), December 31, 199X

Total sales	$15,750
Cost of goods sold	11,250
Gross margin	$ 4,500
Operating expenses	
General and administrative	1,800
Depreciation	300
Other operating expenses	1,050
Total operating expenses	$ 3,150
Net operating income	$ 1,350
Interest expense	90
Pretax income	$ 1,260
Adjustments	
Owner-related items (1)	$ 587
Nonrecurring items (2)	90
Nonoperating items (3)	70
New organization (4)	0
Total	$ 747
Adjusted pretax profit	$ 2,007

Notes to Income Statement

1.a.	Owner's salary and bonus	$300
	Fair market salary	(150)
		$150
b.	Eliminate owners' excess perks including travel, car, entertainment, and insurance	50
c.	Eliminate owner pension expense	30

d.	The seller owns another company that buys raw materials, stores them, and delivers them to the seller's company at a $200,000 profit	200
e.	The owner receives a commission of 1 percent on company sales paid to his marketing company	<u>157</u>
	Total	<u>$587</u>
2.a.	Eliminate nonrecurring bad debts related to the bankruptcy of one customer	35
b.	Eliminate the one time expense of installing and replacing a telephone and voice mail system.	40
c.	Vandalism losses not reimbursed by insurance	<u>15</u>
	Total	<u>$90</u>
3.	Eliminate the following nonoperating items	
a.	Interest expense	90
b.	Gain on the sale of fixed assets	<u>(20)</u>
	Total	<u>$70</u>
4.	No adjustment is needed. The land and the building are part of the corporation, and the owner wants to sell the land and building with the company.	

TABLE 9.2

Seller's Adjusted Balance Sheet (in 000s), December 31, 199X

	Book	Adjustment	Recast
Assets			
Current assets			
Cash	$ 675	$ —	$ 675
Accounts receivable	1,800	(50)[1]	1,750
Inventory	1,688	(88)[2]	1,600
Other current assets	112		112
Total current assets	$4,275	$ (138)	$4,137
Fixed assets			
Land	900	1,000[3]	1,900
Plant and equipment	4,500	1,000[3]	5,500
Total fixed asset, cost	$5,400	$2,000	$7,400
Accumulated depreciation	(1,800)	1,800	0
Total fixed assets, net	3,600	3,800	7,400
Total other assets	819	(819)[4]	0
Total assets	$8,694	$2,843	$11,537

[1]Accounts receivable reserves are increased $50,000 to cover bad debts. Adjusted receivables represent the net realizable value.

[2]Inventory is adjusted downward because $88,000 of inventory is considered obsolete and not salable.

[3]Land, plant, and equipment are adjusted to reflect their fair market value as determined by appraisal or agreed-to value by buyer and seller or estimated by seller.

[4]This represents a nonoperating asset that should be sold or removed from sale. It is a real estate investment and is vacant land.

Liabilities and Equity

Current liabilities			
Notes payable	$ 225	$ (225)[5]	$ 0
Accounts payable	788	—	788
Current portion of long-term debt	337	(337)[6]	0
Accrued expenses	675	(200)[7]	475
Contingent liability— lawsuit	810	(810)[8]	0
Interest payable	90	(90)	0
Total current liabilities	$2,925	$(1,662)	$1,263
Total long-term liabilities	1,575	(1,575)[6]	0
Total liabilities	$4,500	$(3,237)	$1,263
Total shareholder's equity	4,194	6,080	10,274
Total liabilities and equity	$8,694	$2,843	$11,537

[5]Short-term borrowing is paid off at closing.

[6]Long-term debt is paid off at closing.

[7]Accumulated vacation and sick leave pay earned by employees that have not been paid, unpaid sales commissions earned by company's salespersons, and portion of annual property taxes that should be charged to this years that haven't been billed yet.

[8]This is a lawsuit in which the company believes its maximum liability is $810,000. Therefore, this is a one-time liability that will be settled and paid by seller at closing.

10

WHO ARE THE BEST BUYERS?

Why Competitors and Suppliers May Be Your Worst Alternative

You will want as many potential suitors for your business as possible to ensure that you get a good price. You should carefully study the major advantages, disadvantages, and risks associated with selling to:

1. Competitors
2. Employees
3. Suppliers
4. Customers
5. Individual investors
6. Larger private and public companies

Your merger and acquisition intermediary or broker can help you with this. You'll be much better off selling to an experienced buyer because he'll be aware of the myriad complexities involved and can move the selling process along. An experienced buyer will also identify your needs and better meet them than will an inexperienced one.

COMPETITORS AND SUPPLIERS

You should consider selling to a competitor. A competitor knows your industry and probably knows you and your company also. He will probably look at buying your company as an opportunity to grow and expand his company.

There are, however, many risks involved, even when your competitors are ethical people. When your company competes in the same market and shares many of the same customers, there are not many synergies involved. Consequently, your competitor will not pay fair market value. He'll discount the price considerably.

Your biggest risk in selling to a competitor occurs if the deal falls through. Unfortunately, this frequently is the case. When this happens, your competitor has learned your company's secrets. This information may give him a competitive advantage in the marketplace. A competitor will now know enough to destroy your business. I'm aware of one company, not a client, that as a standard practice seeks out new markets, finds out the leader in that market, and then negotiates to buy the company. The buyer makes a bogus offer to buy the company. The phony buyer carefully analyzes the seller and then backs out of the deal. The buyer then enters the market as a start-up company armed with intelligence information from the aborted deal and proceeds to drive the company it attempted to purchase out of business. This company's executives are very good at their trade and feel that they are not unethical, just smart businesspeople. At last count, this would-be buyer had pulled this trick on 20 companies. It is possible, also, that your competitor will spread negative rumors about your company that may or may not be true.

Many competitors are tire kickers, not serious buyers. They view the opportunity to acquire your company as an intelligence-gathering mission. The difficulties lie in figuring out a competitor's true intentions. Consider selling to a competitor only when you can't find another qualified buyer.

Suppliers and vendors fall into the same risk category as competitors and should be considered as buyers of last resort.

EMPLOYEES

Federal tax laws encourage employee buyouts. Most employee buyouts are structured as employee stock ownership trusts (ESOTs), which are trusts established to purchase and hold stock for employees.

There are several reasons why an employee buyout makes sense: (1) it will generate much goodwill with the employees and community, and you will be perceived as a benevolent employer; (2) you can achieve significant tax benefits with an ESOT; and (3) employees are available to acquire your company. Employees usually feel it is their right to own your business.

While these reasons are commendable, employee buyouts have major disadvantages and risks. The big risk is if the deal falls through because you can't agree to price and terms. Because you and the employees are put into an adversary relationship during the negotiating process, a deal that fails will probably cause a strained relationship between you and your employees. Some employees may leave the company as a result. Others will blame you. They will believe that they, not the outside buyer finally brought in, should own the company. Employees are not entrepreneurs. They are not risk takers and prefer job security and a paycheck to risk taking. As a result, employees will expect you to sell for less than market value. They will want other concessions such as owner financing or extra time to put the deal together.

You also lose confidentiality when dealing with employees. Everyone will know you are selling.

Selling to employees is an option you should consider, but it's risky. You won't receive top dollar, and you forfeit confidentiality. If the deal doesn't fly, there will be tension between you and your employees. Sell to employees, but only if necessary, unless you are willing to accept less money and are willing to accept the risks involved.

One last caveat: after the employees acquire the company and something goes wrong, don't be surprised if they bring a fraudulent conveyance action against you. Loyalties are thin, and employees tend to think the former owner got the best of them in negotiations. This will be especially true if, for some reason, your former employees screw up the business and it goes into the tank.

Despite these caveats, more company owners are selling their businesses to employees using an employee stock ownership plan (ESOP). Currently there are more than 10,000 ESOPs covering over 11.5 million employees. An ESOP is a tax-qualified, defined-contribution employee-benefit plan that invests primarily in the stock of the employer. A tax-qualified plan is any retirement plan that meets the requirements of the Internal Revenue Code.

ESOPs may be used for a multitude of purposes, including raising capital and buying out existing owners, as in a leveraged buyout. ESOPs may also be used to keep a potentially dying firm alive rather than face liquidation. For our purposes, this discussion is limited to using an ESOP as a vehicle to help the sale of an owner's interest in his business to employees of his company.

The basic idea of an ESOP is that common stock (or convertible preferred) is distributed to the accounts of employees and eventually passed on to them at retirement or departure from the firm. ESOPs can be leveraged or unleveraged. A leveraged ESOP borrows money to buy stock. Only a firm with a reasonably low debt-to-equity level will be approved by a financial institution for the heavy debt financing that is necessary to set up a leveraged ESOP. An unleveraged ESOP is funded with cash contributions from the company that are used to purchase stock from the company or the current stockholders. If a company's shares are not traded publicly, the purchase price is established by an independent business appraiser. The ESOP cannot legally pay more than the fair market value of the shares.

The ESOP option enables an owner to sell his business to the employees and take advantage of tax benefits. Among these benefits are the following:

- If after the sale at least 30 percent of a private business is owned by an ESOP, the seller can *avoid* current tax on the gain by using the proceeds to buy stocks or bonds of another U.S. industrial company. The ESOP must hold at least 30 percent of each class of outstanding stock or 30 percent of the total value of all outstanding stock. The proceeds must be invested within 3 months before the sale and not later than 12 months after the sale. In addition, the stock must have been owned for at least 3 years prior to the sale to the ESOP. Tax deferral is not available for any gain realized by a C corporation on the sale of stock to an ESOP under Section 1042(c)(7) of the Code. An excise tax of 10 percent can be levied against the proceeds the seller receives if certain conditions are not met.

- If an ESOP owns more than 50 percent of the company, those who lend money to the ESOP are taxed on only 50 percent of the income received on such loans. The borrower (an ESOP) usually gets a break in the cost of capital by 1–2 percent over normal rates.

- A company can *deduct both* principal and interest payments on an ESOP loan. That is right. Principal payments are tax deductible. Generally, a trust is created, and the trustees borrow the money from a lender. The company guarantees payment on the loan, and the trust uses the money from the loan to purchase an owner's stock that is outstanding. The company makes payments to the trust, which in turn pays off the loan. A company sponsoring an ESOP can make deductible contributions of up to 25 percent of an ESOP participant's salary to repay the principal portion of the ESOP loan. There is no limit on deductible plan contributions to repay interest. The percentage of the company purchased by an ESOP depends on how much additional debt the company can service on a pretax basis. Sometimes the company is short on collateral to secure the ESOP loan. When the selling shareholder is electing to defer gain on his sale of stock, he may be willing to pledge a portion of his replacement securities as collateral for the ESOP loan. In this case, more funds can be borrowed; replacement securities are released from encumbrance as the ESOP loan is repaid.

- The dividends that a business pays on the stock held by the ESOP are treated like interest and are a deductible expense.

- Instead of borrowing from a commercial lender, the ESOP can borrow from the company if the company has sufficient cash. A selling shareholder may take back a note with the ESOP. To avoid paying tax on the sale, he can liquidate enough other assets to purchase qualified replacement property within the 15-month replacement period. If the company sponsors a profit-sharing plan, this plan can be amended or merged with the ESOP and all or a portion of the profit-sharing assets can be liquidated and used to supplement the ESOP loan. Borrowing against corporate-owned life insurance policies on key employees is another way to create wealth for the ESOP so it can cash the owner out. Another wealth creator is a refund of previously paid corporate income taxes by creating a net operating loss carry-back from deductible contributions to the ESOP to repay the debt.

Despite the advantages ESOPs offer, they are not appropriate for all companies. Some owners who aren't ready to retire may not want to give up any portion of control. In addition, a company that has an ESOP cannot elect S corporation status. ESOPs are expensive to set up. The legal, accounting, actuarial, and appraisal fees for a small or midsized company can total $50,000 and more. In addition, there are annual expenses, including an annual appraisal. An ESOP is intended to cover all employees, and it requires the owner to disclose certain information about the company, its performance, and its key executives' salaries. The financial condition of the company may not allow it to guarantee the loan for the ESOP. Tax deductions are of value only to a company with taxable income. ESOP debt, like any debt, can be burdensome. The ESOP must permit employees to put securities acquired from the ESOP back to the company. This can result in a cash drain that the company cannot afford.

Employee lawsuits in connection with an ESOP generally result because employees feel an ESOP is being manipulated to the benefit of management. The main problem concerns valuation of the stock.

Selling to Individual Investors

Often a middle manager or senior executive for a company decides that he wants to own a company and run the show. Generally, such buyers are inexperienced in acquiring a company and lack capital. They'll want you to help with the financing, and the front-end money will be slim.

Individual investors are cautious and careful about the selling price and generally very conservative in what they'll offer. They can't afford to offer a high price. Everything they have will be on the line, and they won't have the financial strength to infuse more cash into the business to make it grow. As a result, they will not pay for any future growth of your company. The amount they will pay will usually be based solely on the past performance of your company.

When the company's assets can't be used for borrowing, you'll be asked to carry the financing. The debt will be paid out of the future cash flow of the business. If the business runs into trouble or can't support the level of debt, then the debt won't be paid.

Use caution and carefully evaluate the strengths, weaknesses, and motivation of this kind of buyer.

LARGER PRIVATE AND PUBLIC COMPANIES

Public Companies

A public company generally will pay the most for a company it acquires. Public companies have access to the equity markets and often will pay all cash for a company. Public companies acquire all sizes of companies, ranging from companies with sales of several million to very large companies.

You can easily learn about a public company from its annual reports, 10-K reports, and so on. These companies are a blue-chip source for your company. Don't be frightened into believing that a large public company wouldn't be interested in you. Large public companies acquire small privately-owned companies constantly.

Private Companies

Many medium and large privately owned companies actively acquire companies of all sizes. These companies have the credit available to pay premium prices for companies that suit their fancy.

The major problem with privately owned companies is that they are private and tend to be very secretive with their financial information. Often they won't readily come forward with financial information. Consequently, it is difficult for you to evaluate their potential as a buyer. Many companies project a successful image but are not as successful as they appear. Can they afford to purchase you? Can you work with their top management? Will your company fit in well with their existing operations and planned growth? If answers to such questions are satisfactory, privately owned companies can be excellent buyers because of their management ability and resources available to buy your company.

OTHER SOURCES

Financial Buyers

Financial buyers are investment groups whose members acquire companies for their own account. The two best known groups are leveraged buyout and venture capital groups.

Leveraged buyout companies have various sources of funding; they actively acquire companies in all industries and usually leverage part of the company's assets. They usually want management to remain and won't buy if that isn't the case. Some of these investment groups are financed by the wealthiest families in the state or country. Others are financed by major companies or financial institutions.

Venture capital groups are mostly involved in start-up and early-funding phases of companies and expect high returns on investment because of the risk they take. Recently, some of them have begun to consider buying established companies that have the potential for rapid growth. Because venture capital groups' expected returns are so high, they usually reduce the selling price they will pay.

Investment groups are motivated by high rates of return. Consequently, they are price conscious. They look at many, many deals before investing, and generally won't pay top rates because their return expectations are so high.

Both are viable buying groups, but they don't pay top rates and will look at many deals before they'll settle on one. There are exceptions to this rule. Financial companies that own operating companies are excellent buyers, provided you meet their acquisition criteria. Financial companies have the resources and will pay top dollar. This kind of company can be an excellent source as a buyer for your company.

Foreign Companies

Foreign companies acquire about 15 percent of all medium to large companies in the United States. Foreign buyers often pay a high price because they want to enter a new market and invest here for political and safe haven reasons.

Foreign buyers pay premiums for companies for two reasons. Foreign tax laws are more favorable for acquisitions than U.S. tax law is. Thus foreign companies have a tax advantage over U.S. companies that enables them to pay more. Second, foreigners' return-on-investment expectations aren't as high as those of U.S. companies. As a result, they will pay more for a business.

Companies Outside Your Market or Industry

You will receive a premium for your company from a buyer who wants to enter your industry or market. This is a prime buyer to solicit because he wants to enter and establish himself in your market. If the buyer is a private or public company, this situation can be a real winner for you, resulting in a premium price paid for your company.

If a deal falls through, generally no harm is done because the buyer is not a competitor or in your industry.

How Do You Find the Right Buyer?

Finding the right buyer for your company can be a tough, demanding, and time-consuming task. The market of buyers is fragmented and dispersed. The right buyer may be nearby or located in another city, state, or country. Searching for the right buyer can be like looking for a lost golf ball in the rough. You have to search hard to find it.

This is where a good intermediary or merger and acquisition consultant/broker can assist you. A good intermediary has contacts and a network throughout the United States and overseas. These contacts help him bring the right buyer to the table.

Sellers are usually wrong when they assume which geographical part of the country a buyer will come from. They often think the buyer will come from the general vicinity in which they are located, but this usually is not so.

Buyers generally fall into a couple of geographic categories. When your company's market is local, the buyer can come from the local market or from the regional market. When the buyer is in your region, such as the Midwest, the buyer may want to expand into your local market through an acquisition of a company such as yours.

Sellers are often surprised by where their potential buyers come from. Companies who sell to a regional market generally are sold to companies outside their region or country. An envelope company from Canada may want to expand into the United States by acquiring a regional envelope company. A company that sells its products nationally or internationally could be purchased by anyone in or outside the United States.

You won't always know why a buyer is interested in your company or from which part of the country he will come. It is best to search for buyers throughout the local, regional, and national scene. Sometimes, you'll need to search internationally. When there are many buyers for your company, you have a better chance of selling for the price, terms, and conditions that best satisfies your needs.

Where to Find Them

Here are four ways to identify those elusive potential buyers who will pay a premium for your company:

1. Which companies make a good fit and would be compatible with your company? Identify these companies, as they are potential buyers.
2. Identify similar companies that are not direct competitors but are in related industries. Which companies are making acquisitions in these industries that could have synergies with your company in terms of sales, distribution, products, manufacturing, technology, and so on?
3. Identify the types of companies that have acquired companies in your industry. Perhaps there are similar companies making acquisitions that would have an interest.
4. You can run ads in *The Wall Street Journal* or your local paper. The problem here is that every amateur buyer in the world comes out of the woodwork.

There are many other methods, and your merger and acquisition professional will have hundreds of contacts. He will know how to search out and find that one elusive right buyer. If you are up to it, you can do it yourself. In either case, be patient. You won't find the perfect buyer overnight. Allow a year for the process. Don't listen to anyone who tells you it can be done a lot faster; he is talking about a fire sale and that is not how you cash out and sell your company for the most profit.

CHAPTER
11

NEGOTIATING
THE DEAL

Seventeen Fatal Mistakes Buyers Make and How to Capitalize on Them

You have decided to sell your company, and you have a serious buyer. This chapter covers what is involved in making the deal happen. It will help you negotiate a successful deal.

Let's first focus on several important and fundamental negotiation tactics. Before any discussion of price, it is important that both the buyer and seller make their needs known to each other. However, it is more important for the seller. When an experienced buyer knows your needs, he can make an offer that will meet your needs.

If you are interested more in the total purchase price than in an all-cash deal, and you are willing to carry some financing, make this known. But tell the buyer you expect a higher purchase price as a result. Maybe taxes are an important item to you. Discuss with your buyer how he can help with your tax problem. You may want your son-in-law to remain with the company. Maybe you only want to stay with the company part time and then plan little or no involvement after you have seen to the details of a successful transition. You might want personal loan guarantees removed.

You should sit down and write out your priorities (needs) and rank them from most important to least important. Now you know your priorities and those most important to you. Communicate those needs to the buyer and make sure he understands them. The buyer also needs to express his needs. Remember, a deal won't get done unless both of you satisfy your most important needs. That's why a frank and open discussion on individual needs must be held early on. This initial discussion will also help cement the all- important chemistry that is needed for you to successfully complete the deal.

Since terms drive the deal, it's important to focus on general parameters of the deal before you talk price. That is because you will want more money if you are being asked to carry financing than in an all-cash deal. You'll want to know whether the buyer plans to buy the assets or the stock. If you are hit harder by taxes from an asset sale, you'll want to adjust your price upward accordingly. If the buyer wants you to take stock and the stock isn't the quality you would like, that can also affect your selling price.

So talk needs first, then general terms. Finally, talk price. You'll settle the price and terms issue before you bring your attorney in to negotiate the legal details of the agreement. Your merger and acquisition professional should be actively involved during this process. He should help negotiate with you the price and terms subject to review of your tax and legal advisers. This allows you an out if either your attorney or tax adviser has serious problems with the price and terms of the deal. If you can't agree to price and terms, you don't need to spend money on legal advice. Once you have a verbal agreement on price and terms, the buyer will draft a nonbinding letter of intent, at which time you should bring your lawyer into the picture. Then the two attorneys will negotiate the letter of intent and purchase agreement.

I have mentioned time and again the need for you to be informed about important tax and legal issues. Be sure you are aware of the important tax and legal issues involved in a deal before beginning your negotiations. You should consult with your tax and legal advisers so you have the best information possible. After all, knowledge is power. However, in the early discussion stages with the buyer you don't want or need an attorney at your side. When you have one at your side, the buyer will respond with his attorney. Attorneys are adversarial in nature and set up an immediate adversarial relationship. That gives the buyer an edge. Your greatest negotiation strength is *before* the letter of intent is signed. You don't want the buyer's attorney present in the earliest stages of negotiations. If the buyer allows you to have an attorney at your side, that's fine. But that's not likely to happen, because as soon as you bring your attorney onto the scene, the buyer will too.

For now, negotiate the price. One important caveat is that you negotiate important things first (price and terms); then negotiate the less important things. If you start with some of the lesser items, a sharp buyer will give in to you on several lesser issues and then use those concessions as a lever to make you concede on the most important issues. Again, negotiate price and terms first. If you can't agree to these, you don't have any reason to talk about the remaining issues, and you can save a lot of professional fees. You may just have a tire kicker instead of a bona fide buyer.

Make time work for you. Don't establish a deadline for yourself to get the deal done. Deadlines force you to make unnecessary concessions. Generally, it is best for you to ask the buyer to make the first price offer. If you go first, he'll discount your offer and hope to negotiate somewhere in between. Maybe the buyer will offer more than you had in mind. In this case you could have left a lot of chips on the table. Let the buyer make an offer first.

When you're discussing price, neither party has a strong commitment to the deal, and it is quite easy for one party to back off. Hardball negotiations aren't called for because they can easily cause the other party to walk from the deal. Negotiating a business sale is different from union negotiations, where ultimately both sides have to work together. Negotiating a sale of a company is not like negotiations in a legal suit, in which one side will pay to remove uncertainties.

If both sides approach the deal by looking at needs and terms first, a win-win situation presents itself so you can resolve the price issue. Remember, you are the only one who really knows your bottom line. No one can negotiate this for you.

You need to negotiate price. If you ask for $8 million, the buyer offers $7 million and sticks to his guns, and you accept the $7 million, then the buyer will turn to his adviser and say, "What is going on here? There must be something wrong. What does the seller know that we don't?" The buyer will feel much happier paying something above $7 million and feeling some hard negotiations have taken place.

Don't start out with your lowest and best price. The other side won't believe you, regardless of your sincerity. You must negotiate price.

On the other hand, be careful not to dig a hole for yourself by asking an absurdly high price, much above what you'll settle for. The buyer will recognize a price that is way too high and may just walk away and never make a counteroffer.

When a buyer offers you $7 million and you haven't named your price, a good idea is just to say, "Your price is way too low." See if the buyer will come up. He may offer $7.5 million and you haven't named a price yet. This is wise on your part, because he is bidding against himself. If the buyer won't budge until you counter with a price, fine; give him your price.

Here's another example of some shrewd chess moves. Let's say the buyer offers $6 million and you want $8 million. Making a bunch of small concession moves, such as $100,000, will take too long to negotiate. In the real world, these kinds of deals fall apart. Constant changing of the price proposals—even with small changes—encourages the other side to wait for a concession. It's an attitude of "he made one last week so he'll make one this week." There is no credibility, no finality to a given offer. Make a few bold moves. Don't try to squeeze nickels or you'll lose the pot of gold in the process. Set a reasonable price based on solid valuation techniques and make meaningful concessions at appropriate times.

Remember, you need to have good reasons and a rationale for why you want $8 million for your company. Numbers that you've plucked out of the air carry little weight with the buyer.

When you are at a meeting with the buyer and he offers $6 million but you want $8 million, don't make a concession at this time no matter how much the buyer cries about your being overpriced; don't retreat from your $8 million at this session. If you do, it will undermine your price proposal. Don't waffle that day. Smile and discuss other events, maybe the Super Bowl, but don't concede your position that day.

Never state that your price is fixed and nonnegotiable and that you won't budge from it. Never bluff unless you are willing to accept the fact that the buyer will walk. When you bluff, the other side may believe you and never come back to the table. He won't pay your bluffing purchase price. Leave a little wiggling room for yourself. Saying, "I want $8 million for my company" is better than saying, "My bottom price is $8 million, and I won't budge for a nickel less."

When the price gets close, such as $7 million and $7.4 million, don't offer $7.2 million while the buyer is at $7 million. You'll end up selling at $7.1 million. Let the other side bid first. It is at this point you can give away $200,000 so fast you won't know what happened.

OTHER ISSUES BESIDES PRICE

Your objective should be to solve problems and achieve compromise. Negotiating is compromise. Negotiating is timing.

Several years ago, I was negotiating a teacher's union contract and was representing the board of education. At our first meeting with the union negotiator, both sides' issues were discussed. We agreed to put all our demands on the table first and not to bring other new demands up later. I casually suggested to the union negotiator that since he had the most demands, he should go first. Everyone snickered, including the press and observers in attendance. I listened carefully to each of the union demands and, based on the number of their demands, added a demand to our side that neither the board nor I had intended to pursue. We added that we wanted the teachers to pay for all their dental insurance. Naturally, a huge cry went out. That demand successfully wiped out three of the teachers' main demands. When a number of sessions were completed, the teachers offered to pull three crucial issues off the table if the board would remove the dental insurance issue. What do you think we did?

Negotiations have to be treated like a game. Make thoughtful chess moves. Sometimes you need to make demands just to influence the other side to withdraw some of their proposals. Concede on some issues and hold back others as trading bait.

During negotiations, don't say a certain thing is nonnegotiable. Such a position will kill a deal. Banging on the table is another sure way to kill a deal and make people mad at you.

Nitpicking will also kill the deal. Attorneys by nature look for problems. That is their job. It is not their job to kill a deal because they want to argue and fight over every sentence in the agreement. Keep your eye on the goal and make your attorney focus here also.

Make sure you know who the decision makers are. Who really calls the shots? Don't negotiate with someone who can't make decisions. Otherwise, you'll make most of the concessions while the negotiator runs to the phone to see what he can do. Remember, those farthest from the negotiating table will take the toughest line. This is especially true in cases where you are being acquired by a larger company. No one in that larger company wants to be labeled as the one who gave the ship away.

During negotiations both buyer and seller are going to be concerned about similar questions, such as:

1. Why is the bid price so low? So high?
2. Are they fishing or are they serious?
3. Should we look for other companies or buyers?
4. Are these people qualified? Can they do the deal?
5. How can we make our company look better?
6. How do we reduce or manage risk?
7. Will I pay too much? Will I not get paid enough?
8. Can we negotiate with them? Are we powerful enough to play in their league?
9. Can we live with their top people?
10. Why do advisers get paid so much?
11. What is the worst that can happen?

You'll be nervous when you negotiate. As Ted Koppel says, "Just don't let them see you sweat." Both sides will be nervous. For you, it likely will be the biggest deal of your life. Have clear in mind what you want for your company. Know what your bottom line is. Know what terms and conditions are acceptable. Everyone agrees about the walkaway. A walkaway is a combination of price, terms, and conditions that represents the least you will accept. Without a walkaway plan, you have no negotiating road map. You are the person in charge, so don't let your advisers call the shots. Ask for the options. Make sure you understand them and then be in charge.

One last caveat concerning negotiating the purchase agreement details: a buyer has a major advantage over the seller because it is customary for the buyer to draft the purchase agreement. Some lawyers who will be drafting the contract for the buyer see you as the adversary. They'll try to inflict legal results on you in such a subtle way that you'll never know you were had. Make certain your lawyer drafts the sections of importance to you such as representations and warranties. Don't let the buyer's attorney do it, because it is simply not possible for you to negotiate out everything the lawyer may have put in on his first try.

SEVENTEEN FATAL BUYER MISTAKES

It's not only sellers who make errors in the deal negotiations. Buyers make their share as well. Here is a list of the more common buyer mistakes. See which mistakes you can capitalize on and which you can avoid making.

1. The Buyer Allows Transfers of Liabilities
The buyer agrees to assume seller's known and unknown liabilities. These are agreed to early on in the negotiations and are stipulated in the letter of intent. The seller should try to have the buyer assume both balance sheet and off-balance-sheet liabilities. The latter may include lease commitments, future customer claims, possible litigation settlement payments, and environmental liability.

2. The Buyer Agrees to Reimburse Seller for Legal, Audit, Accounting, Broker, and/or Tax Expenses Before a Letter of Intent Is Drafted and Executed
A seller is in his strongest bargaining position before the letter of intent is drafted and executed. Therefore, the seller should extract as many concessions as possible from the buyer before it is executed. Ask the buyer if he will pay for your legal and brokerage fees. It is customary for the buyer to pay the brokerage fees. But don't expect the buyer to volunteer to pay any of these fees. He won't. Another benefit the seller should ask for before the letter of intent is executed is a high perk package for employment and/or consulting. The buyer gets to tap the seller's knowledge following the acquisition and can fully deduct the payments allocated to the contract.

The payments are ordinary income to the seller that is taxed—at least for now—at about a higher rate than capital gains. This situation is highly desirable to the buyer. Therefore, the seller should ask for a perk package early on, regardless of whether the seller intends to work for the buyer in the long term. Use the perk package as trade bait or leverage later when the negotiations get tough.

3. The Buyer Falls in Love with the Deal and Overpays for the Company

During the valuation phase many buyers assume they are smarter than the seller and will be able to manage the company better and more profitably. Consequently, they pay too much for the company. This is a major error in judgment by the buyer. Buyers also tend to put too much money in the front end of the deal and don't hold enough back for working capital and capital expenditures to make the company grow.

4. The Buyer Agrees to Details Too Quickly and Easily

Buyers should not simultaneously make an offer, negotiate a letter of intent, and agree to detailed representations, warranties, and covenants. However, this error is made all the time by buyers. The buyer has not had enough time to explore the company's condition in detail. The buyer's letter of intent should be brief and nonbinding. It should stipulate the purchase price, how paid, whether stock or assets are purchased, and very little else. Naturally, the seller should pack everything he can into the letter of intent and then, if needed, use some of the items as trade bait later.

5. The Buyer Rushes Due Diligence

The buyer does not do a complete Phase I environmental audit. The buyer should not spend time and money on other due diligence areas until the environmental assessment is done. The audit should indicate that there is no significant environmental liability of which the buyer was not previously aware. After the audit, particular emphasis should be placed on identifying and quantifying contingent liabilities, valuing assets, and determining the future potential of the business.

6. The Buyer Agrees to Covenants and Conditions in the Purchase Agreement Too Quickly

It normally is a mistake for the buyer to agree to particular representations and warranties before the results of due diligence and contents of the seller's disclosure documents have been analyzed. The buyer should insist that conditions be agreed to conditionally.

7. The Buyer Becomes Too Involved in Immaterial Issues

As a result, the buyer becomes angry with the seller and the chemistry between them breaks down. Day-to-day negotiations should be left up to your attorney. Let your attorney be the bad person. The buyer should be involved in material and unresolved issues that arise between counsel. *It is very important for both sides that they maintain good chemistry.* I was involved in a $28 million deal where everything had been agreed to and all that remained was to deliver the money and sign the agreement. The buyer and seller met for lunch privately, and during that lunch the buyer unintentionally insulted the seller. One careless remark killed the deal. The seller died within one year of that meeting and never had an exit plan. The buyer never did acquire another company and missed out on a chance of a lifetime because the deal was a perfect fit. By the way, the seller was three times bigger than the buyer. The buyer would have been the number one player in his market rather than a small player. Small talk and a big head killed the deal.

8. The Buyer Assumes That the Seller Is Willing, and Able, to Fulfill Written Commitments

Contracts enforceable with indemnification are no better than the paper they are written on. A buyer should have a significant portion of the purchase price placed in escrow until liabilities are satisfied or clearly quantified.

9. The Buyer Lets a Deal Drag

The longer it takes to get a deal done, the more likely the deal won't be done at all. Attention spans are short, and when a deal drags, immaterial issues can be blown out of proportion. Keep the deal moving along.

10. The Buyer Believes All the Seller's Assurances

When a party is unwilling to put assurances in writing, it's a sign of insincerity, and the accuracy of any oral assurances should not be relied upon.

11. The Buyer Ignores Key Constituents Such as Customers, Suppliers, and Employees

The buyer doesn't insist on interviewing key constituents of the company because the seller won't allow him to under the terms of a confidentiality agreement. The buyer, often wrongly, assumes that customers, suppliers, and employees will automatically remain loyal after the transaction is completed. The buyer ignores competition and the fact that normally competitors make an all-out onslaught on the seller's customers once the street knows that the company has been sold.

12. The Buyer Acts Under Pressure and Buys a Company That's a Poor Strategic Fit

Many buyers acquire companies that are not a good fit with their company. They misjudge the suitability of the seller in some important area, such as technology or distribution, where they thought synergies were present, when in fact no synergy was present. Again, the culprit is due diligence. Not enough time is taken to carefully examine these issues.

13. The Buyer Acquires a Business in Which the Buyer Has Neither Experience nor Any Real Interest

Later the business runs into trouble because inexperienced ownership makes poor management decisions.

14. The Buyer Assumes Technology Is Proprietary and Therefore Cannot Be Duplicated

This is a common mistake made because of inadequate due diligence.

15. The Buyer Assumes Unwanted Inventory, Equipment, or Real Estate Can Be Quickly Disposed of to Reduce Debt

Disposing of unwanted inventory and equipment usually takes much longer and is sold for less than initial buyer expectations.

16. The Buyer Often Fails to Realize That the Market Is More Mature than It Appears, Leaving Little Room for Growth

The reason is poor due diligence. The buyer didn't really analyze the market or industry as carefully as he should have.

17. The Buyer Is Outnegotiated by the Seller

The buyer fails to retain experienced advisers early in the negotiations and makes too many concessions before a letter of intent is drafted and executed. The seller requires the buyer to put the concessions into a letter of intent and uses some of these concessions as trade-off bait later on.

The seller is always in the strongest negotiating position before the letter of intent is drafted and executed. Consequently, he should extract as many concessions as possible before the letter of intent is drawn up. This is why the seller should not bring legal counsel onto the scene until after the letter of intent has been drafted.

When a seller has legal counsel present, the buyer automatically has his counsel present. Attorneys are adversarial. The seller will never get the same concessions when the buyer has counsel present. The seller, however, can have his merger and acquisition intermediary with him. Naturally, the seller should have legal and tax advice and know the issues before negotiating. But sellers should exclude legal counsel from the critical opening negotiating phases unless the seller is totally uninformed about the key legal and tax issues. If that's the case, he hasn't read this book and is a sitting duck for a sharp shooter to pick him off.

12

FINANCING THE TRANSACTION

Twenty-Five Financing Strategies and More

Ideally, a seller wants to receive all cash for his business without having to worry about helping the buyer finance the transaction. Unfortunately, all-cash deals are the exception rather than the rule. First, the seller may not want all cash at closing for tax reasons. Second, the seller may have a perfectly good buyer who just doesn't have enough liquidity or money to pay all cash. Even if the buyer does have the cash, he may not want to put it all into the transaction. On occasions like this, the buyer will expect the seller to cooperate and aid in getting financing. The buyer reasons that the seller already has a good banking relationship. So why shouldn't the seller help him obtain financing?

What happens to a perfectly good transaction when neither buyer nor seller have good financing sources? What happens when neither party understands the financing resources available? The sale might not come together. The deal has a much better chance of success when both parties are properly advised and knowledgeable about available financing sources, loan criteria, and deal-structuring techniques. The purpose of this chapter is to explain the intricacies involved in financing the deal and to illustrate how to tap the financial markets. This chapter discusses various sources of lenders and their policies. It explains how to structure a deal and provides an example to illustrate the essential techniques.

Anyone considering selling his company should find a purchaser with sufficient financial resources for the seller to cash out at close. Many smaller companies are bought by much larger ones that have the resources to cash out a seller. However, as a practical matter, most companies will be sold to individual investors or to small companies. These, of course, are not cash-rich like the large companies. In these situations, the seller needs to help finance the deal.

I'm working with a company that has just emerged from a Chapter 11 bankruptcy. The business is still hemorrhaging and losing considerable amounts of money. The principals have owned it for more than 19 years and bad luck has jeopardized all their hard work and financial security. This kind of business requires a lot of creativity to sell because there will be few buyers for it and the few there are won't be the most qualified.

The buyer may feel that he doesn't want to pay all cash and will want the seller to carry back some financing. In this instance, the seller becomes a partial banker for the buyer. Seller financing has worked out well for many company owners. The method is straightforward. The buyer makes a down payment and then provides a note for the balance of the purchase price secured by a mortgage on the stock or assets of the businesses. The deal becomes much more complicated when the buyer wants the seller to subordinate and take a junior position in the security to the bank. The buyer wants to use the seller's assets to finance the transaction, and the bank won't lend against the assets without a senior security position. The assets of the company provide the security in the deal, and the seller's security position is behind that of the lender. Negotiations may have gone on for a long time before the buyer springs this expectation on the seller. It is at this point that many deals come apart. The seller says, "I might as well leverage the assets myself as let the buyers do it." This may be a good idea. Cashing out doesn't mean just selling out. It can mean taking cash out of the businesses through financial leverage while remaining in charge. For these reasons, understanding the financing possibilities of cashing out is important not only to the buyer but also to the seller.

What happens when the buyer is short of the capital needed for the down payment? The next section discusses 25 successful techniques that a seller can use to help this kind of buyer. The buyer may be a good one who just can't meet the seller's down payment requirement. The second part of this chapter explains leveraged buyout (LBO) financing strategies, in which the buyer uses the seller's assets to finance the transaction with an institutional lender. It discusses various levels of financing including senior, mezzanine, and equity providers' financing policies and terms. A case history approach illustrates the point. Finally, this chapter provides an LBO example that shows how to finance and structure a deal using third-party financing.

TWENTY-FIVE FINANCING STRATEGIES

Sellers who must help finance the acquisition often are dealing with an inexperienced buyer. Consequently, the more assistance the seller can provide, the more likely the deal will be successful. Let's assume the buyer is short of cash for the down payment. The seller agrees to carry the balance of what the buyer owes, provided the buyer can come up with the cash necessary for the down payment. Here are 25 financing tips that might help the buyer raise the necessary front-end capital needed to accomplish the deal:

1. Installment Purchase

The buyer makes a down payment on the business with the balance paid over a period of years at a competitive interest rate. The buyer puts up anywhere from 15–50 percent of the selling price with the balance paid at market interest rates over time. A note is executed and generally secured by the assets of the business or stock of the newly formed company. A Uniform Commercial Code filing with the secretary of state's office secures the collateral, and a mortgage recorded in the county where the property is secures the real property. Generally, the seller prefers a Contract for Deed over a mortgage because he can get the business back more quickly if the buyer defaults on the payments or terms of the contract.

2. The Blanket Lien

Often the seller is too concerned with security to engage in a full leveraged buyout with a buyer he does not know. In the seller's mind, and rightly so, he can see the buyer taking over the company, carelessly managing it, or stripping it of its assets. This would seriously decrease the company's value and jeopardize its very existence. Generally, a buyer can alleviate these fears by providing more equity to back up the note for the down payment. As security for the note besides the business, the buyer could offer a piece of real estate he owns as additional collateral. Suppose he gives the seller not only the company's assets as security but also his own home or an apartment building as additional security. This is called a blanket lien and enables the seller to take a smaller down payment. If the buyer defaults on the contract, the seller can repossess the business and foreclose on the buyer's property.

The seller can make the request for security outside the business more palatable to the buyer by agreeing to terms in the note that stipulate that if payments have been on time for a specific period, he will release the house or outside equity from the mortgage. The business should have grown and the buyer should have a larger equity share in the business by then. This enables the seller to feel more comfortable with the security. Consequently, he is more willing to release the outside equity used as additional security.

3. The Life Insurance Policy

A seller fears what might happen to his business and the money owed if the buyer should become ill and die. Because of this fear, he can often persuade the buyer to name him as the beneficiary of a life insurance policy that the buyer takes out on himself. If the buyer should die, the policy will completely pay off the amount of the loan that the buyer owes the seller.

4. Raise the Price, Lower the Terms

Suppose the seller and buyer are $100,000 apart on the down payment. One way to break the impasse is for the seller to accept less of a down payment. The reduction in the down payment is then added to the selling price. For example, add $25,000 to the selling price if you reduce the down payment by that amount. In this case, the seller receives more for his business and the buyer can afford the lesser down payment. If the seller doesn't need the cash and is comfortable with the security, this method can resolve the down payment problem.

Since terms drive the deal, the seller could also agree to a lesser interest rate in the early part of the contract. A contract stipulation could be that interest rates will be raised later. Principal payments could also be reduced or delayed. Interest only would be paid the first year or two. Principal payments can be graduated so that each year the amount of principal retired is increased. The possibilities are unlimited. This, of course, is one reason that buyers like seller financing—it can be more creative and flexible than outside financing services. When the seller makes concessions like these, he should insist on a larger purchase price or another concession.

5. The Balloon Down Payment

The buyer has an amount of money coming from an inheritance and isn't going to receive it until six months after the closing of the deal. If the buyer had the money, it would cover the down payment. However, the buyer doesn't have the extra $100,000 he needs. The seller could solve this dilemma by taking a note from the buyer for $100,000 that balloons and is due in six months. The note is due and payable in six months when the buyer should have the inheritance money. Of course, the worry is: What if the buyer doesn't get the money? This arrangement would largely depend on how sure you are that the money will be there. Short-fuse balloon notes have a way of backfiring. The executor of the estate may persuade you that there are no problems and that the money will be available. If so, you may feel comfortable enough to accept this idea. You may prefer to accept the balloon note payment rather than let the deal fall through.

Has the buyer considered all other sources of income? Maybe he has left his job and is expecting a profit-sharing check or severance payment. An insurance settlement for an injury may be arriving soon. If you want to complete the deal, you must think of ways to create wealth for the buyer.

6. Defer Part of the Down Payment with No Mortgage Payments

The buyer offers the seller a note for part of the down payment. The seller defers payments on the installment note until after the buyer pays the down payment note in full. Let's face it. If the business you are selling is less than desirable, you probably can find only one buyer for it. This method allows you to help solve the buyer's down payment dilemma and initial cash flow problems the business may have and close the deal so it works for both parties.

7. Spin Off an Operating Entity

Assume that the seller's business has several operating divisions that operate independently. If the buyer agrees, you could sell a division, keep the money, and reduce the selling price and amount of the down payment. This could be just the thing that makes the deal go.

8. Spin Off a Product Line

Reduce the selling price or down payment by selling off fading, failing, or declining product lines that are not essential to the operation. Reduce the selling price and the down payment with the cash generated from the product line sale.

9. Sell Off Inventory

Sell excess, obsolete, and slow-moving inventory. Run a fire sale. If the seller doesn't want to do this, then the buyer can sell off the inventory, subject to the successful closing of the deal. The proceeds from the sale can finance part of the down payment. The inventory is sold at the time of closing. Once the company is sold, the buyer ships the merchandise to the customer and either collects cash or takes a receivable. A commercial finance company will advance cash on the invoice of the receivable. The advance can then be used for the down payment. This strategy works when the buyer can sell a customer that the seller hasn't sold previously.

10. Partial Liquidation of Assets

When a company has machinery and equipment that are outdated, obsolete, or not needed for the business, the buyer can sell them subject to the deal closing. Normally, the seller should have done this anyway. When the buyer can unload some unwanted equipment at a good price, cash received from the liquidation can be used for the down payment.

11. Sale Leaseback of Machinery, Equipment, and Real Property

You can sell equipment, machinery, and real property to a third party who has the financing arrangements to handle the purchase of the equipment. The third party then leases it back to you. In a sale of this kind, you receive cash for the assets and the business is now subject to a monthly lease payment. Cash produced from the sale can be used as part of the down payment, provided the buyer agrees to allow the sale the assets. He knows that when the deal closes, instead of owning the equipment, his new company will now be making lease payments. It is a way for the owner to pull immediate cash out of the business and still close the deal.

12. Refinance Real Property, Inventory, Machinery and Equipment, and Receivables

You can refinance any one of these assets. You can refinance the building and plant through a mortgage banker, savings and loan, or commercial finance company. You take the money out of the business and the buyer assumes responsibility for making the payments to the finance company. The same applies to inventory, machinery and equipment, and receivables. You can help the buyer finance the deal by allowing him to leverage the assets of your company. Naturally, the seller wants the proceeds of the refinancing. If the buyer needs working capital, you can leave some refinancing proceeds in the business and take a note back from him.

13. Assume Trade Payables

Who is going to pay for the trade payables when the company is sold? Since trade payables are normally due in 30 to 60 days, they must be considered part of the purchase price. By allowing the buyer to assume the trade payables, you could reduce the down payment. This enables the buyer to use supplier credit to finance part of the down payment.

14. Buyer Meets Seller Needs

Assume you plan to buy a new car that costs $25,000. You could allow the buyer to use his credit to purchase the car for you and make the monthly payments. Since your buyer must be a good credit risk and has an established credit reputation, why not let him buy the car for you? Instead of doling out $25,000 for a new car, you allow the buyer to reduce his down payment by this amount. It's really a bootstrap method. If your deal comes down to a point where $25,000 is the difference between doing the deal and not doing it, you might consider this method.

Here is another idea: when the buyer has a motor home, possibly part of the down payment could be made by trading in the motor home for part of the down payment; this works nicely when the seller plans to travel the United States after the sale.

Or the buyer could make an assignment of his country club membership, and the value of the membership could be applied against the down payment. Some thought on your part will result in many other ideas.

15. Allow the Buyer to Assume the Seller's Debt Obligations

You may be under much financial pressure from personal and business obligations, and this may be the reason you're selling the business. Many business owners cannot stand the idea of debt or are tired of the continued debt obligation, whether personal or business. When the seller has an outstanding loan for some real estate he has purchased, the buyer can use his credit to assume the obligation of the monthly payments and release this debt obligation from the seller. This is the same as cash and could be a method to reduce the down payment requirement. This affords greater liquidity to the seller and less drain on his cash.

16. Borrowed Financial Statements

When the buyer's financial statement and cash position is not sufficient to do the deal, the buyer can seek out a strong financial partner who does not put up any money. Because of his accumulated wealth and high net worth, his partner's financial statement and guarantee make it possible to borrow the needed funds from the bank. The buyer can use the strength of the partner's financial statement for loans that ordinarily would not be available to him. He'll have to give up some equity in the company, but it's better than not having any equity at all.

17. Using Talent Not Money

If the buyer is an advertising agency, an accountant, an attorney, or the like, he could provide personal services over the next year to the seller. The value of these personal services could be applied to the down payment.

18. Borrow Against Life Insurance Policy

Does the buyer have cash values tied up in life insurance? The buyer could take a loan out against the cash values and use the money for the down payment. With interest rates as low as they are, it doesn't pay to have money tied up in such low return investments. The buyer may feel he needs this insurance as a protection for his family. What's a better insurance policy than an ongoing, cash-producing business?

19. Use Dead Equity

Let's say you can't complete the transaction because you don't feel the buyer has enough at risk and you want a larger cash down payment than the buyer can afford. In this case, the buyer could offer some comfort to the seller through dead equity that he has in a house, a car, a boat, real estate, and the like.

When the buyer's personal home has a first mortgage on it and some unused equity, the buyer can give the seller a secured position in this dead equity. This may help the seller feel more comfortable and allow him to go ahead with the deal. Say the house is worth $200,000 and has a $130,000 first mortgage against it. This leaves $70,0000 in equity. Let's say the deal hinges on a difference of $50,000 in the down payment. A flexible seller might accept an offer of a $50,000 note, provided the note is secured by the equity in the home. The buyer hopes the seller will accept this additional collateral instead of an additional $50,000 down payment. The terms of the note are negotiable. Other real estate could be considered such as apartment buildings, office buildings, and the like. Dead equity normally cannot be financed through normal financing channels. Often the seller can help the deal work by allowing the buyer to pledge the equity in assets that are already fully leveraged.

20. Two- and Three-Way Exchanges

Swap a smaller business or real estate as part of the down payment on a larger business. This may work when the buyer has a business that the seller can see as something fun that he can do without working so hard. A three-way swap occurs where the seller doesn't want the buyer's business. The buyer finds a third party who will take this business in trade for the assets that the seller wants and will accept from a third party.

21. Liquidating Paper Assets

Sometimes the buyer holds notes or other debt instruments from people who owe him money. He could discount these notes, sell them, and use the proceeds for the down payment.

22. My Talent, Your Cash

The buyer is short of money and hooks up with a partner who believes in the buyer's talents. Here, the buyer puts in the talent and the partner puts in the cash. Now the deal will go because money and talent are present in sufficient quantity to meet the seller's needs.

23. My Equity, Your Cash

The buyer provides equity in his home, business, or property. The partner provides the cash for the down payment. The equity is at risk in making the acquisition, but the partner is the one who puts the cash in. This works well when cash is short, but the buyer has property or stock and doesn't want to refinance the property or sell the stock.

24. My Statement, Your Cash

The buyer has a good net worth on paper, but his assets are all tied up in various investments. He needs cash, so he brings in a partner. The partner puts up the cash for the down payment, and the buyer goes at risk with his financial statement. Because of his equity, his financial statement and personal guarantee make the transaction a workable possibility.

25. Borrow Loan Broker and Intermediary Commissions

Both buyer and seller could have obligations to pay commissions at closing to either a loan broker or an intermediary who is helping with the financing and sale. When there is an impasse regarding the down payment, brokers and intermediaries often will cooperate by deferring the fees owed them, take equity in the transaction, or do both. With their help, the down payment is smaller, and both parties can close the deal. After all, if the deal isn't consummated, the brokers won't be paid.

Now let's look at how to complete a merger or sale of a business when the buyer has the down payment but wants to use the assets of the company to secure third-party institutional financing needed to cash out the seller.

ANATOMY OF THE LEVERAGED BUYOUT

In the previous discussion we talked about seller-assisted financing. Now let's shift our focus to financing sources outside the buyer. One financing trend that surfaced during the 1980s was the increased amount of capital available for financing acquisitions, recapitalization, management buyouts, and so on. The sophistication of the techniques for structuring capital also multiplied. Most of the increases in available capital have come from the private capital markets. The dramatic increase in private capital available for investment has caused significant changes in the way corporate America finances acquisitions. Historically dominated by a handful of large institutional lenders, the number of sources of capital has expanded way beyond normal institutional lending. With more investors in the capital markets, sophisticated financing techniques similar to those enjoyed by the *Fortune 500* companies have become available for smaller companies and businesses

In the past, if a company didn't have the right amount of assets, it was almost impossible to persuade a lender to make a buyout financing loan against it. The 1980s changed all that. Today, financing sources make loans not only because of the underlying asset strength of the company but also on the strength of historical and projected cash flows. During the early 1990s, however, the recession and the excesses of the 1980s resulted in defaults on loans. As a result, cash flow lending came to a halt, and more conservative lending practices returned. The era of the 5 percent equity deals is over. However, as the economy continues to grow and expand, cash flow lenders are coming back into the marketplace and will be a source of capital for years to come. This will occur when the cost of capital is cheap and inflation is low, as it is today. Prospective borrowers, however, can expect to encounter varying terms and conditions between different lenders, and even from the same lender over time.

While leveraged deals in the 1980s involved little equity, today's market mandates that equity occupy 15–25 percent of the capital structure of the company. In the past, a buyer who wanted to purchase a company would go to an asset-based lender such as a bank, finance company, or a savings and loan company. While you can still go to these sources, many other sources will help with an acquisition today, including buyout funds, insurance companies, private investors, pension funds, venture capital companies, and mutual funds. These are all potential sources of financing for an owner who wants to recapitalize his company and take money out or to the buyer who wants to acquire a company. These same sources are the lenders for management buyouts and ESOP financing.

To understand a leveraged buyout, it is necessary to understand the three broad categories of levels of debt. Senior debt, mezzanine or subordinated debt, and equity. All are ways of financing an acquisition. Each has its own return expectations based on the level of risk involved. Table 12.1 summarizes the structure and financing costs associated with a leveraged buyout. Let's take a closer look at each of these.

TABLE 12.1

Terms, Fees, and Returns Expected by a Leveraged Buyout Lender

Level of Debt (% of Capital)	Type Security	Interest	Advance Rate	Term	Up-Front Fees	Interest rate/ Dividend	Equity Required	Total Return Wanted	Typical Investor/ Lender
Senior debt (40–70%)	Working capital revolver	Receivables inventory	70–90% 40–60%	Evergreen Evergreen	1–3% of commitment; 0.5% on unused lines	Prime + 1–2.5% floating	None	NA[1]	Banks, finance companies, S&Ls
Senior debt (40–70%)	Term loan	Assets, stock, cash Flow	70–100% on machinery and equipment 50–70% on real estate	5–10 years/ negotiate amortization	1–3% on total commitment	Prime + 1–2.5% floating	None	NA[1]	Banks, finance companies, S&Ls, insurance companies
Subordinated debt (0–50%)	Privately placed subordinated debt[2]	Usually unsecured or a second lien	NA	5–15 years/ bullet or sinking fund payout	2–4%	Prime + 3–7%	0–30%	15–30%	Buyout funds, finance companies, banks, insurance companies, pension funds, S&Ls

202

Equity (15–25%)	Preferred stock	NA	Convertible to common; sometimes redeemable	None	0–12% Cumulative or non-cumulative	0–100%	>25%	Buyout funds, insurance companies, venture capitalists
Equity (15–25%)	Common stock	NA	Sale of company	None	Residual as paid out	0–100%	>35%	Buyout funds, venture capitalist management, private lenders
Equity (15–25%)	Warrants/options	NA	Sale of company	None	None	5–20%	NA[3]	Management incentives, equity participation by senior sub debt

[1]Return expectations will vary depending on the lender. Large money center banks sometimes syndicate senior loans to smaller regional or foreign banks. The lead bank in a syndicate will charge a syndication fee and retain part of the annual commitment fee and boost its total returns on the small principal balance it books for its own account.

[2]There are also publicly placed and traded issues of subordinated debt that usually involve significant amounts of capital—$50 million or more. This kind of debt is often called a junk bond.

[3]Warrants and options are sometimes issued to senior and subordinated debtholders and management as equity kickers.

203

Senior Debt

Senior debt is characterized as having the senior security interest in the asset being financed. Sometimes it is called a secured first position in the asset. This level of financing is the least risky for the lender, and so the rate of return is less than it is for mezzanine financing. Thus a lender with a senior position in an asset has first claim against the asset should the buyer default in the financing contract. It also has first claim against the asset should bankruptcy occur. The senior lender would share first in the proceeds from an asset sale before any junior debtholder or unsecured debtholders.

The interest rates for senior loans typically have rates tied to the prime rate. Senior debt interest rates range from 1 to 4 percent over floating prime interest rates. Assets that could have senior debt include receivables, inventory, machinery and equipment, and real property. Senior lenders typically will lend 70–90 percent against receivables, 40–60 percent against finished goods inventory, 70–100 percent on machinery and equipment, and 50–70 percent on real estate.

Receivables and inventory are revolving loans used for working capital. These loans are typically evergreen or open ended, and fluctuate in principal amount depending on the value of the collateral at any given time. The loan must be repaid in a single bullet payment. The repayment is made at the maturity of the loan, or three to four years from the closing date. Both the lender and the borrower understand that the credit line will be renegotiated and rolled over at maturity.

Machinery, equipment, and real estate loans are typically term loans financed at 1–4 percent over floating prime rates. Equal principal and interest payments are made throughout the life of the loan. Similar to revolving lines of credit, interest rates on term loans reflect the risk of the loan. As the loan becomes more seasoned, interest rates are reduced as debt is paid down. Senior lenders often will reduce principal payments in the early years of the loan, when the borrower's cash flow is tight. The loan may be extended for up to ten years. Besides plant and equipment and real property, collateral for term loans may include cash flow. This is important for businesses such as service companies that are not asset intensive.

The lender values fixed assets usually at the orderly liquidation value. However, the equipment loan is usually based on the appraised forced liquidation value. Buildings and land are appraised at fair market values. Loan terms are from 5 to 8 years but, as mentioned previously, can extend to 10 years. Building loan terms can be for as much as 20 years.

Some senior lenders will make unsecured loans beyond their normal advance rates on collateral values. These lenders will decide this based on the operating cash flows and other repayment capabilities of the borrower. Repayment could be made from asset sales, product spinoffs, and the sale of unrelated subsidiaries. A senior lender who makes unsecured loans may require a small equity kicker to enhance its return.

Senior lenders charge various fees. For receivables and inventory financing, expect fees to range from 1 to 3 percent of the loan commitment. Senior lenders also charge a fee on the unused line. This is typically 0.5 percent. Term loans have commitment fees of 1–3 percent and no fee on the unused line. Senior lenders also charge breakup fees in case the deal doesn't go through. They may also charge closing fees, arrangement fees, and syndication fees that can add an additional cost of 1–2 percent to the original commitment fee.

Subordinated or Mezzanine Debt

Subordinated debt is debt that is junior to the senior lender. That is, the debt security for the loan is in second place behind a senior lender. If a default occurs, subordinated debtholders wait in line until senior debtholders have been paid. Subordinated debtholders' risk is much greater than is that of the senior lender. Consequently, the rate of return on the loan must be much higher for the subordinated debt lender.

"Sub" debt lenders expect return rates of 15–30 percent. A typical loan would include a premium interest rate and equity participation of 15–30 percent. To get the return needed, equity is granted through conversion features, warrants, and the purchase of common stock. Subordinated debt generally is unsecured but can be secured behind the senior lender. Subordinated covenants will limit the amount of senior debt it will subordinate too.

Default provisions are subordinate to the senior lenders and often require that the subordinate debtholder defer legal remedies for a period. This allows the senior lender to exercise its legal rights and allow time for

the borrower to cure the default. Senior lenders are sensitive to decapitalization of the company. Scheduled repayments on sub debt usually do not
begin until a borrower has repaid or significantly reduced senior debt.
Consequently, sub debt repayment schedules range from 5 to 15 years. Sub
debtholders require 15–30 percent in equity and likely will insist on dividends or redemptions until the borrower pays off or refinances the sub debt.

A company's cash flow is usually tight in the first year or two after the
acquisition. Therefore, sub debtholders sometimes will agree to defer interest payments for a few years until cash flow is better. It is also possible to
defer both principal and interest payments for several years until the company's cash position is strong. Zero coupon bonds and preferred stock both
are used in sub debt arrangements at times. Compensation for sub debtholders is in higher interest rates, although payment may be deferred, a larger
equity position, or both. Sub debtholders expect a rate of return that is com-
mensurate with the risk. This return can come from interest earned on their
subordinated debentures and warrants to buy stock at a nominal price.

Sub debt lenders will take as little as $500,000 in sub debt financing
but prefer much larger placement of funds, typically $1 million and up.
However each lender has many different requirements, such as size of company, industry, geographic location, and so on.

Besides institutional lenders, an owner of a company frequently serves
as the sub debtholder. To get the purchase price he wants, he's often willing to take back paper on terms that are attractive to the buyer. Sometimes
the sub debt is unsecured, below market rates, and with no equity participation. However, all that is negotiable. The seller should try to get terms
similar to those sub debtholders receive.

Equity Financing

Many buyers can't raise the 15–25 percent equity they need to purchase a company, and they must look for an equity investor. An equity
investor could be an individual, small investor groups, or an institutional
investor. Many finance companies will also participate as an equity investor
in an acquisition, as well as leveraged buyout funds and venture capital
firms. Some finance companies and bank holding company affiliates also
provide equity and sub debt.

Institutional equity investors generally want a liquidation preference over senior management and a high return on capital invested. Returns on capital typically range from 25 to 45 percent and sometimes higher. Higher rates of return are dependent on the institutional investors' perception of the risk involved in the company and its position on the balance sheet.

Equity or ownership in a company can take many forms: common stock, options, warrants, and preferred stock are common. Preferred stock can take many forms, while the other forms of ownership are more predictable. Preferred stock has a liquidation preference senior to common stock but is junior to any sub or senior debt. It can be convertible into shares of common stock and can have a cumulative dividend equal to the prime rate. Preferred stock can take on many characteristics of sub debt. For example, preferred stock can have a fixed dividend, an amortization schedule, and no common stock conversion rights. Mezzanine debt, on the other hand, provides for significant deferrals of interest and carry rights to convert into common stock. Whatever the form of ownership an investor takes, the driving force behind an equity investor or a sub debtholder is internal rate of return (IRR). The return must be in line with the perceived risk involved. The return must also meet its IRR standards or expectations.

Professional investors expect to cash out within three to seven years. They will insist on demand registration rights and puts of securities back to the company. They will want covenants that include the right to visit management and inspect the books and records of the company. They will expect detailed financial reporting and other information and the right to attend board of directors' meetings and hold a seat on the board.

Sellers sometimes are equity participants in leveraged buyouts as well. The seller receives substantial proceeds from the sale of the business and participates in the future growth of the company through a minority equity position.

Now let's look at a situation that involves an institutional investor. This investor will make loans for senior and subordinated debt and provide equity if needed. However, before the investor will make a loan, the borrower must meet several lending criteria:

Case Study of Lending Criteria

You need to understand the individual lending criteria of each potential source of financing. This is especially important because of the many different financing sources and the different loan criteria on which each lending source makes its loan decision. Interest rates, fees, loan covenants, and loan advance rates can vary significantly from one lender to the next. The Acquisition Financing Checklist that follows is comprehensive. The checklist should help you understand vital information about the lender and its loan practices. The lender's identity has not been revealed. However, the information provided is real and represents the loan criteria of a large institutional investor. The checklist should help you hone in on what lenders are looking for. Although lending criteria change, you should use this checklist as an example of the kind of information you must know and the kinds of questions you should be asking any financing source you may consider.

This lender claims to function as a one-stop shop for all your financing needs. It is trying to meet every kind of buyout need, including senior, mezzanine, and equity financing. It functions as an investment bank, merchant bank, venture capital firm, small-business investment company (SBIC), commercial bank, and commercial finance company.

It's the 1990s version of a financing superstore. But how easy is it to work with? How costly is its capital? What qualifications do we need to do business with this lender? The checklist will help answer these questions and more.

Use this checklist the next time you are shopping for your buyout financing. It provides important information. For example, item 3 shows that this lender started its leveraged buyout activity in 1980. It is good to know it has been in the business of leveraged buyout financing for a while. It has many years of experience making these kinds of loans and then working with the borrower after the loan has been made. It should be possible to check with a couple of its client's and find out how well the lender treated them particularly when tough times came along. It has 35 merger and acquisition professionals on its staff and has completed 20 financings in the past year. The smallest deal it provided financing for was $5 million and the largest was $28 million. It makes loans for mergers and acquisitions and is a real player in financing deals. Some financing companies claim to be in merger financing, but really aren't. However, item 13 states that if you are looking for less than $5 million in financing, this lender would be the wrong one for you because your loan request would be too small.

**Financing Checklist
(For Illustration Purposes Only)**

Financing Source
    Great American Funding for Your Company
    Robert L. Bergeth
    Senior Loan Officer
    326 Broadway
    Suite 219
    Wyzata, MN 55391

1. **Type of Financing Firm**

    __X__   Investment bank
    __X__   Merchant bank
    __X__   Venture capital firm
    __X__   SBIC
    __X__   Commercial bank
    __X__   Commercial finance company

2. **Affiliation**

    __X__   Parent company: several subsidiaries

3. **Vital Statistics on Financing Source**

    __1980__   Year began LBO activity:
    __35__   Number of M&A professionals on staff
    __20__   Number of acquisitions financed last year
    __28M__   Largest M&A transaction
    __5M__   Smallest M&A transaction

4. Primary Focus of Financing Company

  _X_ Equity investor
  _X_ Mezzanine provider
  _X_ Senior lender

5. Role in Financing

  X___ Yes ____ No Will function only as deal originator
  X___ Yes ____ No Will participate in deals created by others

6. Type Financing Preferred

  _X_ Asset based
  _X_ Cash flow based

7. Type of Transaction Financed

  _X_ Leveraged acquisitions
  _X_ Management buyouts
  _X_ Recapitalization
  _X_ Refinancing
  _X_ Asset purchases
  _X_ Working capital
  _X_ Turnarounds
  _X_ ESOPs
  ___ Other (describe): _____

8. Bridge Financing

  ___ Farm out but will assist
  _X_ Provided
  ___ Bridge financing not provided; must get your own
  ___ Term of bridge loan
  ___ Terms and interest rate on bridge loan
  ___ Largest bridge loan ___ Smallest bridge loan

9. Capital Available and Invested

  __3B_ Capital available for LBO financing
  _2.3B_ Capital invested in LBOs to date

 128 Number of companies invested in to date
 9B Estimated annual sales of LBO companies

10. Sources of Group's Capital

  X   Allocations from parent or affiliated company
____ Funds managed on behalf of limited partners
____ Funds available from various sources through informal commitments
____ Partners or investors own funds

11. Additional Services Provided

  X   Identifying buyout candidates
____ Negotiating transaction with seller
  X   Structuring and financing transaction
  X   Coordinating legal or other accounting services
____ Providing fairness opinions
____ Help recruit management team
____ Strategic and business planning
____ Conduct business valuations

12. Fee Requirements

____ No fee; relies on interest payment only
  X   All fees negotiable
____ No fee; relies on interest payment and capital gain from stock warrants that can be converted into shares of the company
____ Agent fee
____ Arrangement fees
____ Audit fee
____ Breakup fees
____ Closing fees
____ Commitment fee based on a % of the total committed funds
____ Credit facility fee
____ Flat fee
____ Funding fee
____ Interest rate protection (rate caps, collars, swaps)

_____ Service fee
_____ Syndication Fees
_____ Other (describe): _____

13. **Deal Requirements**

  20M Minimum annual sales of company
   5M Minimum size of investment or loan
5–35M Preferred size of investment or loan
  X   Yes _____ No Company must be profitable
  X   Yes _____ No Will look at turnarounds
  X   Yes _____ No Will do deals in Chapter 11

14. **Management**

_____ Management must be in place
_____ Management can be recruited after acquisition
  X   Yes equity is preferred but not required of management
_____ Total amount of equity required by management of buyout financing. Can state as a percentage.
  X   Varies by transaction

15. **Industries Preferred**

_____ Advertising
  X   Business products and services
_____ Computers
  X   Consumer products
_____ Consumer services including retail
_____ Electronics
_____ Finance and insurance
_____ High technology
  X   Industrial chemicals and materials
  X   Industrial machinery and equipment
_____ Low technology
  X   Medical and health related
  X   Publishing
_____ Real estate and construction
_____ Telecommunications

____ Transportation
____ Utilities
__X__ Wholesaling and distribution
____ No preference will consider all areas
____ Other

16. Businesses Will Not Consider

Finance, Oil and Gas

17. Geographic Coverage

__X__ All USA
____ Midwest
____ Northeast
____ Southeast
____ Rocky Mountains
____ Southwest
____ Northwest

18. Senior Lenders' Policies

____ Yes ____ No Fixed rates only
__X__ Yes ____ No Floating rates only

7–8.5% Interest rates are prime plus 1–2.5%

20 % **of total acquisition cost that equity participants should finance**

__X__ Yes ____ No Creditor voting rights

19. How Important Are the Following Lending Criteria?

A. Loan to collateral value ratio   Expected Range _____ to _____

        __X__ Very important
        ____ Important
        ____ Somewhat important
        ____ Not important

B. Cash flow–to–debt service ratio   Expected Range _____ to _____

    ___ Very important
    ___ Important
    _X_ Somewhat important
    ___ Not important

C. Debt-to-equity ratio   Expected Range _____ to _____

    ___ Very important
    ___ Important
    _X_ Somewhat important
    ___ Not important

D. Historical earnings

    _X_ Very important
    ___ Important
    ___ Somewhat important
    ___ Not important

E. Total interest coverage ratio required:

   1.5:1 EBIT/Total interest

20. **Collateral Advance Rates**

   80%   Accounts receivable average
   85%   Accounts receivable maximum
   40%   Raw materials inventory average
   60%   Raw materials inventory maximum
   10%   Work-in-progress inventory average
   25%   Work-in-progress inventory maximum
   50%   Finished goods inventory average
   60%   Finished goods inventory maximum
   80%   Machinery and equipment average
  100%   Machinery and equipment maximum
   50%   Real estate average
   60%   Real estate maximum
   Appraisal Method for Advance Rates
    ____ Orderly Liquidation   ____ Forced liquidation

21. **Terms of Loan Granted on Collateral**

<u>Evergreen</u>   Accounts receivable

<u>Evergreen</u>   Inventory

<u>_7</u> Machinery and equipment maximum years

<u>10</u> Real estate maximum years

22. **Overadvance Rates Beyond Normal Formulas**

<u>10 to 20 %</u> Maximum overadvance beyond normal formulas

<u>2 Years or 24 months</u> beyond normal terms

_____ Years or <u>3 months</u> maximum amortization deferral

23. Mezzanine Providers' Policies

A. Investment criteria

<u>_2:1</u> EBIT/Total interest coverage ratio required

<u>_9%</u> Required current-coupon rate—prime plus <u>3%</u>

<u>22%</u> Total annualized return on investment required

<u>11%</u> To <u>50%</u> ratio of equity/mezzanine

B. Mezzanine financing provided by

<u>__X__</u> Purchasing notes and/or securities in private placement

_____ Other

24. Equity Investors' Policies

A. Investment criteria

<u>__X__</u> Yes _____ No Requires controlling interest

<u>5 to 7</u> Target period to exit investment, in years

<u>2:1</u> EBIT/Total interest coverage ratio required

<u>30%</u> minimum returns on investment required

Under <u>10%</u> to _____ % range of equity offered to management

B. How active is the investor before closing?

__X__   Very active
_____   Active
_____   Somewhat active

C. How active is the investor after closing?

_____   Very active
_____   Active
__X__   Somewhat active

Items 4 and 6 are important because they state the type of financing this lender provides. As you can see from the checklist, it provides senior, mezzanine, and equity financing. It also provides asset and cash flow financing, which the majority of lenders won't provide. Cash flow financing is particularly important for those businesses that have a strong cash flow but no hard assets.

Item 7 shows other financing this lender will provide, including LBOs, management buyouts, recapitalization, ESOPs, and so on. It will even consider financing for companies that need turnaround financing.

Does the lender do bridge financing? If you are a buyer looking to finance an acquisition, you may need bridge financing while you are waiting for long-term financing to be approved. Bridge financing is for a short term and, therefore, can be approved much more quickly than can a long-term loan. Long-term financing takes time, and you may not have time. This lender will provide the short-term funds needed to close a deal fast. This allows the buyer time to get permanent financing. Bridge financing typically is for 6 to 12 months, and most bridge loans have escalating interest rates that give the buyer an incentive to obtain permanent financing as quickly as possible.

If you don't know the type of transactions a lender will finance, you're wasting your time. Putting financing in place is very costly, and the wrong kind of financing can kill a deal. Item 12 lists some fees that this lender charges. As you can see, lenders are quite creative in devising ways to make it profitable for them to arrange an LBO loan. You won't get all this information without visiting directly with the lender. He wants to see that you are a serious candidate for financing.

Some lenders charge considerable fees. Others do not. Some rely on small fees or none at all. Those with small fees rely instead on interest payments and capital gains to increase their return on investment (ROI). The interest rates are important, but you should base the financing decision on the total cost of financing, and this includes both fees and interest. I'd want a lender that would work with me if bad luck fell on me after we closed the transaction. I'd want the lender's patience and help to get me back on my feet. I wouldn't want an inexperienced lender who panicked and pulled the rug out from under me. I'd be willing to pay a little more for an experienced lender's help.

Deal requirements in item 13 are one of the most important initial questions you need to ask. As you can see, this lender will make loans only to companies whose annual sales are $20 million or more and only to those that want to borrow at least $5 million. If you want less than this, this lender won't provide it to you even if you are company with $20 million in sales.

Item 14 tells whether management must put a meaningful amount of equity into the transaction. Some LBO lenders will waive equity requirements for management if they think you have adequate collateral and sufficient cash flow.

Let's assume you want $5 million and are larger than $20 million in sales, but you aren't one of the industries listed in item 15. If so, you are out of luck with this lender. For example, this lender does not provide buyout funding for construction firms. That is why it is important to know which industries lenders will invest in and which ones they won't.

Geography is also important. It is erroneous to think that because your lending source is not in your area of the country that it won't make a loan to you. Item 17 says this lender will make loans throughout the United States. On the other hand, many lenders who do buyout financing prefer you to be nearby so their supervision costs aren't so high. You need to know their policy regarding where they will make loans.

Number 18 deals with the loan policies for a senior loan. You can see that interest rates float and are 1–2.5 percent over prime. You will also notice that the lender expects a layer of 20 percent equities before it will make a senior loan. It also expects to have creditor voting rights. This means they have the right to decide any future financing your company may require.

Item 19 deals with five important lending criteria. This section tells you the loan requirements you must meet for it to make a loan to you. This lender considers the loan-to-collateral coverage ratio very important. The cash flow–to–debt service ratio and the debt-to-equity ratio aren't so important. They do, however, place a much needed emphasis on historical earnings. They expect the interest ratio coverage to be $1.50 for every $1 of earnings before interest and tax payments. This ratio definition may vary by lender, but most lenders define the ratio as pretax cash flow (earnings before interest and taxes plus depreciation) to total principal and interest payments on the debt. The higher the ratio, the more conservative the lender's loan policy. The ratio also enables the borrower to figure out the approximate amount of funds that a given lender will advance. Knowing these criteria also helps you structure your loan package so that you highlight the important parts in your proposal. The loan officer and committee won't wade through a long loan proposal looking for this information. Highlight it in your executive summary section of your loan proposal.

Item 20 in the checklist, collateral advance rates, gives you some idea of the amount of money the lender will lend against your collateral. It is also important to know how they appraise the assets. For example, forced liquidation appraisal is more conservative than orderly liquidation, especially for machinery and equipment, where this appraisal method is used most often. It it is important to know the method of appraisal because it tells you that one method is more conservative than the other. Although advance rates might seem higher with another lender, the method of appraisal will also determine the amount advanced.

Item 21 illustrates the length of the loan for each type of asset financed. Item 22 shows the lender's policy on overadvances. This lender is willing in some circumstances to advance more money than stated in the advance section of the checklist. It will lend 10 to 20 percent beyond normal advance rates and extend terms up to two years longer than its official stated policy. Be sure to check your lender's overadvance policy. Amortization of the loan may be deferred as well by up to three months. This lender's overadvance lending policy is on a case-by-case basis, as it is with most.

Item 23, mezzanine or subordinated financing, shows that this lender requires at least a 22 percent annualized ROI. It requires prime plus 3 percent for its subordinated debentures, and it expects to have a 2:1 EBIT/total interest coverage ratio. It also expects an 11 to 50 percent ratio of equity to mezzanine coverage. This is a good ratio to see how aggressive a lender is. The lender's mezzanine financing is provided by purchasing debenture notes and/or securities from the borrower's company.

Finally, item 24 shows the equity requirements of the lender. It expects to have controlling interest and to exit the investment in five to seven years. Most equity investors expect controlling interest, but many do not. It requires a 2:1 EBIT/total interest coverage ratio and expects a 30 percent ROI. Ownership offered to management is less than 12 percent. The lender is very active before closing and somewhat active after closing. It also wants a position on the board of directors.

The seller should have extensive discussions with the LBO lender to make sure the buyer can obtain the loan and that the lender fully supports him. An LBO is not simple or easy. The seller should make absolutely certain that the buyer intends to do an LBO and has an excellent financial adviser to help him in financing the transaction. If the seller can obtain the price he wants for his business, he may decide to provide the subordinated debt the buyer needs. The seller can make a more attractive offer to the buyer, and with better terms and rates, than a financial company that carries the sub debt financing. Therefore, the buyer will be anxious for his assistance.

Obtaining adequate amounts of financing requires that the buyer not only finance the purchase price but also refinance the assumed debt. He also must consider working capital and fees and expenses associated with the transaction. Does the buyer have the financing or resources to cover all these expenses?

The buyer needs a loan package that an LBO lender will consider creditable and that proves that he is knowledgeable about the seller's company. Buyers often make mistakes in financing by assuming that senior lenders will lend more against the assets than is normally the case. When the buyer can't obtain the financing he needs, the deal either falls through because of lack of funds or the buyer asks the seller to make concessions on the purchase price.

Let's look at a senior lender's worksheet for the assets of a widget manufacturer to see how a lender determines the amount of money it will lend against the assets of a company.

The accompanying Widget Manufacturing Company Senior Debt Worksheet (Table 12.2) shows that the buyer can borrow $6.2 million against its assets. Of this amount, $2.5 million is revolving debt secured by receivables and inventory, and $3.7 million is term. But what if the buyer needed more money than this to satisfy the seller and counted on the lender advancing more money? Until the lender has appraised the assets, it's not entirely certain what the lender will advance against the assets. An experienced lender will have a good idea, but until the appraisal, you won't know for certain.

TABLE 12.2

Widget Manufacturing Company Senior Debt Work Sheet (in $ millions)

Asset/ Collateral	Book Value	Appraised Value	Liquidation Value	Loan Value	Advance Rate	Loan Amount	Rate/ Term
Accounts receivable (AR)	$2.0	$1.9	$1.9	$1.9	80%	$1.5	8.5% revolving
Inventory (I)	2.3	2.3	2.0	2.0	50%	1.0	8.5% revolving
					Subtotal AR/I	**$2.5**	
Machinery and equipment (M&E)	1.7	2.3	1.3	1.3	80%	1.0	8.5% 7 years
Land and buildings (LB)	2.7	4.4	3.4	3.4	80%	2.7	8.5% 7 years
					Subtotal M&E/LB	**$3.7**	8.5% 7 years
					Total Funds Loaned	**$6.2**	

FINANCING THE DEAL—AN EXAMPLE

Now, how does it all come together? Let's assume that Sam has sold his company to Bill. Bill agrees to pay Sam $8.6 million for his Widget Manufacturing Corporation and agrees to assume $2.0 million of Widget's corporate debt. Sam will get $6.1 million at close and will help Bill finance the transaction by carrying $2.5 million in subordinated debt. Sam and Bill agree that interest will be 7 percent and that Bill will make interest payments only the first three years. Bill must make $300,000 annual principal payments in years 4–7 and $500,000 annually in year 8 on until the debt is paid off. The seller, Sam, is happy. He has gotten what he wanted for his business and has a big chunk of his money up front. The first three years Sam gets interest only on the $2.5 million of sub debt he financed. However, that amounts to $175,000 in annual interest payments. That is more than enough to support his lifestyle. From the $6.1 million Sam gets at the transaction's close, he'll pay his taxes and invest the rest.

How does the deal look for Bill? How much did Bill need to put into the deal? Where did the money come from? Bill created a Sources and Uses of Financing Summary that is shown in Table 12.3.

TABLE 12.3

Sources and Uses of Financing for Widget Manufacturing Company (in $ millions)

	Uses	% of Uses	
	$ 8.6	74.8%	Purchase price
	2.0	17.4%	Debt refinancing
	0.3	2.6%	Additional working capital
	0.6	5.2%	Fees and expenses
Total	$11.5	100.0%	
	Sources	% of Sources	
	$ 6.2	53.9%	Senior debt
	2.5	21.7%	Seller subordinated debt
	2.8	24.4%	Buyer equity
Total	$11.5	100.0%	

   Bill lists the costs of the acquisition as $8.6 million for the purchase price and $2.0 million to refinance the existing debt on the company. In addition, he estimates that he will need an additional $300,000 in working capital and $600,000 to cover his expenses and fees associated with the acquisition. These expenses will include any brokerage fees, financing fees, attorney, accounting and auditing fees associated with the transaction.

   His plan of financing is shown under "Sources." Bill plans to use the assets of the company to raise $6.2 million from his senior lender. The details were listed in the Widget Manufacturing Senior Debt Worksheet Table 12.2 referred to previously. Bill's senior lender requires that he put more than 20 percent equity into the transaction or it won't do the deal. Bill and his equity partners bring $2.8 million to the table, which is 24.4 percent of the total sources of funds needed. The seller, Sam, agreed to carry seller financing as subordinated debt to the tune of $2.5 million. This was 21.7 percent of the funds Bill needed to close the deal. Bill's financial backers believe that he can manage the company so that the cash flow from the business will be sufficient to pay off the debt. If Sam had not agreed to provide seller financing, Bill would have sought out a subordinated financing source. Here, the senior lender was prepared to provide the financing if the seller didn't. This would have cost Bill more in interest and a good chunk of equity because the lender required a 22 percent ROI.

   You'll recall from the Acquisition Financing Checklist that the lender, Great American Funding for Your Company, made both senior and mezzanine loans. This lender was prepared to provide Bill with some equity if necessary. Bill knew the lender well and had carefully cultivated a relationship with it. Because Sam provided the subordinated financing, Bill didn't have to give up any equity, and his cost of financing the sub debt was considerably less than if his lender had given him the money.

   Could Sam have pulled money out of his company the same way as Bill and not sold his business? Sure! Did Sam get a raw deal by not doing so? No. Tom sold to an individual who a major finance company has faith enough in that it lent him money and expects him to pay it back.

   There was a time in the 1980s when deals like this were done with a small amount of equity, sometimes less than 5 percent. Today lenders require a minimum of 15 to 25 percent equity. Bill and his equity backers put a lot of money into this deal and have a great deal to lose if the acquisition isn't successful. Tom and Bill both came out winners.

This transaction could have been structured several ways. This was the easiest and least complex method. A wise seller will carefully investigate the buyer's source of financing before the negotiations are too far along. If the buyer can't pay all cash, then the seller should identify his financing source immediately. The buyer's financing source must verify that the buyer is qualified and that it intends to lend money for the transaction. If the lender won't make this commitment, then the seller should pass on this buyer and look for a new one.

We have talked about the lenders. Now where do you find them? That's the subject of last topic of this chapter.

WHERE TO FIND THE BUYOUT LENDERS

The Directory of Buyout Financing Sources, S D C Publishing, 40 West 57th Street, Suite 802, New York, NY 10019, phone: 212-765-5311, is an excellent source of information in your search for buyout financing. S D C is a source for one of the industry's most comprehensive databases on merger and acquisition activity. It also publishes several newsletters that focus on mergers and acquisitions and corporate financing, including *Mergers & Corporate Policy and Venture Capital Journal*. Both newsletters are excellent sources of information about the continually changing world of corporate financing and mergers and acquisitions.

The Datamerge Financing Sources Databank, DataMerge, Inc., One Cherry Center, 501 South Cherry Street, Suite 500, Denver, Colorado, phone: 1-800-228-1372, is a superb database of over 5,000 financing sources that I highly recommend. The database is easy to use and covers all major categories of debt, sub debt, equity, and specialty financing. It covers financing sources for seed capital, start-up capital, expansion capital, acquisitions and buyouts, commercial transactions, and real estate transactions. The company provides you with a floppy disk that has the financing sources and their financing requirements on it. Use your computer to do the screening to find the best source of financing for you. Names, addresses, and telephone numbers are provided.

13

STRUCTURING THE SALE

Nine Powerful Blueprints

Both buyers and sellers face significant risks when a company is sold. When one party can reduce the risk for another, it enhances the chances of a successful deal.

The way a deal is structured can significantly reduce the risk to both sides. Sellers are concerned about security and taxes. They feel they might not get paid or that the payments will be late. Sellers are, also, worried about how much taxes will be owed. They worry about getting a fair price for their business. Sellers worry that the interest rate won't be high enough. Sellers feel they can't go away for a winter vacation without worrying about the buyer mismanaging their business and losing all their hard-earned money.

The buyers worry as well. Can we afford to buy this business? Can we make the debt payments? Is the business as the seller says it is? Where do we get the cash to buy the business? Are we paying too much?

Buyers and sellers can minimize most of these fears through effective deal making. This is true if the seller sets the price and is flexible with terms because terms drive the deal. A seller will receive a higher purchase price when he is flexible on terms and is willing to accept multiple forms of payment.

The following is a discussion of the various forms and types of payment and the problems and opportunities inherent in each. It is important that both buyer and seller understand the impact that goodwill has on the deal in terms of taxes, income, cash flow, and price/earning multiples. I'll start by helping you better understand goodwill as it relates to a transaction between buyer and seller. Then I'll follow with a discussion of the various forms of payment, including cash, stock, installment sale, annuities, convertible debentures, earnouts and royalties, covenants not to compete, and, last, employment and consulting agreements.

GOODWILL AND INTANGIBLE ASSETS

To accountants, the difference between the fair value of an acquisition's identifiable assets and the amount paid for the acquired company is dubbed goodwill. Actually goodwill is a catchall term comprising supposedly value that can't be quantified such as brand loyalty, corporate reputation and superior management.

From 1927 until the Revenue Reconciliation Act of 1993, goodwill could not be written off for tax purposes. It was amortized, and showed up on the income statement as an expense, thus reducing reported income. However, for tax purposes, goodwill could not be used as a tax deduction. The Revenue Reconciliation Act of 1993 simplifies the tax law, and thus ends the ongoing costly conflict between business and the IRS about which intangibles can be written off for tax purposes and which can't. The new tax law reduces the uncertainty not only about which intangibles can be written off, but also how fast they can be written off. Under the new law all intangible assets, including goodwill, must be written off or amortized over 15-years, regardless of the business. The capitalized cost of specific intangible assets referred to as section 197 intangibles must be ratably amortized over a 15-year period beginning in the month the business is acquired. The 15-year amortization period applies regardless of the actual useful life of an amortizable section 197 intangible. No other depriciation or amortization deduction may be claimed on a section 197 intangible that is amortizable under this provision.

As a result of 1986 changes in United States tax law designed to slow the pace of takeovers, the goodwill write-off measure in the 1993 tax law won't apply to situations where a company wants to buy another company outright by purchasing its stock. *The tax benefit will go only to companies that buy the assets of another company.* As a result, most of the benefits of the new law will go to those companies who want to sell divisions, product lines, or chunks of a business. The law will also encourage the sale of business services or professional practices where most of the purchase price is intangibles. In this case, the buyer can write-off intangibles over a 15-year period if the assets of the company are purchased.

The new law certainly encourages some transactions. For example, one obvious business sector that will benefit is any company that has a branded product line that it wants to sell. Goodwill can represent up to 80 percent of the transaction's cost. Under the new law, goodwill can be written off over 15 years. Larger companies that have divisions that they want to sell will benefit. For example, a company that has a division of proprietary plastic products that it wants to sell, could benefit tax-wise under the new tax law.

The following are some of the Section 197 intangibles that can be amortized over 15 years under the new law when a businesses' **assets** are acquired:

Goodwill. Goodwill is defined as the value of a trade or business that is attributable to to the expectancy of continued customer purchasing, whether due to the name or reputation of a trade or business or to any other factor.

Going concern value. Going concern value is the additional ingredient of value of a trade or business that attaches to a property by reason of its existence as an integral part of a going concern. Going concern value includes the value that is attributable to the ability of a trade or business to continue to function and generate income without interruption notwithstanding a change in ownership.

Workforce in place. Workforce in place includes the makeup of the workforce including its experience, education and training. It also includes the terms and conditions of employment and any other value placed on employees or their attributes. Thus, the portion of the purchase price attributable to the existence of a highly skilled workforce is amortizable over 15 years. The cost of acquiring an existing employment contract or relationship with employees or consultants, including any key employee contract, is also amortizable over 15 years.

Information base. Section 197 intangibles include business books and records, operating systems, and any other information base including lists or other information with respect to current or prospective customers. Technical manuals, training manuals, data files, and accounting or inventory control systems can be amortized over 15 years. The cost of acquiring customer lists, subscription lists, insurance expirations, patent or client files, or lists of newspaper, magazine, radio or television advertisers can also be amortized over 15 years.

Know-how. This includes any patent, copyright, formula, process, design, pattern, know-how, format, or other similar item.

Customer based intangibles. Customer based intangibles include the market composition, market share, and any other value resulting from the future sale of goods or services resulting from relationships with customers in the ordinary course of business. Typical examples include customer base, circulation base, undeveloped market or market growth, and insurance in force. The deposit base of a bank including checking accountants are also included.

Supplier based intangibles. The portion of the purchase price attributable to the existence of a favorable relationship with persons that provide distribution services such as favorable shelf or display space at a retail outlet, the existence of a favorable credit rating, or the existence of favorable supply contracts are all section 197 intangibles.

Any license, permit, or other right granted by a governmental unit or agency. This includes liquor licenses, taxicab medallions, airport landing or take-off rights, regulated airline routes, and television or radio broadcasting licenses.

Franchises, trademarks, and trade names; copyrights, and patents or interest in those copyrights or patents. A franchise is an agreement which gives one of the parties to the agreement the right to distribute, sell, or provide goods, services, or facilities within a specified area. The renewal of a franchise, trademark, or tradename is treated as an acquisition of the franchise, trademark, or tradename. These are all amortized over 15 years and are all section 197 intangibles. Copyrights and patents, when acquired in a business acquisition, are treated as section 197 intangibles and are amortized over 15 years.

Covenant not to compete. Section 197 intangibles now includes covenants not to compete. Any amount that is paid or incurred under a covenant not to compete made in connection with the acquisition of business or trade is chargeable to the capital account and must be amortized over the 15-year period. For the purposes of the new law, when either stock or assets are purchased, covenants not to compete must be amortized over 15 years. This is quite different from the law which was in effect before the 1993 tax law. Covenants not to compete prior to the 1993 tax law, were generally written off over the life of the covenant. For example, if the covenant not to compete was for six years, then the covenant was generally amortized over six years. Under pre-1993 tax law, whether a covenant not to compete was amortizable, and if so, over what period, had been held by the courts to be dependant on a number of factors. Was there a business purpose for the covenant? What amount of the purchase price can be properly allocated to it? Can the covenant be separated from goodwill? Was the purpose of the covenant to protect the business from competition or was it to protect the value of purchased assets? These questions and other considerations caused numerous disputes with the IRS. The new law does away with many of these conflicts by allowing covenants not to compete to be amortized over 15 years. Of course, the covenant not to compete can be shorter, such as 6 years; however, the buyer must amortize the cost of the covenant over 15 years, not 6 years as pre-1993 tax law allowed.

In addition, any agreement that requires the former owner of a trade or business to continue to perform services, or provide property or the use of property, that benefits the business or trade is considered to have substantially the same effect as as a covenant not to compete. This is provided so that when the amount paid to the former owner exceeds reasonable compensation for the services actually rendered, then the excess compensation shall be treated as covenant not to compete and amortized over 15 years.

An amount paid under a covenant not to compete which actually represents additional consideration for the acquisition of stock in a corporation is not a section 197 intangible and must, under present law, be added to the basis of the acquired stock when the stock is sold rather than assets.

Purchase price of business is allocated to section 197 intangibles under the residual method. Under pre-1993 tax law, the purchase price of a business was allocated under a so-called *residual method* imposed by the Internal Revenue Service. This method required that all assets of an acquired trade or business be divided into the following four classes: (1) Class I assets, included cash and cash equivalents; (2) Class II assets, included U.S. government securities, readily marketable stock or securities, foreign currency, and certificates of deposit; (3) Class III assets, included all furniture, fixtures, land, buildings, equipment, other tangible property, accountants receivable, covenants not to compete, and intangible assets other than goodwill and going concern; and (4) Class IV assets included intangible assets in the nature of goodwill or going concern value. The purchase price of an acquired business (reduced by the amount of the assets included in Class I) was allocated to the assets in Class II and III, the excess was allocated to goodwill and going concern value that could not be amortized.

Thus, under pre-1993 tax law, allocations to intangibles other than goodwill and going concern value continued to cause disputes with the IRS regarding (1) their existence, (2) their value, and (3) their useful lives. The 1993 Revenue Reconciliation Act resolved all three of these issues by recasting the way in which the residual method is applied. All amortizable section 197 intangibles are now treated as Class IV assets subject to the 15 year amortization rule. Goodwill and going concern are also amortizable over 15 years.

The residual method under the new law applies not only to the purchase of a company, but also where a Code Section 338 election is made to treat a stock purchase as an asset purchase. The residual method also applies to buyers for the purpose of determining the basis of the acquired assets. It applies to sellers, also, for the purpose of determining their gain on each of the separate assets sold.

CASH IS KING

Cash is immediate, and everyone knows its present value. All cash, however, plays into the hands of the tax man. Consequently, many sellers don't want all cash; some have estate plans they want considered. Further, most buyers do not have the financial resources or the desire to pay entirely in cash.

Taking shares of stock in the buyer's company as an installment sale is the only way to defer taxes into the future. Therefore, many sellers will take the risk of accepting stock in preference to an equivalent amount of cash or take an installment payment as part of the purchase.

STOCK IS RISKY

A selling company can accept stock as consideration from a public or private company. The most common uses of stock for the seller's company is the example of public companies.

The seller who is considering accepting payment in stock must remember that he is trading an investment in his own company for an investment in the acquiring company. A seller's future success and fortune will be dependent on the stock market and the management abilities of the acquiring company. Before a seller should accept stock from a buyer, many questions need answers, such as: Is the stock marketable? Can the stock be sold in the public markets? Can you sell 100 percent of the stock when you want to, or are there restrictions preventing you from doing so? Is the stock registered? This means that, at some specific time in the future, stock that was accepted by the seller as part of the purchase price must be registered with the Securities and Exchange Commission. This enables him to sell it in the open market. If registration rights are not granted, there is usually a two-year waiting period before the stock can be sold. A lot can happen to the price of stock during that period.

Registration is a costly procedure for buyers, so they may be reluctant to go forward with the registration procedure. The buyer may also place some restrictive covenants on the stock. The most common restrictive covenant is one that limits the seller's ability to sell the stock. The covenant may say that a seller cannot sell any stock for a time, or that he cannot sell more than a certain number of shares of stock within a specific period. The buyer does this to prevent selling pressure in the stock that might deflate the price of the company's stock.

It is possible to protect the stock from restrictive covenants. To guard against a decline in stock value, the seller could purchase stock price insurance or sell the stock short.

Companies with high price/earning multiples like to use stock in a transaction because it requires relatively few shares to complete the deal and dilution of shares is small.

As a seller you may want cash, in which case the buyer's common stock may be issued to institutional investors, whose cash will then be used to pay you. If the buyer is a public company, a new stock issue in the public market or a rights offering to existing shareholders can be used to raise the cash also.

Nonmarketable stock is often used in transactions involving buyers who are private companies. The seller usually becomes an employee of the merged companies and may become an officer or member of the board of directors.

When the company is privately held and there is no ready market for the shares, other mechanisms can be employed for the common shareholder to ensure liquidity.

A right to "put" shares back to the company may be employed. Here the company buys out a shareholder's interest. The value of the shares may be set by a formula, a fixed dollar amount, or a multiple of earnings. It also may call for an independent appraisal. Generally, the right to sell stock back to a company can be exercised only during a finite period. This restriction protects the company from being threatened by a massive call on its capital. The company may reserve the right to "call" its shares that might not be convenient to the seller at the time.

A company may have plans to go public, or it may wish to remain private. Both courses of action could have a major influence on the value of the stock the seller obtained in the transaction.

The seller could also receive a sweetener in warrants or options to purchase a specified number of shares of the buyer's common stock at a given price.

Finally, the buyer may agree to make a loan against the stock the seller got from the buyer in the deal. For example, the seller wants to cash out of his stock after two years. The company could agree to make a loan on part of the stock with the stock pledged as collateral.

There are many ways stock can be used as part or all of the consideration in a transaction. Be sure you understand that you may be stuck with poor quality stock. This can be true whether the buyer is a public or private company. There are many public companies whose stock is of little value today but was previously a high flier.

SELLER FINANCING—THE INSTALLMENT SALE

An installment sale contract can be a very good vehicle for both buyer and seller. Some sellers prefer an installment transaction over an all-cash purchase price because deferring tax over a period is to their advantage. Typically, however, an installment transaction occurs because the buyer refuses to pay all cash. To complete the transaction, the seller must help the buyer by providing more attractive terms. If the seller refuses to help with financing, he may have to accept a major discount for cash.

As an example, let's consider a transaction with a purchase price of $7 million and a down payment of $2 million. That leaves $5 million to be financed for five years at 10 percent per annum. The deal is structured so that the seller receives a $1 million principal payment annually for five years. The first year interest payment would be $500,000 (10 percent of $5 million). A selling stockholder pays a capital gain tax on the annual principal payment, and the interest payment is treated as ordinary income.

The terms can be structured in many ways. You could have an interest-only payment of $500,000 for three years and then step the principal payments up each year and have a balloon payment after ten years. Of course, there are variations to this, but the key is to meet the needs of the parties involved.

The seller says all this is fine, but he worries about whether the buyer will run the business in the ground and leave him high and dry. The seller wonders, "Can the buyer make the note payments?" There are risks to the seller when he takes a note from the buyer, but generally, the risks aren't as great as it may seem. The seller will soon see how he can eliminate the risk. A buyer will argue that he is taking a calculated risk when he gets your company and he wants you to have some risk as well. If the seller won't take some risk, the buyer argues, maybe the company's future isn't what the seller claims it is.

Be sure your lawyer has drawn an agreement that makes the sale irrevocable and allows you the right to sell or assign all or part of the buyer's note. The agreement should stipulate the specific collateral behind the buyer's promise to pay. When you have the right to sell all or part of the buyer's note, and you have solid collateral, then you can sell all or part of the note to a lending source. Otherwise, if the buyer closes or devalues the business, you would have no recourse, no business, and no money. For these reasons, the seller has every right to expect a premium for his company when he is asked to help finance the sale.

Collateral for Installment Notes

Collateral or security for an installment note usually results in much discussion and negotiation. Often no collateral is required if the buyer is creditworthy.

Usually, the installment note is collateralized by the assets of the seller's business, or the stock of the seller's business, or both. Sellers usually prefer assets to stock as collateral. The reason is although the stock may be in escrow serving as collateral for the loan, the buyer has use of the assets and can pledge the assets as collateral for another loan for his own immediate benefit. If the assets are mismanaged, the stock may become worthless. The buyer, of course, prefers to pledge no collateral. When he must pledge, he wants to pledge the stock of the selling company, not the assets.

When the note to the seller is secured by the assets of the business, sometime the note's collateral is subordinated to other senior secured debts of the company. The note payable may or may not be personally guaranteed by the buyer.

The seller and the buyer can usually reach a mutual understanding when the buyer wants to pledge part of the seller's assets with a lender to raise the down payment or majority of the purchase price.

The seller may ask for assets of the buyer outside the company as additional security for the note. Of course, the buyer will resist this.

The seller may insist that the buyer maintain a minimum net worth level in the selling company after the acquisition. For example, net worth levels might be 125 percent of the note. The seller and buyer could also agree that some percentage of future earnings are retained in the company until the loan is paid off.

Installment notes resulting in seller financing are a common method used in financing the sale of a business. However, much negotiation and discussion will center on the subject of security for the seller so that he is assured he will be paid.

A seller wants to smell the roses, wintering in a warmer climate with his friends. He doesn't want to worry about the business being run into the ground or about not being paid after all his years of hard work. The buyer must address this basic need or an installment sale won't work out.

ANNUITIES AS COLLATERAL

Instead of using the assets as collateral for an installment note, a superior method is to use an annuity as security. The buyer can secure the note by using a single-payment premium prepaid annuity. This is an insurance product that can be used to guarantee the buyer's note. The buyer purchases the annuity from an insurance company that, in turn, guarantees the payment of the installment note to the seller. Here the seller looks to the insurance company, rather than the buyer, for payment. The assets of the company are unencumbered. A key point is to make sure the insurance company guarantees the yield on the annuity for the length of the installment note. Think of this as **collateral substitution**. Instead of using the assets of the corporation as collateral, your buyer uses an annuity. He can purchase this product at a considerable discount from its face value. Therefore, it's a good deal for both of you. The seller has security and peace of mind knowing he's protected and will be paid by a major insurance carrier than the buyer. The buyer has the assets unencumbered so that he can use them to raise some cash for the annuity and down payment. Because he is buying the annuity at a discount, in essence he is paying less for the company.

When one or more balloon payments are involved, your buyer can use another form of collateral substitution. Assume there are three balloon payments coming due as follows:

10 years $200,000
15 years $200,000
20 years $200,000

Balloon payments, such as those just discussed, could help with tax or estate problems for the seller or could be deal enhancements or pot sweeteners to make the deal fly.

Security is the issue for the seller. Will he get paid his balloon payments when they are due? Will the buyer even be alive then? What if the payments are made by the U.S. government? End of worry for the seller. Here is how it works.

At close, the buyer purchases U.S. government bonds called zeros or strips in the seller's name. Zeros or strips are similar to the old Series E bond. The bonds are purchased at a discount from the face value. The holder of the bond receives no interest during the life of the bond but at maturity receives the face amount. Since there are no coupon payments, these bonds sell at a large discount from their par or face value. The one drawback is that interest accrues and the IRS requires that the holder make annual tax payments although he does not receive any actual interest payments. Here is an example:

Balloon Payment due in	Balloon Payment Amount	Acquisition Cost	Yield
10 years	$200,000	$ 99,140	7.4%
15 years	200,000	59,600	7.9
20 years	200,000	39,400	8.0
Total	$600,000	$198,140	

Thus, for about $200,000, the buyer can secure $600,000 in payments for the seller. The seller can sleep well knowing the payments are coming from the United States government. The buyer can look to his own cash and the assets of the company that are free and clear from any seller's security interest in them to buy the zero for the seller.

Zero coupon payments are especially helpful in situations where the seller wants deferred payments for tax or estate purposes. Zeros are also effective when a sweetener is needed to induce the seller to accept the buyer's offer.

When a buyer uses annuities and zero coupons as collateral for the installment note and balloon payments, sellers can rest easy and go on with their life. The U.S. government is going to be making the payments and not the buyer. From the buyer's standpoint, it is a sweetheart deal. This is because an asset-based lender will lend him the money when the assets are pledged as security. This enables him to buy the annuity and zero coupon for the seller.

CONVERTIBLE DEBENTURES

A convertible debenture is a bond or note that, at a definite and specific date, may be converted to stock, cash, bonds, or a combination of these things. When a buyer has the credit and assets to back up the issuance of convertible debentures, and assuming the convertible rights are for cash or stock, this is an excellent offer and one a seller should strongly consider. It is practically impossible to lose with this one.

The buyer conserves cash, and the seller has the best of both worlds. If the stock goes up, he will convert the debenture to stocks. If the stock goes down, he will convert to cash. This is a mutually beneficial situation for both parties.

Generally, only large companies offer convertible debentures. Should you sell to a large company, be sure that the debenture allows you to convert to either cash or stock.

EARNOUTS AND ROYALTIES

Rarely do buyers and sellers agree that the company is worth the same amount. Usually, they agree after some hard negotiations. Sometimes a buyer and seller just can't agree to a selling price. This may happen because the two parties view the company's future earning potential differently. The seller may feel that the company is poised for significantly higher earnings in the future than demonstrated in the past. The buyer, however, may not accept those rosy forecasts.

Future sales and earnings improvements may be a result of a new product that is ready to go on the market. Or sales and earnings growth may result because earnings are understated, when accounting policies are designed to minimize taxes. Our seller wants to be compensated for this improvement in financial performance. Our buyer, on the other hand, is prudent, conservative, and cautious and doesn't want to pay for that projected growth until it happens. The buyer believes it may happen and wants it to happen. That is why he wants to buy the company. But he isn't as certain as the seller is about the earnings forecast.

Thus an impasse occurs between what the buyer will pay and what the seller wants. This difference can be resolved through an earnout or royalty.

A buyer will pay royalties when he questions earnings that a new product is expected to produce over time. How successful will the new product be when it hasn't been tested in the marketplace? The technique used here is that the seller will retain ownership of that product and the buyer will pay royalties as a percentage of gross sales. The buyer and seller both should prefer having the royalty based on gross sales. It's easy to measure. The seller doesn't have to worry about accounting gimmicks that reduce royalties when the royalty is based on another number, like net profit or a gross margin. A buyer should like this because he won't have the seller looking over his shoulder after the deal is done and he is managing the company. The royalty can vary from 0.5 percent to 15 percent based on the industry. You can conduct research to find out royalty arrangements for your industry. You can also negotiate and arrive at a percentage.

An earnout makes sense when the two parties can't agree on the selling price. The earnout gives the seller the right to receive additional monies if the company reaches certain earnings or sales goals. Earnouts can also act as an incentive for the seller to continue as part of the management team. This assures the buyer that the sellers will remain motivated to reach those sales and earnings goals.

One caveat: be careful if the earnout is structured as a bonus. If the earnout involves substantial sums, the IRS could make a claim of unreasonable compensation. In which case, the payments would not be deductible to the corporation as a business expense but would be treated as nondeductible dividends.

The seller should insist that the earnout measurement be tied to gross sales or revenues. Gross sales are better than profits because it is more easily measured and cannot be easily distorted or misstated. When the sellers remain as part of the management team, the buyer may insist that an earnout, based on revenues, be subjected to the maintenance of designated profit margins. This is meant to eliminate the incentive for the seller's management to develop profitless sales simply to achieve the earnout.

To illustrate, let's assume that the company's sales have averaged $10 million over the past three years. You are sure that growth will be 15 percent annually over the next five years and your conservative buyer will only accept a 5 percent growth rate.

One scenario among many possible solutions is listed in this example:

Year	5% Sales Growth Buyer's Forecast	15% Sales Growth Seller's Forecast
Base year	$10,000,000	$10,000,000
Year 1	10,500,000	11,500,000
Year 2	11,025,000	13,225,000
Year 3	11,576,000	15,209,000
Year 4	12,155,000	17,490,000
Year 5	12,763,000	20,114,000
Five-year total	$58,019,000	$77,538,000

Let's say the purchase price dispute between the buyer and the seller is $400,000. The difference between the seller's sales expectation and buyer's forecast is $19,519,000. Two percent of $19,519,000 is $390,000. The two parties could agree that the buyer will pay a 2 percent success bonus to the seller on sales above a 5 percent growth rate. After five years, the seller would receive $390,000 if his sales numbers were reached. The buyer could also insist on a cap of some dollar number because he wouldn't want to pay more than $390,000.

A seller may want the earnout money placed in escrow on an annual basis, or he may want it to be paid annually. There are many ways to structure the deal to each party's satisfaction.

The buyer often expresses concerns in an earnout that he may be obligated to make a larger payment than anticipated if the acquired company has erratic sales or earnings. The earnings or sales could grow, decline, and then skyrocket. A buyer may be obligated to pay the earnout if sales or earnings improve because of the buyer's hard work rather than because of any impending growth by the seller's company at the time of the acquisition.

You can address the foregoing concerns by placing a cap or ceiling on the total amount of the earnout if the buyer is worried about paying too much. Limits could also be placed on the amount of any single payment. The earnout could be delayed and paid after three years or five years, and so on. Earnings or sales that fall below the previous period could be penalized.

In the end, the buyer may decide it is better to pay a higher fixed price and avoid an earnout.

The seller has some concerns as well. He may worry that the company won't be managed in the same way. For example, the buyer may cut back on overhead, sales force, or capital expenditures. This could prevent the company from achieving its targets that make an earnout possible for the seller.

The seller may not believe that he will get a good accounting from the buyer. He may worry about creative accounting practices. In the case of a large corporate buyer, the seller will be concerned with the unreasonable allocation of the parent company expense burden that could depress earnings and his earnout, if the earnout is based on earnings.

When everything is said and done, the amount of the earnout may not be substantial enough to bother with. Earnouts sound good at first, but you need to determine carefully whether an earnout is the best solution. Generally, a seller should avoid an earnout unless the earnout is a part of a purchase price premium that he is holding out for.

COVENANT NOT TO COMPETE

A covenant not to compete generally prohibits a seller from engaging in a business similar to the one he has sold to the buyer for a specific time and over a specific geographical area. In addition, a seller must represent a viable competitive threat to the buyer. Obviously, a seller of advancing age and poor health might not pose a competitive threat.

Covenants not to compete can be for as many years as agreed to by both buyer and seller provided the time period is reasonable. From a tax standpoint, the buyer must amortize the covenant over 15 years, even though the agreed to covenant might be for only 5 years. This is the tax law regarding covenants not to compete that was enacted in the Revenue Reconciliation Act of 1993. Income the seller receives from the covenant is treated as ordinary income in the year received. See the discussion on goodwill and intangibles at the beginning of this chapter for a more detailed discussion of the tax consequences and history.

The seller is usually willing to accept a covenant not to compete because the buyer's request that the seller not compete with him is reasonable. The buyer is protected from the seller competing with him over the life of the covenant. In addition, the buyer is getting an interest free loan from the seller when the covenant is part of the purchase price. This helps offset the fact that the buyer can't write off the covenant not to compete any faster than 15 years.

The main drawback from the seller's standpoint is that income received from the covenant is treated as ordinary income. When a taxpayer is in the 39.6 percent federal tax bracket he'll pay a considerable amount more in taxes than if this income was capital gain tax that has a maximum rate of 28 percent.

EMPLOYMENT AND CONSULTING AGREEMENTS

Often the buyer wants the seller to stay on and manage the company. Many companies won't acquire another company unless the management stays on. Usually, when the seller owns the company, the buyer will want the seller to stay around and help with the transition. This is where consulting and employment contracts come in. The buyer may pay more for the business knowing it will be secure for a while longer. It raises his comfort level to have the seller stay on for a transition period.

It is advisable to make employment agreements and consulting agreements separate from the purchase agreement documents.

An employment agreement is a personal services contract. If this contract is embedded in the documentation of the deal, it can be a deal breaker for the seller. Generally, in cases of fraud or misrepresentation, lawyers look at the employment contract to help the buyer get out of the deal.

Both buyer and seller, however, enjoy real advantages in having an employment agreement. Let's take an example of a seller named Sam. Sam has owned his business for 20 years and has become accustomed to having the company pay for the perks he has enjoyed.

When Sam is asked, "What are you going to miss most of all after you sell your company and retire?" he'll often talk about the perks: the fishing and hunting trips he took with customer friends, the car, the annual trade convention in Hawaii, his country club membership, his airplane, and his suite at football and basketball games. It is not unusual for Tom to enjoy $30,000 to $60,000 a year in perks.

An employment contract is one way to continue to provide Sam with many of these perks. Sam knows the cost of his perks will double after the sale because he'll be paying for these perks with his after-tax money and not pretax company money. These perks can be a part of the total package paid for his company. The continued perks can be sweeteners that will help shelter some seller's income from the tax man. This expenditure is a regular business expense and doesn't show up on the balance sheet. The buyer can dangle out three to five years of perks and make the seller's exit less painful. The employment contract and perk package allow the seller a transitional period to adjust financially and psychologically to his new life-style.

By providing $30,000 to $60,000 worth of perks to the seller over five years, the buyer can knock $150,000 to $250,000 off the purchase price. A seller retains his perks, which would cost him $300,000 to $600,000 or more with after-tax dollars. The buyer has the services of the seller and takes a normal business deduction. The buyer has received an interest-free loan, in essence, with no effect on his balance sheet when he pays for the perks as part of the purchase price.

It is virtually impossible to provide anyone but an employee with a perk package. Therefore, a seller who is retained as part of the management team should insist on a generous perk package. By the way, the history of an entrepreneur staying on as an executive with a large company after the acquisition is not good. Usually a parting of the ways occurs within 18 months. The bureaucracy is too confining, and disagreements about policy cause the death of the relationship.

Consulting Agreements

Consulting agreements are an advantage to the seller because he can have continued involvement in the business and help ensure the continued success of the business. Sometimes the seller can obtain a higher purchase price for the business when a consulting agreement is part of the deal. Payments are ordinary income to the seller.

The buyer views a consulting contract as an opportunity to capitalize on the knowledge and wisdom of the seller. He knows that a lot of the business knowledge is in the seller's head and not on paper. The consulting agreement is tax deductible, and there are no interest payments owed. Part of the purchase price can be the consulting agreement, and payments are deferred from the close until the agreement calls for payment.

Consulting agreements are usually worded so that the seller receives a specific amount of money on a monthly, quarterly, or annual basis. In return, the seller's services are available to the buyer for a specific number of hours or days each month. The consulting contract may require that the seller's services be available to the buyer at the buyer's discretion. Therefore, a consulting agreement should be such that the payments to the seller are made even if the buyer doesn't use the seller's consulting services. An agreement should also specify that the consultant will receive certain hourly payments when the consulting time is exceeded.

The contract should be separate from the selling documents. The failure of the consulting agreement should not void the sale. A consulting agreement should allow the seller to set up a separate consulting company. This is wise because it allows the seller to provide the buyer with his own consulting services or with substitute services of a like quality. The seller doesn't want to have to come home from a winter vacation because the buyer needs his consulting services. The danger here for the seller is if circumstances such as his health, a management dispute, or a misrepresentation claim comes up, he doesn't want the consulting agreement or deal to come apart because he hasn't performed his agreed-to consulting service. With a consulting agreement, the seller should have the right to continue to provide the services through another person.

Here is a good way the seller can defer some taxes on the consulting agreement to which the buyer should agree as well. It is based on the principle that taxes aren't paid on borrowed money. Our seller doesn't have to pay taxes on this money because he is borrowing it from his newly created consulting company.

Here is how it works:

A buyer prepays several years of consulting services to the seller's consulting company. The seller then borrows the money from his consulting company. He pays taxes only when he actually provides the consulting service.

Let's say that your not-to-compete agreement is for three years and the agreement calls for $200,000. You have a seven-year consulting agreement that is set up so that at the end of the third year payments escalate from a small amount of $10,000 a year to $100,000 a year in years 4 through 7. The buyer prepays the entire seven-year contract at close to the seller's consulting company. The seller then borrows the money from his consulting company and does not pay taxes on that money until he actually earns it. A seller has the use of the money up front from the beginning for investment or whatever. This is a very good way to provide a seller with a lot of tax-sheltered money up front. It is especially important for a seller who doesn't need cash for his immediate use and doesn't want to pay taxes on that cash at the ordinary income tax rate.

14

INNOVATIVE STRUCTURING

Eight Surefire Techniques That Save Taxes and Increase Profits

Tax laws constantly change. Discuss with your tax adviser the merit of any of the tax-deferral methods suggested here.

COLLATERAL SUBSTITUTION

A buyer often won't pay all cash and will want to leverage part of the assets of your company as a means of paying for your company. He will want you to allow him to pledge the assets of your company as collateral for a loan from a lender. Further, he may ask you to subordinate your interest in the assets to the lender. You may not want to do this.

You fear that he'll run the business into the ground and you won't get paid for all your years of hard work. Your junior position to the lender won't mean much if the buyer botches the deal. Further, you need to consider the tax ramifications besides your risk. One way to hurdle this collateral problem so that it's a winning situation for both of you is for the buyer to purchase a single-premium immediate annuity from a highly rated insurance company. The buyer will name you its annuitant and benefactor.

Let's say you are 60 years old and are to receive $8,384 a month for ten years as part of the terms of the annuity. The life insurance company is guaranteeing and making the payments. If the buyer runs your company into the ground, you'll still be paid by the insurance company. The total payments in this example are $1,006,085 over ten years. If you should die before the payments have been made to you, the insurance company will pay your beneficiary the same income amount for the balance of the ten-year period.

Seventy-two percent of the monthly income in this example is not taxable. You receive $6,003 of the $8,384 and do not pay tax on it. The percentage of income not taxable is effective until the net investment in the contract has been recovered, when the remaining income is taxable.

The advantages to you are obvious: security and a greatly reduced tax burden. You know you'll get paid because a blue-chip insurance company is insuring the payments. You can retire and smell the roses knowing you won't have to worry. You will be paid.

The buyer will like providing you with an annuity. By allowing him to leverage your assets to buy the annuity for you, you're enabling him to acquire your company. Further, he'll be buying the annuity based on the present-day value of money. So the $1 million he owes you won't cost $1 million but something less, based on the current interest rates. Currently, when interest rates are low, the cost to the buyer in this example would have been approximately $720,000. This is a good deal for both of you. Your tax advisers can help you arrive at an equitable arrangement in which the taxes are paid by both of you.

Your security in the deal is the insurance company. You do not have a security interest in either stock or the assets of your former company. As a result, you don't have to worry about what happens to the company. One exception is the matter of fraudulent conveyance that is discussed in Chapter 14. Be sure you read about fraudulent conveyance.

The buyer will like the deal because he can use your assets to acquire the company. Naturally, you'll help him in arranging a loan with an asset-based lender so he can acquire your company and do it risk-free for you.

Sale-Leaseback Tax Shelter

Generally, a seller will have the physical facility housing his business outside the corporation. If this is your situation, you have been well advised. Your company most likely has a lease arrangement with you, and you are using the lease payments to make principal and interest payments on your factory or building. You are taking some depreciation and interest expenses to shelter part of the income you are receiving from your company. If this isn't the case, then you should sell the facility to yourself and lease it back to the new owner at fair market rental rates. The technique of a sale leaseback can work for other company assets as well.

The buyer needs to cooperate with you to maximize the benefits for you. Remember, the key to doing a deal is knowing what your needs are and making them known to the buyer. You help him buy your company by being flexible, and he helps you. As you know, terms drive the deal. Here is how it works.

Sam owns a corporation, and the corporation owns a $1 million building. Bill wants to buy the corporation. The first step Sam must do is to buy the building from his corporation at fair market value (not book value). Sam, as an individual now, owns the building.

Sam gives the corporation a promissory note for $1 million. He then has the title to the building, and the corporation has the note from Sam. Bill's new corporation signs a new lease with Sam as an individual. The lease is a 15-year triple-net CPI lease that requires the tenant to pay all taxes, repairs, and utilities. The CPI portion is the Consumer Price Index, which means that Bill's lease payments are indexed for inflation.

Bill, now the owner of the corporation, signs the lease with Sam. Sam then sells the lease at a discount to a pension fund or insurance company. The insurance company pays Sam enough cash for the lease so that even when discounted, the cash covers the purchase price of the building. Sam receives $1 million from the insurance company for the lease.

Bill's new corporation (Sam's former company) now makes the lease payments to the insurance company. Sam uses the $1 million to redeem the note from his corporation. The corporation has the $1 million, while Sam owns the building and has the full tax benefits of owning a building. Depreciation from the building helps shelter some of the income Sam will receive from Bill for his company, especially if it involves a note. The company has the $1 million that can then be used for a major down payment on the purchase price paid by Bill.

In summary, Sam has the building to shelter the ordinary income he receives for his company. The deal must be done on an arm's-length transaction with the buyer because otherwise the IRS will call it a sham and disallow it. With the buyer in the deal, it works as an arm's-length transaction. This wouldn't work with your wife or brother-in-law.

A CONSULTING AGREEMENT AS A TAX SHELTER

Generally, a seller is well advised not to sign an employment contract. An employment contract is a personal-services contract. When an employment agreement is part of the purchase agreement, it can be used by the buyer as a deal breaker. The buyer can plead misrepresentation and use the employment agreement as a means to get out of the deal. Usually, the seller just stops performing on the employment agreement. The buyer then goes to court and asks the judge to set aside the entire transaction because of nonperformance under the employment agreement. Entrepreneurs do not make good employees. Generally, an entrepreneur and the acquiring company have serious disputes over the way the company is run. This usually happens within 18 months. When this happens, the seller wants out.

When you need to remain with the company under the terms of the purchase agreement, you should not include the employment agreement as part of the purchase agreement. You'll also want the employment agreement to continue to pay your perks and fringe benefits. This includes not only your salary, but your car, trade show attendance, country club dues, insurance, artwork, a condominium, and so on. Better for the company to pay your $10,000 country club dues and deduct those expenses than for you to have to earn $17,000 to keep $10,000 after taxes to pay for it.

When you have a consulting agreement, it usually is not possible for you to have your perks paid for by the company. You can turn your consulting company into another beautiful tax shelter, however. Consulting agreements normally allow the seller to set up another company, but you must do this before you close the deal.

Now your consulting company has an agreement to provide consulting services to your old company. It must enable you to provide like quality services. The consulting agreement with your new consulting corporation is not a personal services agreement. When you are in Florida for the winter or you are sick, you may not want to provide the services called for in the contract. With a properly drafted consulting contract, one of your consultant associates can provide the services, and you can still meet the terms of the contract.

Here is an excellent tax-planning tool when you use a consulting company. It is based on the principle that you do not pay taxes on borrowed money. You don't pay taxes because you will be borrowing the money from your consulting company.

You'll agree to a noncompeting agreement with the buyer for three years. Covenant-not-to-compete payments are ordinary income to you. Since you are receiving covenant-not-to-compete ordinary income for the first three years, you want very little consulting income the first three years. Then, beginning in the fourth year, you'll want a lot of consulting money. Consulting income is ordinary income to you and deductible to the buyer.

As an example, let's assume you have a ten-year consulting agreement with payments of $10,000 due annually the first three years and then $100,000 annually for years 4 through 10. You, therefore, have a ten-year consulting contract with your former company worth $730,000. Then, let's assume that the buyer prepays the entire $730,000 of the consulting agreement at close to your consulting company. You then borrow the money from your consulting company to use or invest as you wish. You have a loan from your company that you will pay back as you see fit, and you won't pay taxes on that money until you earn it.

In this example, if you need or want a lot of money at close, you can do so without triggering a big tax bite because the tax is deferred until you earn the money.

LOOK UP IN THE SKY! IT'S A ZERO? IT'S A STRIP?

No, it isn't Superman and it's not a World War II Japanese airplane or the Las Vegas Strip. It's a U.S. Treasury bond, and it works like the old Series E savings bonds. You buy them for a discount off face value and hold them until maturity. Then you collect the face amount. Discounts from face value depend on the interest rate and the length of maturity.

Assume you and the buyer can't agree on the purchase price. So you say, "Look, I'll do the deal, but I want a balloon payment of $250,000 in 5 years, a $500,000 payment in 10 years, and $1 million payment in 20 years. The payment due in 20 years is to go to my children and grandchildren. The payment in 10 years and 5 years is to be paid directly to me." You do this for tax-shelter purposes, knowing your grandchildren will need it for college and going into business. They'll be in a lower tax bracket than you, and you won't need the money.

The buyer (Bill) balks and refuses to go along with your plan because he says it will cost too much. You say, "Bill, it won't. Let me show you why. Bill, I want you to buy a U.S. government savings bond called a zero or strip. Since you'll be paying for this zero at close, you'll be using the present-day value to acquire it. You'll get it at a big discount off face value. Further, I want the face value fixed and guaranteed. It's from the insurance industry, and the one I want is called a future values certificate." The insurance company buys the zeros, and you make the deal with the insurance carrier.

The example that follows best illustrates how it works. Remember, the U.S. government is guaranteeing and making the payments to you, not the buyer. Bill is purchasing the zero from the government for your benefit along with your children's and your grandchildren's. Bill is purchasing the zero at a big discount from the face value. These debt instruments pay no interest over the lifetime of the instrument. That is why they are discounted off the face value so steeply.

Maturity Date	Face Value at Maturity	Discount from Face Value	Cost to Buyer	Yield to Maturity
5 years	$ 250,000	25%	$187,500	6.2%
10 years	500,000	50	250,000	7.4
20 years	1,000,000	80	200,000	8.0
Totals	$1,750,000	63.6	$637,500	

For $637,500 Bill has purchased $1,750,000 of bonds for you and your family. This is a way to provide for your family in the future. The 5-year bond can go to your son, daughter, or wife, for example, if you don't want it. The possibilities are limitless.

A key disadvantage for you is that the IRS won't wait 10 or 20 years for its cut. The interest is taxed as it accrues. Each year you own zeros, you must report and pay tax on the interest. Your investment is assumed to have been earned that year.

The tax on the interest assigned to your children or grandchildren can be paid by you. Since your children will likely be in the 15 percent tax bracket, their tax liability will be less than yours. You and your wife each can give $10,000 to your children annually. There is no tax liability to them for the gift that can then be used to pay their tax liability. You and your wife can make a $20,000 gift to each child annually. That will cover their taxes when your kids are in the 15 percent tax bracket. If you have 20 children and grandchildren, you and your spouse together can give away $400,000 annually and never have to fill out a gift tax form. That will go a long way to reduce your estate tax liability down the road when you aren't here anymore.

There is a way to beat this, however. Don't buy federal bonds; buy tax-free zeros issued by municipalities. These are investments that dodge the federal tax liability entirely. Because the interest is tax-free if it is paid periodically, there is no federal tax liability in having the accruing income assigned to you annually. It's tax-free!

You may have to sweeten the offer for Bill to get him to go along. You can assume more tax liability or let him use the assets of your company to leverage the deal. You can agree to an asset sale rather than a stock sale. The options are endless. A smart seller can achieve a much larger selling price with fewer taxes than an uninformed one.

CONVERTIBLE BONDS OR DEBENTURES

A standard debenture is a general debt obligation, usually subordinated, that is backed only by the reputation of the issuing company; that is, it is an unsecured bond. As an interest-bearing security, a standard debenture obligates the company to pay the holder a specific amount of money at intervals. The principal amount of the loan is repaid at maturity.

A convertible debenture is a bond that can be exchanged at a future date for a specified number of common shares at a preset price. Terms of the debenture can be that the debenture amount can be converted into common stock, for example, at 15 percent higher than market price.

Let's say a public company wants to acquire you. You like the company and know it has a good future. The public company wants you to help finance the transaction and offers you a debenture. You agree but insist it be convertible to common stock. You lock in a steady interest return on the bond (debenture) and still enjoy the appreciation value of the company's stock. The IRS is willing to go along because the bond interest is taxable. If you opt to convert to stock, the transaction is not taxable because your basis in the bonds simply shifts to the stock. When you sell the stock, you pay the tax man.

Debentures are excellent tools for you to use, but only if you have the conversion-to-stock feature. Better yet, you should have the debenture convertible to either stock or cash. You'll have the best of both worlds: cash, if the stock goes down in value, and stock, if the value of the stock goes up.

Bring in a Partner

This method allows you to sell your business for a premium and allows the buyer to acquire your company for nothing down. That is why you can command a premium. It's a reverse of the collateral-substitution method.

The technique here is that you find a large qualified buyer who uses his borrowing ability to purchase 49 percent of your company. Your company, in return, promises to pay off the buyer's loan. However, the buying company guarantees and obtains the loan so the loan is not secured by your company's assets.

You pocket the loan amount and enjoy it today. Your company pays the loan off over five years. The buying company can then have the right to buy you out after the loan is paid off or after several years. You can also jointly agree to sell the company in its entirety after five years, with you receiving 51 percent and the buyer 49 percent of the proceeds.

You receive a higher price for your company and you get cash now, but you need to stay with the company for a few years. The buyer uses his borrowing power and receives 49 percent of the company without any of his own capital invested.

This is a way for you to sell your company for a premium. The key is finding the right buyer and being willing to wait up to five years to cash out entirely. It also is a way for you to become much more liquid now.

An LBO

A leveraged buyout uses many techniques outlined in this chapter. An LBO is an excellent way to sell your company for more than the earnings allow. This is especially true for an asset-intensive company with low profits compared with the value of the assets.

An ideal LBO company has slow or flat growth. It is also a low-tech company in a mature, fragmented market. It has lots of assets but not too much debt.

Let's say this describes your company and a buyer wants to buy your company. With this approach, he'll use the assets of your company as collateral to do the deal. Because your earnings don't justify a high selling price, you decide to sell to him. The buyer, on the other hand, is a fireball. He sees that product line X produces $200,000 a year in profits and requires $2 million of the assets to support those profits. Product line Y produces $600,000 a year in profits and requires $3 million of the assets.

The buyer liquidates product line X for $2 million, which he then uses to pay the asset-based lender. Part of the $2 million is reinvested in new equipment needs for product line Y. The debt is reduced and the company continues to grow, paying off the seller over time.

Your asset-intensive, low-profit company has provided you now with a better than expected purchase price. The buyer purchases your company using the assets of the company to collateralize the loan, that he then uses to buy the company from you. The business is now less asset intensive and more efficient. Sometimes part of the company is sold to provide needed cash to reduce debt levels to acceptable standards.

The result is that you receive a high price compared to the earnings of the company; the buyer purchases the company for a smaller down payment than normal, and the company is then more efficiently organized than before.

You could do the reorganizing yourself. Generally, sellers don't. You are bored and tired of the business and aren't up to it. Maybe you are emotionally attached and can't let go. You see the opportunities but just don't have the desire to put forth the effort and take the risks required to take advantage of the opportunities. Sell to an LBO buyer, and he'll do it for you.

How The Kids Can Buyout Dad Without Any Cash

You now want out of your family business and want to sell to your two grown kids who want to buy your business. The problem is that they don't have any money. What should you do? Sell them your business anyway. Here's how to do it. Your problem is that all of your assets are tied up in your business. Your corporation owns most of your assets, including excess cash, investments, land, and building. These assets, however, are not needed to run the business. Let's examine this puzzle more closely and see how you might sell your business to your grown children although they have no cash to buy it with.

Bob, who is married to Beth, owns 100 percent of Maxima Machine Corporation, Inc. that is worth $3,040,000. Maxima Machine has 3,040 shares of common stock that are worth $1,000 a share. Bob's son and daughter Todd and Stacey have been running the business for the past few years and Bob is confident that they will be good managers without his presence.

Bob sets up the following five-step plan: (1) Bob gives 40 shares of stock worth $40,000 to Todd and Stacey. Todd and Stacey each receive 20 shares worth $20,000. (2) Beth joins in the gift tax return, making the $40,000 a tax-free gift. (3) Bob sells his remaining 3,000 shares to Maxima Machine Corporation for $3,000,000. (4) Maxima Machine Corporation pays for the shares with $250,000 in cash, $550,000 in real estate, and a note for $2,200,000 payable over 15 years. Interest is prime plus 1 percent. (5) Bob resigns, retires and moves with his wife, Beth, to their dream vacation home.

What is the result? Todd and Stacey now own 100 percent of Maxima Machine Corporation, 50 percent each. Bob collects three things from the company: rent for the real estate he leases back to the corporation, and interest and principal payments on the $2,200,000 note. Bob pays only the capital gains rate of 28 percent on the stock profits and only as he collects the principal. He pays ordinary income tax on the interest received. The example is very flexible and can be changed in many ways to fit the objectives of most family businesses.

15

LEGAL TRAPS

The Shark Bites After The Sale Too!

You need a deal-oriented attorney to help put the transaction together. He must have deal-oriented experience because a mistake could be costly, and there are many potential legal traps you'll need to avoid. You'll pay for a good, experienced, deal-oriented attorney, but he'll save you a lot of money in the end. You can't afford to pay a less knowledgeable attorney to learn at your expense.

When you begin the sales process, you should negotiate the price. You are the only person who knows the details of what has happened to date in all those meetings with the buyer. You are also the only one who knows your acceptable bottom-line price. Further, you have built a positive relationship with the buyer and you will want to maintain this relationship. Remember, you may choose to work for the buyer, so protect your relationship. (See Chapter 11 for specific instructions about negotiation strategies and tactics that you'll need in the early phases of the negotiating process.) There is a right and wrong time to bring an attorney into the negotiation's picture. Failure to understand when to have an attorney at your side during negotiations and when not will place you at a significant disadvantage in the early stages of negotiations.

The pages that follow discuss some important legal issues involved in a transaction. By being aware of the important legal issues, you can discuss your needs and wants with your attorney during the letter of intent and purchase agreement phases of the deal. You'll also be made aware of some significant legal pitfalls that I hope you'll avoid.

Your deal-oriented lawyer and the buyer's lawyer negotiate the conditions of sale. There are several reasons for this. First, the final documentation must be clear and defendable in a court of law. It must protect both you and the buyer. Second, when the negotiations hit a snag and the going gets tough, you'll want your lawyer to be the bad guy. You blame your attorney for the condition in the contract or why you won't agree to some condition. It's your attorney, and he won't let you agree to what the buyer wants. You want to remain the good guy so the deal goes through. If you and the buyer get angry with each other, the deal will be off. You must maintain the chemistry between you and the buyer.

When you negotiate price and terms, it is quite common for buyers to pay all professional fees for both parties involved. However, don't expect the buyer to offer this. He won't. You raise the issue. If the deal doesn't go through for some reason, both parties pay their own professional fees.

Letter of Intent

The seller is always in the strongest negotiating position before the letter of intent is signed. Therefore, the seller should try to extract as many concessions as possible before signing any letter of intent. The letter of intent may be an unnecessary expense and time factor. This is the case when the initial draft of the acquisition agreement can be prepared quickly, or when the parties appear to have a high level of trust in each other.

A letter of intent is usually drafted by the buyer and includes the important terms of the deal; ideally, the letter ends negotiations on price and terms.

The letter of intent bridges the time gap until the purchase agreement can be executed and the buyer does due diligence.

A letter of intent is also useful to commit and inform other players to a transaction, including lenders, other stockholders, and sometimes important customers and suppliers.

The letter of intent should also establish a timetable in which the buyer must complete his due diligence investigation of the seller.

The seller generally wants the buyer to put up a significant qualifying deposit. This separates the contenders from the pretenders. However, the buyer will generally want a binding agreement and a no-shop clause for the deposit requirement. This, in essence, takes the company off the market. The letter of intent may sometimes be binding, anyway, if the seller perceives that there are few qualified buyers and he is comfortable in making all anticipated representations and warranties about his business. Unless the amount of deposit is significant, the seller should not agree to a no-shop clause or a binding agreement.

Typically the letter of intent includes the purchase price, terms of payment or a formula to determine the purchase price, and a general description of the stock or assets to be purchased by the buyer and those retained by the seller. It also includes noncompetition covenants or special employment agreements.

The letter of intent should have a binding confidentiality and nondisclosure agreement. The confidentiality portion must prohibit the buyer from revealing any information about the proposed sale of the business. Further, the nondisclosure part must prohibit the buyer from disclosing or using any of the seller's proprietary information or trade secrets. The seller should take all protective measures and limit the business information revealed to the buyers. As the deal progresses to the near-close phase, the seller can release the more sensitive information. This should be done only in the later stages when the seller is sure the deal will close.

Once you sign the letter of intent, the buyer will begin his due diligence process, and he'll draft the final purchase agreement. The negotiations over the buyer's draft are what makes or break the deal. Letters of intent and final purchase agreements can be long and detailed or short, consisting of as few as five pages for simpler transactions, excluding exhibits.

There are two important legal doctrines that both you and your attorney should be aware of. If he is a deal-oriented attorney, he'll know about them. The first important legal trap is called the **sale-of-business doctrine**; the second is called **fraudulent conveyance**.

Sale-of-Business Doctrine

Sellers are well advised to be careful about the representations they make. It is most important to make full, complete, and truthful disclosures about the business they are selling. A seller can be sued by the buyer in state and federal courts for fraud should there be material misrepresentation of fact. A seller must be totally truthful and hold nothing back.

For many years, securities law specialists believed that securities laws did not apply to the transfer of stock of a privately held company. The reasoning was that although the transfer involved shares of stock, it was in reality a means of conveying ownership. However, this so-called sale-of-business doctrine has been rejected by the U.S. Supreme Court and presumably will be rejected by the state courts as well.

This means that if you sell your company and take part or all of the purchase price in stock from the buyer's company as payment, you can be sued by the buyer for fraud. The Supreme Court ruled that this kind of transaction comes under the jurisdiction of the Securities Act of 1933.

This is a good place to remind you of two important points. First, be sure to give full disclosure of all material and relevant facts both orally and in a written sales document. Second, be certain you have a deal-oriented attorney who will set out the facts in detail in a purchase agreement.

Fraudulent Conveyance

If you structure a deal so that you create a fraudulent conveyance, both you and the buyer will regret it. Fraudulent conveyance occurs when a company enters bankruptcy and can't pay its creditors. Fraudulent conveyance is a legal idea that comes out of the sixteenth-century English Statute of Elizabeth. Presently there are four statutory schemes under which fraudulent conveyance risks may arise: the bankruptcy code, which has national application; modern versions of the old English Statute of Elizabeth; the Uniform Fraudulent Conveyance Act; and the Uniform Fraudulent Transfer Act. The Uniform Fraudulent Transfer Act has been adopted by over 25 states.

Fraudulent conveyance is based on the concern of creditors when ownership of a business changes hands. Unsecured suppliers, especially smaller suppliers, do not normally demand quarterly or monthly financial statements and do credit reviews of their customers. Some may monitor the change of ownership. Suppliers may even change the terms and conditions on which they have been extending credit to your company. Generally, your suppliers will continue extending credit to the buyer after you sell him your company without a review of the credit of the new buyer. Concern about fraudulent conveyance arises because these suppliers rely on the continued creditworthiness of the business you have sold.

When a buyer leverages the seller's assets to purchase a company, the potential exists for a fraudulent conveyance. Should this newly acquired company fail because it can't support the debt payments, a fraudulent conveyance is created because one or both of you should have known that too much debt was placed on the company.

For example, you are selling a company that has $15 million in sales and $1 million in pretax income. The future looks rosy for your company, and you persuade the buyer and his lenders that sales are going to be way above expected industry growth. The buyer, consequently, takes on significant debt to purchase the company, using the selling company's assets to secure the acquisition debt. Subsequently, sales fall way below expectations and the buyer can't meet his debt payments. You have just created a condition under which you could be charged with fraudulent conveyance. You would be unwise to project your company's future sales increases above and beyond normal industry growth.

Anything you or the buyer does in structuring the deal's terms so that the company is burdened with debt beyond its capacity to pay that debt runs the risk of a fraudulent conveyance. If the company goes bankrupt after the sale, a bankruptcy judge or trustee can declare the sale a fraudulent conveyance. If that happens, the seller may be required to put all the proceeds of the sale back into the company. The buyer will have to restore all the assets to the company and return all the money borrowed to buy the company. The lender will lose its senior security position in the assets that it lent against. All this happens so that the unsecured creditors will have a fair, equitable shot at the assets of the company in the event it is liquidated in bankruptcy.

Your potential liability for a fraudulent conveyance can be as long as six years after the sale. Most buyers will not be aware of this, but ignorance of the law will not remove the obligation or responsibility for either buyer or seller. You can see why it is important that you do all you can to be certain the company thrives and survives after you have sold it.

You can also see why it is important to have a deal-oriented attorney and accounting firm. A key question they must answer for you is this: "Have I put together the deal so that if the new owner goes bankrupt our deal cannot be charged with fraudulent conveyance?"

WHAT IS tHE BULK SALES ACT?

When a buyer purchases your company's assets, you must comply with Article 6 of the Uniform Commercial Code (UCC) to protect the buyer from the claims of your creditors. The buyer will insist on this. To comply, the buyer will require you to furnish a list of your creditors, signed and sworn by you. You and the buyer must prepare a schedule of the property to be transferred. In addition, your creditors will need to be notified a certain number of days before the buyer takes possession of the assets or pays for them, whichever comes first. The list of creditors must be preserved for six months following the transfer. Details may vary depending on the state in which you are located. Some states, such as Minnesota, have repealed their bulk sales transfer laws and rely on the Uniform Fraudulent Transfer Act to protect unsecured creditors.

The buyer and seller may waive compliance with the Bulk Sales Act. When this is done, the buyer will want the seller to indemnify him against any claims made by the seller's creditors.

Test your lawyer by seeing if he knows the law on bulk sales transfers. If he doesn't, forget him. He isn't a deal-oriented attorney. By the way, most deals waive the bulk sales requirements, and the seller indemnifies the buyer against creditor claims. Notifying creditors of a sale just raises too many red flags.

WHAT IS A UCC FILING?

You'll have to file and record financial statements and security interests in collateral, such as business assets, with the secretary of state's office.

In Minnesota, for example, this is called a UCC-1 filing. A UCC-11 is a request for information about those fillings and is available for a nominal fee.

Ask your attorney about a UCC-1 filing. If he doesn't know about it, he isn't a deal-oriented attorney.

THE PURCHASE AGREEMENT

Your attorney and your buyer's attorney will draft and negotiate the various terms and conditions in the purchase or merger agreement. You must have some knowledge and understanding of several key sections in the agreement, especially the parts dealing with representations, warranties, and indemnification.

Attorneys, by their nature, training, and experience, see the worst in every situation. They also are adversarially oriented. As a result, an unskilled attorney can kill a deal that should have been consummated. There will be trade-offs, and both parties will need to negotiate many elements in the agreement. You want a deal-oriented attorney who knows the areas of the agreement that are important and should not be compromised. He also knows those areas where you need to compromise. You need an attorney you can trust, respect, and control. You must trust his judgment but remain in charge. You must be able to control him, not let him control you. After all, your company and future are on the line.

The concluding section of this chapter contains an outline of some conditions that may or may not be included in the purchase agreement. You'll want to review them so you'll have a feel for what is ahead of you.

The section of the agreement that will be very important to you is the part dealing with representations, warranties, and indemnifications.

The purchase agreement can favor either the buyer or seller in some important areas, depending on how the agreement is drafted. Here are some examples:

1. The extent to which selling shareholders will receive cash at the time of closing. Cash paid would be net of any unpaid taxes.
2. The extent to which buyers will bear the burden of the selling company's liabilities, disclosed and undisclosed.

    a. Will the agreements be drafted so that the buyer inherits all of the selling company's liabilities?

    b. Or will the agreement be drafted in a way that the buyer assumes only specified liabilities and the remainder are left with the selling company or its shareholders?

    c. Who will be responsible for significant contingent liabilities such as environmental cleanup, product liabilities, tax deficiencies, and threatened or pending lawsuits?

    d. Who will be responsible for hidden liabilities such as underfunded pension plans, burdensome long-term debt covenants, or labor problems?

3. The extent to which sellers will be required to give representations and warranties.

    a. The representation and warranty section of the agreement could contain only a few representations and warranties concerning the selling company. The section could, also, be qualified frequently with reference to knowledge (defined as actual knowledge without independent investigation) and materiality. The section also could be restricted to certain people such as shareholders and not be a broad coverage of many people such as employees, officers, directors, and others.

    b. The buyer, of course, will want extensive representations and warranties without any qualification as to materiality and with only occasional reference to knowledge.

    c. A good seller provision would be that none of the representations or warranties survive the closing and that there is no indemnification for breach after closing.

4. Indemnification is the legal mechanism by which the seller will be liable for any breach of the covenants, representations, and warranties made by the seller in the purchase agreement.

    a. The seller should try to limit the time under which a buyer can make a claim under this provision.

    b. An indemnification section should have both a floor and a ceiling in terms of the amount of money a buyer can put a claim in for. Furthermore, a seller could also try to have a per-claim deductible rather than an aggregate claim. The buyer, however, may want provisions requiring the sellers to deposit part of the purchase price with a third-party escrow agent. The buyer could insist on holding back part of the purchase price (to be paid later with interest). He also may want a security interest in certain seller assets. The buyer, for example, could absorb the first 5 percent of the selling price of the company. Indemnification aggregate claims could be limited to 25 percent of the selling price.

c. A seller's indemnification obligations should be several (rather than joint) and in proportion to his respective holdings of shares of stock. Otherwise, the buyer will go after the deepest-pocket shareholder for all the indemnification obligation. The buyer may seek to have obligations of the sellers as a group be joint and several rather than joint only. This would be defined so that each seller would be responsible for all the buyer's adverse consequences (instead of only for his allocable portion) if the sellers as a group failed to perform their obligations. This would protect the buyers from having to proceed against all the sellers to collect all owed to them.

d. The buyer could also not have the right to recoup its losses against any buyer notes issued instead of seeking indemnification from the selling shareholders.

5. The buyer's obligation to close the transaction could, also, be subject to minimal conditions such as

a. Compliance with the seller's representations, warranties, and covenants.

b. Absence of a material change in the business.

c. Delivery of any side agreements.

d. Delivery of an opinion of the seller's legal counsel.

6. The buyer could, also, not have any closing condition concerning its ability to secure financing for the transaction. The same applies to any right to cancel the purchase agreement after signing if the buyer is not satisfied with the results of its business, legal, and accounting due diligence review. A buyer, of course, will want just the opposite.

7. Upon execution of the purchase agreement, how much earnest money will the buyer be required to put up? How much are liquidated damages if the buyer doesn't go through with the deal?

8. When the buyer takes certain liabilities of the seller in an asset sale, the seller should insist that all third parties enter a novation agreement with the buyer. This means that if the buyer fails to satisfy the assumed liabilities and obligations, nonconsenting third parties to whom the seller owed the liabilities and obligations will not have a cause of action against the seller.

9. The seller should be aware that any stock that the seller accepts from the buyer in the deal usually cannot be traded for at least two years. Further, there may be restrictions even longer if the buyer does not maintain a public market for the stock. Restricted stock is often difficult to sell and is subject to a substantial discount. Stock registration rights come in two basic forms. Demand registration rights require the buyer to register the shares for a resale at some future date. Piggyback registration rights entitle the shareholders to include their shares as part of any future registration offering conducted by the buyer. Either way, federal and state securities laws make it possible for shares to be sold into the market for cash.

Representations, Warranties, and Indemnifications

The greatest potential liability a seller will have in the purchase agreement will be in the sections dealing with representations, warranties, and indemnifications. Once the buyer has acquired your company, often he'll begin to complain about one or more issues. For example, one representation you may have agreed to in the purchase agreement is that the inventory conveyed to the buyer is salable, fit for its intended use, and free of any defects in workmanship. The buyer may find some inventory is not salable and will expect you to pay for it.

A buyer will usually have an acquisition attorney who insists that one of your representations and warranties be that all your representations are true and correct. In case of a breach of any representation, warranty, or covenant, the seller will indemnify and hold the buyer harmless from any cost, liability, or expense that might arise. You may also end up giving the buyer the right to offset any bad inventory against the money you'll be collecting from him under installment sale terms. The buyer may negotiate so that part of the sales price is escrowed at closing for a period as security in case he discovers undisclosed liabilities after the close. A buyer can then use the escrow as a means to have his claim satisfied.

If the buyer feels defrauded, he can sue you under federal and state securities laws. This applies when you have taken a buyer's stock as a form of payment. The buyer can also claim intentional infliction of emotional distress.

To prove fraud, the buyer must show the existence of an untrue representation that is material to the value of the business and that you knew about. He can also claim you concealed a material fact. You could be held responsible for what you should have known but didn't know.

Most purchase agreements contain a seller's representation that there are no actions, suits, or proceedings pending, to the seller's knowledge, threatened against or involving the seller, or brought by the seller, or affecting any of the parts of the company the buyer acquires. This means that if the buyer discovers after the close of sale that you were served with a lawsuit alleging the manufacture of defective products, the buyer can allege that you should have said that the representation was true "except for" or "other than" the product liability claim. Make sure these "except-for"s are included in the schedules attached to the purchase agreement.

Indemnity provisions are the most disputed items in negotiations. A seller should insist on and limit the time that a buyer can make an indemnification claim. Two years or less is reasonable. One way to restrict your exposure to an indemnification claim would be to have an indemnification clause that says that aggregate claims must exceed a certain dollar amount, such as $100,000. Thus, if the aggregate claims for which the buyer wishes indemnification do not exceed $100,000, no indemnity is possible. The buyer has a right to indemnification only for amounts more than $100,000. This prevents the buyer from beating you over the head with nuisance lawsuits using the indemnification issue. You should also have a ceiling. An example could be that the maximum claim the buyer can make under indemnification will not exceed a certain percentage of the purchase price, such as 25 percent.

You, as a seller, should insist that the buyer indemnify you for any breach of his representations and warranties. However, indemnification is primarily a legal protection used by the buyer. This section of the purchase agreement is very important, and you should thoroughly understand its meaning.

A wise seller carefully shows via schedules or exhibits appended to the purchase agreement all facts concerning the business. It is also wise to have written attorneys' opinions relating to matters of law contained in the representations and warranties. This puts the attorneys on the hook, also. The same would apply to your accounting firm. They are representing you and you are relying on them for documentation, advice, and counsel by which a buyer may later sue you. Make them responsible along with you.

You should make sure that buyer representations and warranties are contained in the purchase agreements as opposed to just the security agreements. This will better protect you from a breach by the buyer.

Also make sure that there is an ending date for your representations or warranties. Obviously, the closing date would be best, but normally you can negotiate a year or two. When there is no end date, when the representations and warranties survive closing and the consummation of the deal, then the statue of limitations is the period. In some states, the statue of limitations is six years. Be careful here! You don't want six years.

A typical purchase agreement will cover many topics, including a description of the assets and liabilities. The agreement also covers the price and terms of the deal, representations and warranties of both buyer and seller, and an indemnification section spelling out how damages are decided in case of a breach by either party. However, your greatest liability and concern rest with those representations and warranties you'll make to the buyer. The seller's representations and warranties reveal all pertinent facts concerning the business. Furthermore, the representations and warranties shift to the seller the risks of untrue statements concerning those facts. These provisions give the buyer a basis for ending the agreement or possibly renegotiating its terms. In other words, the representations and warranties can be used as a club against you. The most important representations are those regarding financial statements, litigation, taxes, and undisclosed liabilities. You can bet that your buyer's attorney will insist on your representing these.

Listed next are some typical representations and warranties the buyer will ask you to make. Depending on the job your attorney does, there can be as many as 30 or more representations. For you, the fewer representations the better. The entries listed are the more common representations:

1. Your financial statements must be complete and correct. Further, your financial statements must present fairly the financial conditions and results of the operation of your business for the dates and periods indicated. Often a pro forma, adjusted, balance sheet is prepared for the time of close and is used to decide the purchase price. For example, the pro forma would compute the adjusted tangible assets. Insist on generally accepted accounting practices (GAAP) in the adjusted tangible asset determination. This will keep arguments about accounting methods to a minimum and save you money.

2. There is no litigation, proceeding, or governmental investigation existing or pending. Further, seller has no reasonable grounds or knowledge to be aware of any litigation, proceeding, or governmental action.

3. Regarding employment of labor, seller has complied with all federal and state laws and local ordinances relating to employment of employees, that is, wages, hours, employee benefit plans, and pension plans.

4. Regarding product liability, no claims based upon the theory of product liability have been made or threatened against seller.

5. Regarding corporation assets, a schedule is attached that lists and describes each asset. Unless specified, the corporation is the sole owner of each asset. None of the assets is subject to any liens or encumbrances except as stated in the schedule of assets.

6. The corporation's liabilities. Attached is a schedule of liabilities that lists and describes the corporation's debts and liabilities. Included are the name and address of each of the corporation's creditors, the amount owed to each creditor, and the last date on which the debt or liability must be paid or discharged.

Many other warranties and representations can be asked for relating to taxes, accounts receivables, supply of raw materials, customer lists, proprietary rights, real property, and so on. The list can be quite comprehensive. Naturally, the buyer's attorney will try to have many of these items in the purchase agreement. You'll do your best to resist and keep them to a minimum.

Buyer Representations

Here is an example of the type of representation and warranties that a buyer typically would make to a seller.

The buyer represents and warrants that he has inspected and knows the condition of the corporation's premises, inventory, furnishings, fixtures, equipment, and other physical assets. The buyer further represents and warrants that he has examined the corporation's books of account and other business records. Furthermore, the buyer is satisfied that they properly reflect the corporation's past and present earnings and financial condition. The buyer further represents and warrants that he has not relied upon any representations by the seller or others as to the corporation's past or present earnings or its prospects of future earnings.

Covenants Made by Seller

There are several covenants that a buyer will want the seller to make in the purchase agreement. A covenant is a legally binding promise or contract that an indemnification provision will cover. The following are examples of the kinds of covenants that might be included in the purchase agreement:

1. A promise to conduct the seller's business, before closing, only in the ordinary and regular course of business. This prevents the seller from being a good guy and handing out raises or bonuses to employees.
2. A covenant to allow the buyer access to the seller's books, records, and properties during his due diligence investigation.
3. A promise by the seller to pay certain acquisition costs such as attorneys', accountants', and brokers' fees.
4. Inclusion of a covenant not to compete that provides for legal damages or injunctive relief in case of a breach of a covenant. The enforceability of this covenant will require that the covenant be limited in scope, that is, geographical territory and duration. Further, the buyer will want to amortize the covenant; therefore, a dollar value must be assigned to the covenant.

Payment and Security

To close the deal, seller financing may be required. When this is the case, the seller should require a promissory note that describes the terms and contains certain default and acceleration clauses for the notes. A seller should not allow the buyer to hold back installment payments to cover claims or losses for which the seller is liable. The buyer will usually want this set- off. A buyer, at a minimum, should be required to make payments into an escrow account until any set-off dispute is resolved.

When the seller is required to carry back financing, the seller should obtain a security interest in the best collateral possible that is independent of the business being sold. Examples of collateral might be letters of credit, insurance annuities, third-party secured guarantees, and/or second mortgages on personal or commercial property.

The seller should receive a security interest in the business. The goal should be for the seller to step in and take over the business quickly when there is a default.

When assets are sold, the security interest should cover all the assets sold and all the assets that the buyer gets and uses in the business until the debt is paid in full. When there is a stock sale, the security interest should consist of a pledge of the stock sold plus a pledge on all business assets.

Compliance with Federal and State Securities Laws

Most small merger and acquisition transactions involving nonpublic corporations are structured so stock registration under both federal and state securities laws can be avoided.

The sale of stock by the shareholders of a closely held company is generally exempt from the registration requirements of the Federal Securities Act of 1933. The sale of stock to the buyer is not a distribution of securities, and the shareholders will not be issuers, underwriters, or dealers for the purposes of the 1933 act. Further, the buyer is considered a sophisticated investor with access to relevant information. He does not need the protection of the registration requirements of the 1933 act.

State laws vary with respect to registration requirements. For example, in Minnesota certain transactions are exempt from securities registration under Minnesota Statutes 80A.15, Subd. 2(1). The exemption for securities issued applies to transactions in which selling shareholders must vote on the transaction. The following three types of transactions are exempt: (1) a merger of the selling corporation, (2) a stock-for-stock exchange, and (3) a stock-for-asset exchange. Other exemptions could occur for isolated sales and a private offering exemption. Thus it is usually possible under many states for the buyer to exempt from registration any securities issued to the seller when the shareholders of the seller vote on the transaction.

Each state has its own securities laws applying to the issuance of securities.

Transfer, Sales, and Use Taxes

Most states impose transfer or sales taxes on the sale of real property and on the sale of tangible personal property not for resale. Most states don't impose a sales tax on inventory but do impose a sales tax on the sale of machinery and equipment, furniture, tools, dies, and the like.

To avoid a sales and use tax, depending on state law, it may be better to structure the acquisition as a stock transfer or merger, which is generally immune from sales taxes. However, some states impose a stock transfer and/or stock issuance tax.

Cancellation or Abandonment of Agreement

Every purchase agreement will have a provision explaining how one or both parties can get out of the deal and what conditions must be present to end the agreement. Usually, the agreement will provide that the deal may be canceled by mutual consent of both parties' boards of directors. The agreement may also say that the deal is canceled in the event that the transaction cannot be closed before a specific date. The agreement may also specify that the deal is voided if a condition required before closing doesn't happen. For example, if the shareholders fail to approve the deal or if the buyer fails to obtain financing.

Once the buyers have a purchase agreement executed with the sellers, the buyers will want to be sure the deal is done. They don't want the seller talking to other buyers. Because the buyer has difficulty enforcing a no-shop provision in the agreement, attorneys for the buyer often will insist on breakup fees. A large breakup fee makes it very difficult for the seller to walk away from the deal.

Another tactic preferred by buyer attorneys is to use a lockup option. The seller shareholders agree to grant the buyer an option to acquire their individual shares in case of a third- party offer to purchase the seller. The mere existence of a lockup option granted by the selling shareholders to the buyer will generally be enough to discourage any would-be new suitors who would want to acquire the seller.

Other Legal Considerations

The buyer and his attorneys will investigate the seller's material contracts and legal proceedings; they'll review the stockholder and director minutes and find out or verify the presence of any third-party liens and encumbrances. They will search or conduct searches of Uniform Commercial Code, judgment, bankruptcy, and tax liens. The results of the legal diligence will be used to tailor specific provisions in the purchase agreement, primarily concerning a seller's representations and warranties. For example, perhaps a major tax liability is found out that had not been previously revealed. Perhaps neither party was aware of a serious infringement on a patent or trademark.

When there are serious actual or contingent liabilities, the deal may have to be repriced or even aborted. A buyer's legal counsel will conduct a thorough search as early as possible in the diligence phase.

Liability for Selling Corporation Indebtedness

Generally, when a buyer purchases the seller's stock, the seller's creditors will have legal recourse only against the selling corporation's assets and not the new buyer's personal assets. However, where a merger occurs, most state corporation laws allow the seller's creditors legal access to both buyer's and selling corporation's assets.

When the buyer purchases the selling company's assets, the bulk sales provisions of the Uniform Commercial Code, Article 6 generally allows the seller's creditors to sue the buyer for up to six months after the acquisition. Creditors usually can't sue when notice was given to all the seller's creditors and certain other procedures were followed.

Even if the parties have complied with the notice and other requirements of the bulk sales laws, courts increasingly have held the buyer responsible for some or all of the seller's debts and contingent liabilities (especially tort liabilities for defective products). The common law doctrines of de facto merger and successor liability make the buyer responsible when the seller's business has been transferred to the buyer as a going concern and the seller goes out of existence. This is especially true when the seller's shareholders receive an equity interest in the buyer.

When the buyer purchases the seller's assets or merges with the seller, the buyer may have transferee liabilities for the seller's federal income tax obligations (Code Sec. 6901). He also may be responsible for the seller's state and local taxes under special state-transferred liabilities statues.

Environmental Issues

Under federal environmental laws and some state laws, the seller will be liable indefinitely for any environmental problems caused by the seller at any of his facilities. After the sale of the company, it becomes difficult to sort out how much of the environmental problem was caused by the seller and how much was caused by the buyer. The seller should have an environmental audit done at the time of the sale. The reason for doing so is to record permanently the condition of the property at the time of the sale.

GENERAL STRUCTURING CONSIDERATIONS

There are many considerations regarding stockholder and minority stockholder rights.

A seller's stockholder profile will frequently influence the buyer's approach to structuring the acquisition. When the seller is closely held, the buyer probably can negotiate directly with all the sellers' shareholders to acquire 100 percent of the stock. When there are many shareholders, this may not be possible. Then a merger with the seller or a purchase of the assets of the company may be more practical.

The types of sellers' assets can strongly influence the way the deal will be structured. When the seller has difficult-to- transfer assets, the purchase of the seller's stock or a merger of the buyer's subsidiary into the seller will normally make unnecessary the need for an asset sale. Difficult-to-transfer assets include large numbers of vehicles, parcels of real estate, or important contracts, leases, licenses, and the like, which prohibit assignment. On the other hand, some agreements or licenses are specifically drafted to require the other party's approval for even a change in control of the seller or a merger involving the seller. An example is the sale of controlling interest in a seller's stock.

Directors' and Shareholders' Responsibility

All mergers or sales of stock or asset transactions normally are subject to the majority approval of the boards of directors of both buyer and seller. Directors owe fiduciary duties of care and loyalty to both their corporation and its shareholders. Directors who plan to sell significant amounts of stock must be careful to ensure that their personal interests do not conflict with those of the seller himself and his minority shareholders. When directors exercise their responsibilities in a fiduciary manner and act in good faith, they should not have a problem with the sale of the company.

Besides approval by the seller's and buyer's boards of directors, many merger and acquisition transactions will require shareholder approval. When the buyer purchases all or most of the assets, state law generally requires the approval of the seller's shareholders. For example, Minnesota Statutes 302A.661, Subd. 2, require a majority vote of the seller's shareholders. The specific provisions of corporate law and the selling corporation's charter vary with respect to the vote percentage and may be much higher.

Approval by the shareholders of each of the constituent corporations to a merger or exchange of securities must also, as a rule, be approved by a majority vote of shareholders. States vary with respect to this requirement. For example, Minnesota Statutes 302A.613, Subd. 2, show that shareholders are entitled to written notice, not fewer than 14 days before the shareholder meeting, saying that the purpose of the meeting is to consider the proposed plan of merger or exchange of stock. The shareholders must receive a copy or short description of the purchase agreement. In certain limited cases, when the buyer is much larger than the merged corporation, the seller shareholders' approval may not be required.

Generally, no vote of selling shareholders or buyer shareholders is required where the buyer acquires the sellers' stock. Exceptions would arise when the buyer's charter requires the approval of the buyers' shareholders and when the buyer is issuing more stock than is authorized under its charter. Then, the buyer shareholders are required to vote to authorize the new stock issuance. Generally, a vote is also required if the buyer's stock is publicly traded.

Dissenters' Rights

The corporate laws of most states provide for dissenting shareholders' rights in case of a sale of all or most of the seller's assets that are not done in the usual or regular course of its business. The same applies to a merger with another corporation.

Dissenting shareholders may obtain cash for the fair market value of their shares under a court-supervised appraisal.

Because of the voluntary nature of a stock acquisition, statutory dissenters' or appraisal rights, do not apply. That is, a seller shareholder is not compelled to sell his shares to the buyer These rights entitle the selling company shareholders to sue to recover the fair market value of their stock.

Purchase Agreement Summary

There are, of course, many other sections to the purchase agreement. Each is different depending on the deal. You should consider having an arbitration clause to settle disputes. This can be a lot cheaper and faster to settle than lengthy litigation.

This section was meant to review some potential pitfalls after the deal is done. I hope it made you aware of the need for a deal-oriented attorney.

You should insist that all language in the purchase agreement be written in plain English. You'll save money, time, and aggravation after the deal is done when the contract is clear. Why let attorneys argue about its meaning two or five years from now? Insist on English, not legalese.

One last admonition: The party who drafts a contract always has the advantage. Since the buyer usually drafts the contract, insist on having your attorney draft those sections that affect you the most.

The outline of the purchase agreement that follows is quite comprehensive. Most agreements contain fewer provisions. However, this outline should give you an idea and a feeling about the covenants, warranties, and conditions that you may be required to negotiate or agree to.

OUTLINE OF A COMPREHENSIVE PURCHASE AGREEMENT

1.	Introduction
2.	Sales of Stock and Consideration
2.1	Transfer of Stock
2.2	Consideration
3.	Representations and Warranties of the Company and Seller
3.1	Organization
3.2	Authorization
3.3	Capitalization
3.4	Title to Securities
3.5	Financial Statements and Projections
3.6	Undisclosed Liabilities
3.7	Accounts Receivable
3.8	Inventory
3.9	Tax Returns and Audits
3.10	Product and Service Warranties and Reserves
3.11	Customers and Suppliers
3.12	Property Owned or Leased
3.13	Intellectual Property, Patents, and Trademarks
3.14	Assets Necessary for Business
3.15	Debt

Schedules

12. Patents and Trademarks
13. Nondisclosed Agreements
14. Conflicting Interests
15. Agreements That Are Noncancelable
16. Other

Exhibits

1. Employment Agreement
2. Counties and Cities in Which Seller Is Not to Compete
3. Other

16

DUE
DILIGENCE

What The Buyer Will Be Looking For

A wise buyer will investigate and scrutinize both you and your company very carefully. I'll describe some buyer's concerns. What he will be looking for. You can take corrective action on those areas needing fixing before you sell. Do not try to hide these problems. Point them out to the buyer and offer a solution. Remember, buyers understand there is risk involved in a deal. They'll be more concerned with assessing and managing the risk. They fear the unknown—what you haven't told them. If they understand the risk and know how to manage it they'll be frightened away from the deal only if they really aren't serious about purchasing your company.

During the due diligence phase, your buyer will raise many concerns. What follows are the more common problems involved in a deal as viewed from the buyer's perspective.

WHAT SHOULD THE BUYER INVESTIGATE?

Litigation

Experienced buyers and their advisers know that few firms are free of litigation. The most common liability concern is product liability. The buyer knows that product liability claims often show up long after the deal is done. You will need to address this area to allay any fears the buyer may have. Show him your liability exposure in terms of legal costs and claims paid over the past five years. If you have a good record here, you'll want to emphasize it. Show what corrective action you have taken when you've had to.

Dressed-up Financial Statements

A buyer and his advisers will analyze what you may or may not have done with your financial statements. For example, maybe you deferred repairs, maintenance, and research and development expenses. Perhaps you may have unduly low reserves or estimates for such things as bad debt, sales returns and allowances, warranties, and slow-moving and excess inventories.

Your buyer will be concerned with your accounting methods; that is, did you expense or capitalize certain items and by that increase or decrease earnings? He will be concerned about how you account for inventory such as last-in, first-out (LIFO) or first-in, first-out (FIFO) accounting. Your buyer knows LIFO is conservative for earnings and shows less inventory value than FIFO.

The point is, you will need to address your buyer's fears and worries. Be forthright and you'll build the trust and respect needed to close the deal.

Inventory Undervaluation and Overvaluation

A key source of overvalued inventory is unrecorded inventory obsolescence caused by product overruns, changing technology, and maturing or discontinued products. New product development is another contributor. Undervaluation usually results from excessive, obsolescent write-downs or inaccurate inventory counting.

Receivables

Receivables may not be collected at recorded amounts because of doubtful accounts, cash and trade discounts, dated receivables, and sales returns and allowances. You may not have adequately reserved for these items.

Credibility Check

Some acquirers will investigate to find out your credibility and character. A buyer will want to know the character of the person(s) they are dealing with. They're looking for a solid gold reputation because you may be a seller who wants to stay on and run the company after the acquisition.

Tax Contingencies

Tax contingencies represent a big problem area for buyers because most companies are very aggressive when preparing their tax returns. A private company may not have had a recent audit. A buyer is concerned about a tax audit that could be triggered. The result of a tax audit could result in a big tax exposure to him after he has acquired your company. The sale triggers the audit, and he doesn't want your tax liabilities.

Unrecorded Liabilities

Unrecorded liabilities can include vacation pay, sales returns, allowances and discounts, pension liabilities, lost contracts, and warranties.

Lost Contracts

Lost contracts and business relationships after the acquisition can include important suppliers, customer contracts, favorable leases, and licenses.

Insurance

Discontinued and reduced insurance coverages, and significantly increased insurance rates, are red flags. So is an increasing ratio of insurance expense to fixed assets.

High Employee Turnover

A high employee turnover rate, employee militancy, and labor problems all are red flags.

Sales

A significant percentage of earnings obtained from problem business segments such as sales from declining products, unstable foreign markets, short-term government contracts, and the like is a red flag.

Customers

The buyer knows he may lose some of your customers after the acquisition. As a result, reliance on a limited number of customers or one or two major customers is a big red flag.

Management Capability

Buyers like to see a well-run organization with happy employees. They like to see strong management that knows the business and has financial controls in place. Financial controls include pricing and costing policies and procedures, budgeting systems and controls, and purchasing policies and procedures. In other words, they like to see reports based on facts that allow management to maintain control and manage the operation. A wise seller must understand the need for management to appear strong and capable.

Future Expenditures

Significant future expenditures might include plant relocation or expansion and replacement of aging property, plant, and equipment. The needs for significant new product development or installation of a new computer are other expenditures that could affect the deal. These conditions will significantly affect the price a buyer will pay for your business.

Pension Fund and Health Benefits

When a selling company has many employees in their late fifties who are soon eligible for health and retirement benefits, the buyer will ask you to reduce the sales price. The retirement of many employees can cause a drain on the buyer's cash flow when he has to pay the unfunded pension and postretirement health benefits.

On the other side of the fence, many pension funds have surplus funds that serve to make the acquisition less expensive. If this is the case, be sure to make your buyer aware of this.

Financial Ratios

The buyer will compare your company's various financial ratios with industry averages. He will want to know how your company stacks up against industry averages. You should know as well. If you stack up positively, use it as a selling tool. If not, show what you are doing to bring key ratios up to industry standards.

Related-Party Expenses

Your son-in-law, whom you have set up in a business you financed, does business with you. Instead of buying directly from a vendor, you let your son-in-law buy from the vendor and then resell to you at a profit. Your son-in-law's employees do the machine maintenance work on your equipment without charge. These are the kinds of complicated internal accounting problems that affect the quality and predictability of earnings. Buyers are very nervous when they see many of these internal accounting complications.

Be sure you understand what accounting nuances you have used and have them documented and fully explained.

Product Sales and Marketing

Your buyer will analyze many product sales and marketing factors. These include:

- Sales, profit, and backlog by product line
- Major products, new product development, and obsolescence
- Annual and monthly sales histories that examine long-term trends and seasonal or cyclical trends
- Government sales
- Marketing and sales organizations, including special compensation arrangements
- Sales planning and forecasting methods
- Advertising and promotion expenditures and methods
- Market shares and product analysis of key competitors
- Product life cycles and technological obsolescence
- Competitive strategies and competitors
- Key factors for success, including threats and barriers to entry
- Customer attitudes and buying power
- Price and profit margins for every product or service line

The buyer, especially a sophisticated one, will compare industry averages to learn about your company's performance. Product obsolescence can significantly impact a transaction. When a buyer's due diligence discovers a competitor who has just introduced a new and better line, the buyer will not pay a premium for the line even though the product is very strong and should command a premium. The buyer knows that, although your sales trends have been good, the competitor's new product with new technology or application will ultimately make your product line obsolete. As a result, the buyer will substantially discount what he would have offered. Buyers, therefore, will want to do marketing intelligence. In addition, they will compare their marketing intelligence with inventory turnover and use by each item of inventory to detect slow-moving, excess, and obsolete inventory. Buyers don't want to be forced into the costly mistake of scrapping inventory after the acquisition because of declining or slow-moving product lines.

Buyers will analyze your market and industry very carefully, or at least they should. They will call the editors of trade magazines to get current information. They'll call your association. Don't assume the buyer won't know what is happening in your industry and market. A sophisticated buyer will.

Manufacturing and Distribution

The buyer will review the following:

- Each production facility, including name, location, owned or leased, book value, fair market value, capacity, employees, present condition, and alternate uses
- Manufacturing processes and efficiency
- Suppliers of raw materials
- Physical distribution methods
- Present methods of distribution (direct sales, dealerships, wholesalers or jobbers, in-house sales force or independent reps)
- Special geographic selling areas covered
- Production equipment (owned and leased) by type, manufacturer, condition, age, date purchased, prices, and stock number and all tooling, jigs, dies, and related fixtures, if any.

As you can see, the buyer's due diligence is detailed and systematic. For you, it will be time consuming and exhausting.

WHAT SHOULD THE SELLER INVESTIGATE?

The seller must be prepared to deal with these and many more questions. The buyers and their advisers will not likely overlook these concerns. When you properly plan the sales process, the effort involved should be routine, thus allowing you to concentrate on fine-tuning the sales agreement and continue to manage the company. Sales planning generally is inadequate, however, and you can feel overwhelmed by the amount of questions and information the buyer wants you to dig up and respond too.

You should investigate thoroughly who the buyer is and whether that buyer is best able to capitalize on your company's strength; further, do you have good chemistry; and does the buyer have any skeletons of his own? It's even more important to investigate your buyer if you plan to remain on as part of the management team. It's also critically important when you help with the financing or take stock of the acquiring company. You probably won't need to cover all the concerns listed in this chapter. However, you can use some as a checkpoint when you investigate the buyer. Buyer investigation is often a weak area for sellers. Don't let that be your situation.

One last concern you should know about is called a Z score, and it's taken from statistics. Sophisticated buyers and lenders sometimes use this Z score to figure out a company's future financial strength.

Professor Edward Altman of New York University has developed a Z score formula for private companies. Here is the formula:

$$\frac{(0.7 \times \text{working capital}}{\text{total assets})}$$

$$+ \frac{(0.8 \times \text{retained earnings}}{\text{total assets})}$$

$$+ \frac{(3.1 \times \text{earnings before interest and taxes}}{\text{total assets})}$$

$$+ \frac{(0.4 \times \text{book value of equity}}{\text{total liabilities})}$$

$$+ \frac{(1.0 \times \text{sales}}{\text{total assets})}$$

Compute your company's Z score and be ready to give it to your buyer and buyer's lender when they ask for it. Altman concludes that a Z score of 1.23 or less suggests the potential for bankruptcy within two years. A Z score of 2.90 or more shows continued operations. This assessment applies to closely owned companies and not public companies. Z scores that fall between will result in the buyer doing a lot more due diligence with your financials. A Z score, according to Altman's research, has been a good predictor of a company's potential for insolvency during the next two years. Many lenders and buyers will compute their Z score as a part of their analysis. Be ahead of the game by computing your Z score first. When you have good Z scores, flaunt them.

17

SWEET DREAMS

The Deal Is Done. What Now?

Congratulations! You've sold your company, and it turned out to be mutually beneficial for both you and the buyer. When you first set out on this adventure, you just didn't realize how time consuming and difficult it would be. However, you did your homework. You studied the chapters of this book and started out even and maybe a little ahead of the buyer.

You weren't outsmarted or outwitted. And while there were a few surprises, you most often knew what was coming and knew how to deal with the problems as they arose.

You paid several thousand dollars for good tax and legal advice, and you're glad you did. Your merger and acquisition consultant was competent and knowledgeable. He brought a qualified party to the table and helped you negotiate a successful deal. You made a lot of money in the transaction because you weren't a neophyte and you didn't make neophyte mistakes.

It was hard work and nerve-wracking at times, much more than you thought it was going to be. You are glad you took the time to develop the selling memorandum recommended in this book. It paid off handsomely for you. It was hard work, but in the end it was worthwhile.

You prepared your company for sale and removed contingent liabilities. The deal was simple and straightforward for the buyer.

You negotiated hard and long. You had no idea until you read this book how many items would have to be negotiated. However, you negotiated well and are satisfied with the price and terms you received for your business. Yes, you would have liked to have had more money and, yes, you gave away some things you wished you hadn't; when everything is considered, you did a whale of job considering it was the first company you ever sold.

You applied a few deal-structuring techniques and saved a ton in taxes. The IRS is frowning, but it was satisfied because it still made some dough in the process.

You recast your financials and showed the buyer the true earning power of your company. You did a great job with the sales tool and showed the strength of your company in the industry. The buyer was glad to see the industry growth and your position in the marketplace.

You are really glad you had a deal-doing attorney because you're sure you'll be paid and will avoid future legal hassles from the buyer.

You have been honest with the buyer and haven't misrepresented anything to him. You can sleep well at night and be at peace. You told him about the problems and the opportunities. You showed how the problems could be managed. Consequently, he thought the risk was acceptable.

You're pleased you took the time to figure out what your company was really worth. When the buyer brought up arguments about value, you had answers. You pointed out those factors that added value to your company. The buyer respected you because you were informed and well prepared for your meetings.

You understood the importance of chemistry between you. You felt insulted and became angry on occasion; however, you kept your cool and never blew up at the buyer or his advisers. You were surprised at your restraint, but you knew you couldn't blow your cool or the deal would be off.

You walked away from the business you had worked at for 20 years for a cool $1.5 million at close. The buyer still owes you $4 million. However, you are relaxed and stress free because you know you will receive the $4 million from a major, rock-solid, 100-year-old insurance company as an annuity paid over 10 years. When you couldn't agree on price, you suggested the buyer purchase a zero coupon for you from a municipal government for $1 million due in 20 years. He took you up on the deal because it cost him only $200,000. You're glad you knew about this technique because it made the deal fly and helped you pocket a lot more money.

You have a great consulting contract, and are only 60 years old. If all goes well, you probably can enjoy another 20 years or so. Sure you are feeling a little blue and sad. After all, this was your baby that you had seen grow up. Now your baby has left home and isn't your responsibility anymore. You don't need to worry about him anymore.

What are you going to do? You've never had this much money and freedom before. You'll figure this one out. For now, just enjoy yourself. Go on that trip you have always wanted. See the sights. Visit your son whom you don't see often enough. Rebuild some old friendships that you haven't had time for. Get involved in your local church. The minister has been after you for years to take a more active part. Now you can.

Aw, life is so grand. Enjoy it while you can.

I hope you have enjoyed this book. Let me know. I'd like to hear from you. If I can be of help, write or call.

Robert Bergeth
International Mergers and Acquisitions
326 South Broadway
Suite 219
Wayzata, MN 55391
(612) 541-4803

THE
DICTIONARY
FOR MAKING
A DEAL

Accelerated depreciation A depreciation method that writes off the cost of an asset at a faster rate than write-off under the straight-line method.

Aging accounts receivable The analysis of accounts receivable according to the length of time they have been outstanding.

Annuity Payments of a fixed amount for a certain number of years.

Balance sheet A financial statement stating the assets, liabilities, and ownership of a business organization.

Balloon payment A debt that is not fully amortized, with the final payment due larger than the previous payment.

Bond A long-term debt instrument.

Book value The accounting value of an asset, generally the purchase price.

Bulk sales act A state law intended to protect the creditors of a business that is being sold by requiring that creditors be notified of the sale.

Capital asset An asset with a life, generally of more than one year, that is not bought and sold in the ordinary course of business.

Cash flow A company's operating earnings before it pays interest and taxes, sometimes called EBIT. Cash flow is sometimes known as earnings before interest, taxes, depreciation, and amortization, called EBITDA.

Capitalization The aggregate value of ownership capital, as represented by equity capital and funded debt.

Capitalization of income Estimating the present value of a business by reducing future cash flows to present worth.

Chattel mortgage A mortgage on personal property, not real property.

Collateral Assets that are used to secure a loan.

Condition A provision in a contract that can suspend or rescind a principal obligation.

Covenant A clause of a contract or formal contract concerning acts that one will or will not perform.

Default The failure to pay interest or principal on debt when it comes due.

Discounted cash flow A method for arriving at value by discounting the future cash flows to arrive at present value.

EBIT Earnings before interest and taxes.

Equity The net worth of a business, including capital stock, paid-in capital, and retained earnings.

Equity capital The capital of a business that has been furnished by the stockholders as ownership, as opposed to borrowed capital, furnished by the corporate creditors.

Equity financing Raising ownership capital for a corporation from the sale of common or preferred stock. There is no obligation to repay the funds raised.

Fair market value The price that would be paid by a buyer and a willing seller, where both have reasonable knowledge of the facts and neither is under time constraints.

FIFO accounting A system of writing off inventory into cost of goods sold; items purchased first are written off first; referred to as first in, first out.

Going concern The concept that a business is operating and expects to continue doing so.

Income statement A financial statement that measures the profitability of the firm over a period of time; all expenses are subtracted from sales to arrive at net income.

Indemnity A security against loss or damage.

Insolvency Inability to meet debt obligations.

Intangible assets The assets of a business that have value but are not tangible property.

Internal rate of return The rate of return on an asset investment. IRR is calculated by finding the discount rate that equates the present value of future cash flows to the cost of the investment.

Joint and several contract A contract in which one party consists of two or more individuals. When sued, a party can name any one of them, all of them together, or any group of them.

Junk bonds Securities issued by a company either rated below investment grade or too new to be rated; also known as high-yield bonds or subordinated debt.

Letter of credit An instrument issued by a commercial bank in which the bank substitutes its own credit.

Leveraged buyout An LBO is a transaction in which an investor buys a company with borrowed funds, using the company itself as collateral. The debt can equal as much as 85 percent of the purchase price and is repaid from the company's cash flow or from the sale of assets.

Liability A debt or obligation of a business.

Lien A lender's claim on assets that are pledged against a loan.

LIFO accounting A system of writing off inventory from cost of goods sold; items purchased last are written off first; referred to as last-in, first out.

Liquidation The winding down of a business by the conversion of its assets into cash, followed by distribution to the owners and creditors.

Liquidity A firm's cash position and its ability to meet maturing obligations.

Net worth The capital and surplus of a firm.

Note A written, signed document stating time, place, and payment of how a debt is to be paid.

Novation An agreement for the discharge of an obligation by the debtor to his creditor by the substitution of a new creditor.

Overcapitalization When a corporation's earnings are not large enough to yield a fair return on the amount of invested capital.

Paid-in capital The sum that has actually been received by the corporation in consideration for its stock.

Pledge To place assets of the company as security for a debt to a lender.

Preferred stock Stock given a preference over other stock of the same corporation, generally, with respect to dividend payments.

Present value The value today of a future payment, or series of payments discounted at the appropriate interest rate.

Price/earning ratio The ratio of price to earnings.

Pro forma A forecast or projection that shows what would happen if certain assumptions are realized.

Recapitalization A voluntary rearrangement of the capital structure.

Representation A statement of fact made by one party in order to induce another party to enter into a contract.

Restructuring Usually a negotiated settlement in which bondholders of companies that have defaulted on their debt, or are about to, accept less than 100 cents on the dollar.

Retained earnings The portion of a company's earnings not paid out in dividends. The amount appearing on the balance sheet is the cumulative of the retained earnings for each year throughout the company's history.

Secured loan Money obtained from a lender on the basis of collateral to be forfeited upon default on the loan by the borrower.

Securities General name for stocks, mortgages, bonds, or certificates evidencing ownership or creditorship in a corporation.

Security agreement A contract that creates a security interest or lien on personal property.

Straight-line depreciation A method of depreciation that takes the depreciable cost of an asset and divides it by its useful life to determine the annual depreciation expense.

Synergy The concept that the whole is greater than the sum of the parts.

Tangible assets Physical as opposed to intangible assets.

Tangible net worth The book value of a business less any intangible assets.

Tender offer Any offer to buy a class of securities from the present owners, usually at a premium to the market price.

Terms Details of an agreement such as price, payment schedule, interest rate, due date, and so on.

Title Legal ownership.

Unsecured loan A loan where no security or collateral is used to guarantee payment of the loan.

Warranty An assurance by the seller that the business is as represented or promised.

Working capital The excess of a company's current assets over its current liabilities.

BIBLIOGRAPHY

Alderman, David. "Evaluating a Company's Management Team." *Journal of Business Valuation,* 1987 (Proceedings of the First Joint Institute of Chartered Business Valuators and the American Society of Appraisers, October 1986), pp. 129–137.

Beehler, John M. "Corporate Estate Freeze Valuation Rules Under the Proposed Section 2701 Regulations." *Taxes* (January 1992), pp. 12–19.

Bibler, Richard S., ed. *The Arthur Young Management Guide to Mergers and Acquisitions.* New York: John Wiley & Sons, 1989.

Billings, B. Anthony and Leonard G. Weld. "Taxable Business Acquisitions: Issues and Answers." *CPA Journal* (June 1990), pp. 42–48.

Blackman, Irving L. *The Valuation of Privately Held Businesses.* Chicago: Probus Publishing, 1986.

Blassberg, Franci J. and John M. Vasily. "Tightening the Noose on Fraudulent Conveyance." *Mergers & Acquisitions,* (November–December 1991), pp. 42–48.

Bonovitz, Sheldon M. "Impact of the TRA Repeal on General Utilities." *Journal of Taxation* (December 1986), pp. 388–397.

Burke, Frank M., Jr. *Valuation and Valuation Planning for Closely Held Businesses.* Englewood Cliffs, NJ: Prentice Hall, 1981.

Brown, Gregory K. and John E. Curtis. "Disposing of a Closely Held Business Through a Tax-Deferred Sale to an ESOP." *The Journal of Taxation* (October 1992), pp. 236–241

Clegg, Barry F. and John A. Satorius. *Annotated Business Acquisition Agreements.* Minneapolis: Minnesota State Bar Association, Corporate Document Series, 1991.

Commerce Clearing House, Inc. "Corporate and Securities Law, Accounting, Fraudulent Conveyance, Antitrust Reporting, and Other Nontax

Considerations in Taxable and Tax-Free Acquisitions." *Tax Transactions Library,* Vol. F5. New York: The Author, 1992.

Commerce Clearing House, Inc. "Mergers, Acquisitions and Leveraged Buyouts." *Tax Transactions Library,* Vol. F1. New York: The Author, 1992.

Commerce Clearing House, Inc. "Pro-Seller Stock Purchase." *Tax Transactions Library,* Vol. F6. New York: The Author, 1992.

Commerce Clearing House, Inc. "Special Considerations in Taxable and Tax-Free Acquisitions Involving an S Corporation." *Tax Transactions Library,* Vol. F3. New York: The Author, 1992.

Conway, Richard J., Jr. "State Environmental Laws: Growing Forces in M&A." *Mergers & Acquisitions* (September–October 1991), pp. 64–68.

Cox, Vaughn. *How to Sell Your Business for the Best Price: With the Least Worry.* Chicago: Probus Publishing, 1990.

Craig, Darryl, Glenn Johnson, and Maurice Joy. "Accounting Methods and P/E Ratios." *Financial Analysts Journal* (March–April 1987), pp. 41–45.

Crandall, Arthur L. *Valuing Businesses and Professional Practices with Revenues Under $20 Million.* New York: American Institute of Certified Public Accountants, 1988.

Dal Santo, Jacquelyn. "Valuation Concerns in the Appraisal of Covenants Not to Compete." *The Appraisal Journal* (January 1991), pp. 111–114.

Dema, Richard J. and Duncan Harwood. "Tapping the Financial Benefits of an ESOP." *Journal of Accountancy* (April 1992), pp. 27–37.

Desmond, Glenn M. and John Marcello. *Handbook of Small Business Valuation Formulas.* Los Angeles: Valuation Press, 1987.

Diamond, Stephen C. *Leveraged Buyouts.* Homewood, IL.: Dow Jones-Irwin, 1986.

Faber, Peter L. "Acquisitions and Liquidations Involving S Corporations After Tax Reform." *Practical Accountant* (September 1987), pp. 98–114.

Faltermayer, Edmund. "The Deal Decade: Verdict on the '80s." *Fortune* (August 25, 1991), pp. 58–70.

Feakins, Nicholas L. "Relevance of Financial Analysis to Standard Appraisal Methodology." *Business Valuation Review* (September 1987), pp. 105–115.

Feinberg, Andrew. "What's It Worth?" *Venture* (January 1988), pp. 27–31.

Fisher, Anne B. "The Big Drive to Reduce Debt." *Fortune* (February 10, 1992), pp. 118–124.

Fox, Steven A. *Keys to Buying and Selling a Business*. Hauppauge, NY: Barrons, 1991.

Fredrick, Scott E. "Unleashing Property Values to Finance M&A Deals." *Mergers & Acquisitions* (January–February 1990), pp. 51–56.

Gaffaney, George. *Sale of a Business in Minnesota*. St. Paul, MN: Butterworth, 1991.

Gisser, Michael V. and Gonzalez, Edward E. "Family Businesses: A Breed Apart in Crafting Deals." *Mergers & Acquisitions* (March–April 1993), v27: pp. 39–45.

Haines, Lionel. *How to Buy a Good Business: With Little or None of Your Own Money*. New York: Times Books, 1987.

Harmon, Edward B. "16 Fatal Flaws That Can Undermine an Acquisition." *Mergers & Acquisitions* (January–February 1992), pp. 36–38.

Henning, Gene H. "Completing an Acquisition." Minneapolis: Rider, Bennett, Egan & Arundel, 1988.

Herbert, Lerner J., Godbout, James C., and Herndon, Diane P. "The Corporate Provisions of the Omnibus Budget Reconciliation Act of 1993." *The Tax Advisor* (September 1993), pp. 551–558.

Israel, Charles J. "Spotting the Warning Signs of Product Liability Woes." *Mergers & Acquisitions* (November–December 1990), pp. 31–35.

Johnson, W. A. "Dissenter Shareholder Valuations: A Study of Cases and References." *Business Valuation Review* (March 1988), pp. 9–17.

Kibel, H. Ronald. *How to Turn Around a Financially Troubled Company*. New York: McGraw-Hill, 1982.

Kiesche, Elizabeth S. "No Cash, No Credit, No Megadeals." *Chemicalweek* (November 27, 1991), pp. 20–30.

Klueger, Robert F. *Buying and Selling a Business.* New York: John Wiley & Sons, 1988.

Kramer, Yale. *Valuing a Closely Held Business, Accountant's Workbook Series.* New York: Matthew Bender, 1987.

Kuppinger, Roger. *Everything You Always Wanted to Know About Mergers, Acquisitions and Divestitures but Didn't Know Whom to Ask.* The Author, 1986.

Leung, T. S. Tony. "Tax Reform Act of 1986: Considerations for Business Valuations." *Business Valuation Review* (June 1987), pp. 60–63.

Levine, Sumner N. *The Acquisitions Manual: A Guide to Negotiating and Evaluating Business Acquisitions.* New York: New York Institute of Finance, 1989.

Levinton, Howard and Robert A. Snyder, Jr. "Negotiating Strategies When a Client Wants to Sell a Closely Held Corporation." *Taxation for Lawyers* (January–February 1986), pp. 204–211.

Lindsey, Jennifer. *The Entrepreneur's Guide to Capital: The Techniques for Capitalizing and Refinancing New and Growing Businesses.* Chicago: Probus Publishing, 1986.

Managan, Joseph F. "Tracking Product Liability in Corporate Acquisitions." *Best's Review: Property-Casualty Insurance Edition* (June 1993), v94: pp. 72–74.

Marren, Joseph H. *Mergers & Acquisitions: Will You Overpay?* Homewood, IL: Dow Jones-Irwin, 1985.

McMullin, Scott G. "Discount Rate Selection." *Business Valuation News* (September 1986), pp. 16–19.

Mergers & Acquisitions. "Sorting Out the M&A Market Trends of the 1990s" (January–February 1992), pp. 14–22.

Meyer, Charles H. "Acquisition Structures—Integrating the Tax, Legal and Accounting Analysis." Minneapolis: The Author, 1989.

Michel, Allen and Israel Shaked. "The LBO Nightmare: Fraudulent Conveyance Risk." *Financial Analysts Journal* (March–April 1990), pp. 41–50.

Michel, Allen and Israel Shaked. *The Complete Guide to a Successful Leveraged Buyout.* Homewood, IL: Dow Jones-Irwin, 1987.

Miller, Merton H. "Leverage." *The Journal of Finance* (June 1991), pp. 479–488.

Minnesota Small Business Assistance Office and Fredrikson & Byron, Attorneys at Law. *Buying and Selling a Business in Minnesota.* Minneapolis: Minnesota Small Business Assistance Office and Fredrikson & Byron, 1991.

Minnesota State Bar Association. "An Introduction to the Valuation of Closely-Held Businesses & The Use of Financial Experts in Litigation." Minneapolis: The Author, September 1991.

Mintz, Gilbert. "The Shock Waves from Fat Goodwill Write-offs in Technology Deals." *Mergers & Acquisitions* (January–February 1992), pp. 32–35.

Mullaney, Michael D. and Richard W. Bailine. "Corporate Acquisitions after the Tax Reform Act of 1986." *Tax Adviser* (April 1987), pp. 212–225.

Pratt, Shannon P. *Valuing a Business: The Analysis and Appraisal of Closely Held Companies.* Homewood, IL: Business One Irwin, 1989.

Prusiecki, John F. "Tax Aspects of Agreements for Taxable Acquisitions of Corporate Businesses." *The Journal of Corporate Taxation* (Autumn 1991), pp. 203–217.

Rechtin, Michael D. "Intellectual Property: Ticking Time Bombs for the Unwary Buyer." *Mergers & Acquisitions* (January–February 1992), pp. 28–31.

Reed, Stanley Foster, and Lane and Edson, P.C. *The Art of M & A: A Merger Acquisition Buyout Guide.* Homewood, IL: Business One-Irwin, 1989.

Reik, John W. "Acquisition Financing: The EBIT Multiple Trap." *The Journal of Commercial Bank Lending* (February 1991), pp. 29–36.

Reilly, Robert F. "The Valuation and Amortization of Noncompete Clauses." *The Appraisal Journal* (April 1990), pp. 211–220.

Research Institute of America. *The RIA Complete Analysis of the Revenue Reconciliation Act of 1993 with Code Sections as Amended and Committee Reports.* New York: The Author, 1993.

Rock, Milton L. *The Mergers and Acquisitions Handbook.* New York: McGraw-Hill, 1987.

Schmehl, John W. "How Liquidations and S Elections May Avoid the Impact of TRA '86." *Journal of Taxation* (July 1987), pp. 30–38.

Silton, Lawrence C. *Taking Cash Out of the Closely Held Corporation: Tax Opportunities, Strategies, and Techniques,* 4th ed. Englewood Cliffs, NJ: Prentice Hall, 1988.

Silver, A. David. *The Middle-Market Business Acquisition Directory and Source Book.* New York: Harper Business, 1990.

Smidansky, K.J. "How ESOPs Can Be Used to Dispose of a Closely Held Business." *Tax Accountant* (May 1993), v50: pp. 297–303.

Spilka, George. "Acquisition Mind Game." *Pit & Quarry* (July 1990), pp. 44–48.

Star, Marlene Givant. "Smaller Targets Spotlighted." *Pensions & Investments* (May 27, 1991), p. 28.

Stockdale, John J. "Comparison of Publicly-Held Companies with Closely-Held Business Entities." Business Valuation Review (December 1986), pp. 3–11.

Taylor, William. "Crime? Greed? Big Ideas? What Were the '80s About?" *Harvard Business Review* (January–February 1992), pp. 32–45.

Teitelbaum, Richard S. "LBOs Really Didn't Pay, Say the Chiefs." *Fortune* (August 26, 1991), pp. 73–76.

Tinio, Ferdinand S. "Valuation of Stock of Dissenting Stockholders in Case of Consolidation or Merger of Corporation, Sale of Its Assets, or the Like." 48 *A.L.R.* 3d 430 (1973, Supplements 1979, 1986).

Torchen, Frank. "How Lenders Tightened the Pursestrings for M&A." *Mergers & Acquisitions* (July–August 1991), pp. 23–27.

Tuller, Lawrence W. *Getting Out: A Step-by-Step Guide to Selling a Business or Professional Practice.* Blue Ridge Summit, PA: Liberty Hall Press, 1990.

"Valuing a Closely-Held Business: What a Buyer Will Pay." *Small Business Report* (November 1986), pp. 30–35.

Viner, Gary and Neil Cohen. "Scouring Mid-Sized Targets for Their Hidden Values." *Mergers & Acquisitions* (July–August 1990), pp. 55–60.

Zuber, George and Schector, David. "Avoiding or Resolving Purchase Price Disputes." *The CPA Journal* (March 1993), v63: pp. 28–32.

APPENDIX

Merger and Acquisition Attorneys

Attorneys who specialize in merger and acquisitions are listed by state along with their names, addresses, and telephone numbers.

Mr. Bruce Gagnon
Atkinson, Conway & Gagnon
420 L Street, Suite 500
Anchorage, AK 99501
(907) 276-1700

Mr. Louis Anders, Jr.
Burr & Forman
420 20th Street North, Suite 3000
Birmingham, AL 35203
(205) 251-3000

Mr. Paul Benham
Friday, Eldredge & Clark
400 West Capitol Avenue
Little Rock, AR 72201
(501) 376-2011

Mr. P. Robert Moya
Quarles, Brady & Sannin
Route 1, East Camelback Rd, Suite 400
Phoenix, AZ 85012
(602 230-5500

Mr. Alan Barton
Paul, Hastings, Janofsky & Walker
555 South Flower Street, 23rd Floor
Los Angeles, CA 90071
(213) 683-6140

Mr. Robert Denham
Munger, Tolles & Olsen
355 South Grand Avenue, 34th Floor
Los Angeles, CA 90071
(213) 683-9100

Mr. Ronald Fein
Stutman, Treister & Glatt
369 Wilshire Boulevard, Suite 900
Los Angeles, CA 90010
(310) 556-8000

Mr. John Brooks
Luce, Forward, Hamilton & Scripps
600 West Broadway, Suite 2600
San Diego, CA 92101
(619) 236-1414

Mr. Cameron Baker
Petit & Martin
101 California Street, 36th Floor
San Francisco, CA 94111
(415) 434-4000

Ms. Margaret Gill
Pillsbury, Madison & Sutro
235 Montgomery Street, Suite 1699
San Francisco, CA 94104
(415) 983-1528

307

Mr. David Butler
Holland & Hart
555 17th Street, Suite 2900
Denver, CO 80202
(303) 295-8000

Mr. Garth Grissom
Sherman & Howard
633 17th Street
Denver, CO 80202
(303) 297-2900

Mr. John Lewis
Ireland, Stapleton, Pryor & Pasco
1675 Broadway, Suite 2600
Denver, CO 80202
(303) 623-2700

Mr. David Chipman
Gager & Henry
30 Main Street
Danbury, CT 06810
(203) 743-6363

Mr. James Lotstein
Cummings & Lockwood
185 Asylum Street
Hartford, CT 06103
(203) 275-6700

Mr. Richard McGrath
Cummings & Lockwood
10 Stamford Forum
Stamford, CT 06904
(203) 327-1700

Mr. David Brown
Covington & Burling
1201 Pennsylvania Avenue, NW
Washington, DC 20044
(202) 662-6000

Mr. Stuart Carwile
Wiley, Rein & Fielding
1776 K Street, NW
Washington, DC 20006
(202) 429-7000

Mr. William Coleman, Jr.
O'Melveny & Meyers
555 13th Street NW, Suite 500 W
Washington, DC 20004
(202) 383-5300

Mr. R. Franklin Balotti
Richards, Layton & Finger
One Rodney Square
Wilmington, DE 19899
(302) 658-6541

Mr. A. Gilchrist Sparks
Morris, Nichols, Arsht & Tunnell
1201 North Market Street
Wilmington, DE 19899
(302) 658-9200

Mr. Bowman Brown
Shutts & Bowen
201 South Biscayne Blvd, Suite 1500
Miami, FL 33131
(305) 379-9107

Mr. Michael Jamieson
Holland & Knight
400 North Ashley Drive, Suite 2300
Tampa, FL 33602
(813) 227-8500

Mr. Robert Rasmussen
Glenn, Rasmussen & Fogarty
100 South Ashley Drive, Suite 1300
Tampa, FL 33602
(813) 229-3333

Mr. David Baker
Powell, Goldstein, Frazer & Murphy
191 Peachtree Street, 16th Floor
Atlanta, GA 30303
(404) 572-6600

Mr. F. Dean Copeland
Alston & Bird
1201 West Peachtree Street
Atlanta, GA 30309
(404) 881-7443

Mr. Edward Harrell
Martin, Snow, Grant & Napier
240 3rd Street
Macon, GA 31202
(912) 743 7051

Mr. Mark Nye
Racine, Olson, Nye, Cooper & Budge
201 East Center, Suite 172
Pocatello, ID 83204
(208) 232-6101

Mr. John Bitner
Bell, Boyd & Lloyd
70 West Madison Street, Suite 3200
Chicago, IL 60602
(312) 372-1121

Mr. Frederick Hartmann
Schiff, Hardin & Waite
7200 Sears Tower, 233 South Wacker Drive
Chicago, IL 60606
(312) 876-1000

Mr. Jack Levin
Kirkland & Ellis
200 East Randolph Drive
Chicago, IL 60601
(312) 861-2000

Mr. John Wyse
Seyfarth, Shaw, Fairweather & Geraldson
55 East Monroe Street, Suite 4200
Chicago, IL 60603
(312) 346-8000

Mr. Robert Reynolds
Barnes & Thornburg
11 South Meridan Street
Indianapolis, IN 46204
(317) 638-1313

Mr. Nelson Vogel, Jr.
Barnes & Thornburg
100 North Michigan Street
South Bend, IN 46601
(219) 233-1171

Mr. Darrell Morf
Simmons, Perrine, Albright & Ellwood
115 3rd Street, SE, Suite 1200
Cedar Rapids, IA 52401
(319) 366-7641

Mr. Steve Zumbach
Belin Harris Lamson & McCormick
7th & 666 Walnut Street, 2000 Financial Ctr.
Des Moines, IA 50309
(515) 243-7100

Mr. Robert Edmonds
Goodell, Stratton, Edmonds & Palmer
515 South Kansas Avenue
Topeka, KS 66603
(913) 233-0593

Mr. A. Robert Doll
Greenebaum, Doll & McDonald
3300 First National Tower
Louisville, KY 40202
(502) 589-4200

Mr. Paul Haygood
Stone & Pigman
546 Carondelet Street
New Orleans, LA 70130
(504) 581-3200

Mr. Campbell Hutchinson
Stone & Pigman
546 Carondelet Street
New Orleans, LA 70130
(504) 581-3200

Mr. L. Richards McMillan II
Jones, Walker, Waechter, Poitevent & Carrere
202 St. Charles Avenue
New Orleans, LA 70170
(504) 582-8000

Mr. Norman Bikales
Sullivan & Worcester
One Post Office Square
Boston, MA 02109
(617) 338-2800

Mr. Donald Evans
Goodwin, Procter & Hoar
Exchange Place
Boston, MA 02109-2881
(617) 570-1000

Mr. Kenneth Novack
Minz, Levin, Cohn, Ferris, Glovsky & Popeo
One Financial Center
Boston, MA 02111
(617) 542-6000

Mr. David Lougee
Mirick, O'Connell, DeMallie & Lougee
1700 Mechanics Tower, Worcester Center
Worcester, MA 01608-1477
(508) 799-0541

Mr. Bryson Cook
Venable, Baetjer & Howard
1800 Mercantile Bank & Trust Building
Baltimore, MD 21201-2987
(410) 244-7400

Mr. Joseph Delafield
Drummond, Woodsum, Plimpton & Mac-Mahon
245 Commercial Street
Portland, ME 04101
(207) 772-1941

Mr. Bruce Birgbauer
Miller, Canfield, Paddock & Stone
150 West Jefferson, Suite 2500
Detroit, MI 48226
(313) 963-6420

Mr. Charles McCallum
Warner, Norcross & Judd
900 Old Kent Building, 111 Lyon Street, NW
Grand Rapids, MI 49503-2489
(616) 459-6121

Mr. Ronald Pentecost
Fraser, Trebilcock, Davis & Foster
1000 Michigan National Tower
Lansing, MI 48933
(517) 482-5800

Mr. Stanley Efron
Henson & Efron
400 Second Avenue South
Minneapolis, MN 55401
(612) 339-2500

Mr. John French
Faegre & Benson
90 South Seventh Street, 2200 Norwest Center
Minneapolis, MN 55402-3901
(612) 336-3000

Mr. Keith Libbey
Fredrikson & Byron
900 Second Avenue South,
1100 International Center
Minneapolis, MN 55402-7000
(612) 347-7000

Mr. E. Clifton Hodge
Phelps & Dunbar
200 South Lamar, Suite 500, Box 23066
Jackson, MS 39225-2567
(601) 352-2300

Mr. Edward Wilmesherr
Butler, Snow, O'Mara, Stevens & Cannada
Deposit Guaranty Plaza, 17th Floor
Jackson, MS 39225-2567
(601) 948-5711

Mr. John Bancroft
Morrison & Hecker
2600 Grand Avenue, 1700 Bryant Building
Kansas City, MO 64108
(816) 691-2600

Mr. Howard Mick
Stinson, Mag & Fizzell
1201 Walnut, Suite 2800
Kansas City, MO 64141
(816) 842-8600

Mr. Don Lents
Bryan & Cave
1 Metropolitan Square, 211 North Broadway,
Suite 3600
St. Louis, MO 63102-2186
(314) 259-2000

Mr. Paul Pautler
Thompson & Mitchell
One Mercantile Center, Suite 3400
St. Louis, MO 63101
(314) 231-7676

Mr. John Dietrich
Crowley, Haughey, Hanson, Toole & Dietrich
490 N. 31st Street, Suite 500
Billings, MT 59101
(406) 252-3441

Mr. Larry Dagenhart
Smith Helms Mulliss & Moore
227 North Tryon Street, P.O. Box 31247
Charlotte, NC 28231
(704) 343-2010

Mr. Braxton Schell
Schell, Bray, Aycock, Abel & Livingston
230 North Elm Street, Suite 1500
Greensboro, NC 27401
(919) 370-8800

Mr. William Schlossman, Jr.
Vogel, Brantner, Kelly, Knutson, Weir & Bye
502 First Avenue North
Fargo, ND 58102
(701) 237-6983

Mr. Doug Christensen
Pearson, Christensen, Larivee & Fischer
24 North Fourth Street
Grand Forks, ND 58206-1075
(701) 775-0521

Mr. Robert Routh
Knudsen, Berkeimer, Richardson, & Endacott
1000 NBC Center
Lincoln, NE 68508
(402) 475-7071

Mr. John Aiello
Giordano, Halleran & Ciesla
125 Half Mile Road, P.O. Box 190
Middletown, NJ 07748
(908) 741-3900

Mr. Bart Colli
McCarter & English
Four Gateway Center, 100 Mulberry Street
Newark, NJ 07102-0652
(201) 622-4444

Mr. Bruce Shoulson
Lowenstein, Sandler, Kohl, Fisher & Boylan
65 Livingston Avenue
Roseland, NJ 07068-1791
(201) 992-8700

Mr. Richard Barlow
Montgomery & Andrews
201 3rd Street NW, Suite 1300
Albuquerque, NM 87125
(505) 242-9677

Mr. Robert Anderson
Anderson, Pearl, Hardesty & Lyle
245 East Liberty Street, 3rd Floor
Reno, NV 89501
(702) 348-5000

Mr. Richard Beattie
Simpson, Thacher, & Bartlett
425 Lexington Avenue
New York, NY 10017-3909
(212) 455-2000

Mr. Meredith Brown
Debevoise & Plimpton
875 Third Avenue
New York, NY 10022
(212) 909-6000

Mr. Stephen Fraidin
Fried, Frank, Harris, Shriver, & Jacobson
One New York Plaza
New York, NY 10004-1980
(212) 820-8000

Mr. William Wynne, Jr.
White & Case
1155 Avenue of the Americas
New York, New York 10036
(212) 819-8200

Mr. Alan Underberg
Underberg & Kessler
1800 Lincoln First Tower
Rochester, NY 14604
(716) 258-2800

Mr. Charles Beeching
Bond, Schoeneck & King
One Lincoln Center, 18th Floor
Syracuse, NY 13202-1355
(315) 422-0121

Mr. Edmund Adams
Frost & Jacobs
2500 Central Trust Center, 201 East 4th Street
Cincinnati, OH 45201-5715
(513) 651-6800

Mr. Timothy Hoberg
Taft, Stettinius & Hollister
1800 Star Bank Center
Cincinnati, OH 45202
(513) 381-2838

Mr. Leonard Meranus
Thompson, Hine & Flory
312 Walnut Center, Suite 1400
Cincinnati, OH 45202-3675
(513) 352-6700

Mr. George Aronoff
Benesch, Friedlander, Coplan & Aronoff
1100 Citizens Building, 850 Euclid Avenue
Cleveland, OH 44114-3399
(216) 363-4500

Mr. Robert Markey
Baker & Hostetler
3200 National City Center, 900 E. 9th St.
Cleveland, OH 44114
(216) 621-0200

Mr. John Beavers
Bricker & Eckler
100 South Third Street
Columbus, OH 43215-4291
(614) 227-2300

Mr. G. Robert Lucas II
Vorys, Sater, Seymour and Pease
52 East Gay Street
Columbus, OH 43216-1008
(614) 464-6400

Mr. Richard Chernesky
Chernesky, Heyman & Kress
10 Courthouse Plaza Southwest, Suite 1100
Dayton, OH 45401-3808
(513) 449-2828

Mr. James Baehren
Fuller & Henry
One SeaGate, 17th Floor
Toledo, OH 43603-2088
(419) 247-2500
[[Author: Is SeaGate one word or two?]]

Mr. James White, Jr.
Shumaker, Loop & Kendrick
North Courthouse Square, 1000 Jackson
Toledo, OH 43624-1573
(419) 241-9000

Mr. Theodore Elam
McAfee & Taft
Two Leadership Square, 10th Floor
Oklahoma City, OK 73102
(405) 235-9621

Mr. Lon Foster III
Crowe & Dunlevy
1800 Mid-America Tower, 20 North Broadway
Oklahoma City, OK 73102
(405) 235-7700

Mr. John Johnson, Jr.
Gable & Gotwals
2000 4th National Bank Building, 15 West 6th St.
Tulsa, OK 74119-5447
(918) 582-9201

Mr. Arlen Swearingen
Gleaves Swearington Larsen & Potter
975 Oak Street, 8th Floor
Eugene, OR 97440-1147
(503) 686-8833

Mr. Richard Roy
Stoel Rives Boley Jones & Gray
Standard Insurance Center, 900 Southwest
5th Avenue, #2300
Portland, OR 97204-1268
(503) 224-3380

Mr. J. Gordon Cooney
Schnader, Harrison, Segal & Lewis
1600 Market Street, Suite 3600
Philadelphia, PA 19103
(215) 751-2000

Mr. Vincent Garrity, Jr.
Duane, Morris & Heckscher
One Liberty Place, Suite 4200
Philadelphia, PA 19103
(215) 979-1242

Mr. William Klaus
Pepper, Hamilton Scheetz
3000 Two Logan Square, 18th & Arch Streets
Philadelphia, PA 19103-2799
(215) 981-4000

Mr. James Hardie
Reed Smith Shaw & McClay
James H. Reed Building, Mellon Square, 435
6th Avenue
Pittsburgh, PA 15219-2009
(412) 288-3131

Mr. C. Kent May
Eckert Seamans Cherin & Mellott
USX Tower, 600 Grant Street, 42nd Floor
Pittsburgh, PA 15219-2887
(412) 566-6000

Mr. William Newlin
Buchanan & Ingersoll
USX Tower, 600 Grant Street, 58th Floor
Pittsburg, PA 15219-2887
(412) 562-6000

Mr. John Corrigan
Adler Pollock & Sheehan
2300 Hospital Trust Tower
Providence, RI 02903
(401) 274-7200

Ms. Susan Smythe
Buist, Moore, Smythe & McGee
Five Exchange Street, P.O. Box 999
Charleston, SC 29402-0999
(803) 722-3400

Mr. Thomas Foye
Bangs, McCullen, Butler & Simmons
818 St. Joseph Street
Rapid City, SD 57701
(605) 343-1040

Mr. David Knudson
Davenport, Evans, Hurwitz & Smith
513 South Main Avenue
Sioux Falls, SD 57101-1030
(605) 336-2880

Mr. Samuel Chafetz
Waring & Cox
Morgan Keegan Tower, Suite 1300, 50 North
Front Street
Memphis, TN 38103
(901) 543-8000

Mr. Robert Tuke
Farris, Warfield & Kanaday
3rd National Financial Center, 424 Church, #1900
Nashville, TN 37219
(615) 244-5200

Mr. J. Rowland Cook
Johnson & Gibbs
100 Congress Avenue, Suite 1400
Austin, TX 78701
(512) 322-8000

Mr. William Volk
Jenkins & Gilchrist
2200 One American Center, 600 Congress
Avenue
Austin, TX 78701
(512) 499-3800

Mr. Dan Busbee
Locke Purnell Rain Harrell
2200 Ross Avenue, Suite 2200
Dallas, TX 75201-6776
(214) 740-8000

Mr. Tad Smith
Kemp, Smith, Duncan & Hammond
2000 State National Plaza
El Paso, TX 79901-2800
(915) 533-4424

Mr. Wm. Franklin Kelly, Jr.
Vinson & Elins
2500 First City Tower, 1001 Fannin Street
Houston TX 77002-6760
(713) 758-2222

Mr. T. William Porter
Porter & Clements
Nations Bank Center, 700 Louisiana, Suite 3500
Houston TX 77210-4744
(713) 226-0600

Mr. Don Allen
Ray, Quinney & Nebeker
79 South Main Street, P.O. Box 45385
Salt Lake City, UT 84145-0385
(801) 532-1500

Mr. Arthur Scibelli
McGuire, Woods, Battle & Boothe
Tyson Corner, 8280 Greensboro Drive, Suite 900
McLean, VA 22102
(703) 712-5445

Mr. C. Porter Vaughan III
Hunton & Williams
Riverfront Plaza, East Tower, 951 East Byrd Street
Richmond, VA 23219
(804) 788-8200

Mr. Franklin Flippin
Glenn, Flippin, Feldman & Darby
200 First Campbell Square
Roanoke, VA 24001
(703) 224-8000

Mr. Stewart McConaughy
Gravel and Shea
Corporate Plaza, 76 St. Paul Street
Burlington, VT 05402-0369
(802) 658-0220

Mr. Richard Dodd
Preston Thorgrimson Shidler Gates & Ellis
5000 Columbia Center, 701 Fifth Avenue
Seattle, WA 98104-7078
(206) 623-7580

Mr. Thomas Ragatz
Foley & Lardner
First Wisconsin Plaza, 7th Floor, One South Pinckney
Madison, WI 53701-1497
(608) 257-5035

Mr. William Abraham, Jr.
Foley & Lardner
First Wisconsin Center, 777 East Wisconsin Avenue
Milwaukee, WI 53202-5367
(414) 271-2400

Mr. Conrad Goodking
Quarles & Brady
411 East Wisconsin Avenue
Milwaukee, WI 53202-4497
(414) 277-5000

Mr. Roy LaBudde
Michael, Best & Friedrich
100 East Wisconsin Avenue, Suite 3300
Milwaukee, WI 53202-4108
(414) 277-5000

Mr. John Jenkins, Jr.
Jenkins, Fenstermaker, Krieger, Kayes & Farrell
Coal Exchange Building, 401 11th Street, 11th Floor
Huntington, WV 25726
(304) 523-2100

Mr. Donn McCall
Brown & Drew
Casper Business Center, 123 West First Street, #800
Casper, WY 82601
(307) 234-1000

HOW TO MAXIMIZE VALUE AND CASH OUT
FOR THE MOST PROFIT

Because of the mistakes made in selling a business, much time and potential profit is lost. There are, however, many techniques and strategies that can magnify the profits sellers receive for their businesses, thus, avoiding the costly mistakes that are made in so many deals. International Mergers and Acquisitions is prepared to help sellers in all phases of their merger and acquisition needs. Our contacts are worldwide. Since 1969, we have been providing professional services to companies that are considering cashing out. We help companies analyze strengths and weaknesses, identify possible buyers, and assist with negotiations. *Our primary mission is to maximize the value business owners receive from the sale of their companies.* We can help in the following areas:

Appraisal and valuation assistance. IMA will help establish a range of values for your company.

Help in evaluating the sale or merger of the company, and/or other means of helping the owner cash out. This could include additional financing, ESOP, joint ventures, leveraged cash out, recapitalization, merger, or sale.

Aid in preparing the business plan or selling prospectus.

Search for and identify the best buyers and assist with the negotiations. We use our national and international contacts and our industry savvy to bring the right buyer to the negotiating table. Then we help with the negotiations until the deal is completed.

Arrange financing for a merger, sale, restructuring, sale leaseback, equipment leasing, etc.

Conduct strategic business, market, and acquisition planning. We help companies figure out their merger and acquisition strategies. This includes identifying strategic objectives that will be accomplished by an acquisition. We help identify, analyze, and evaluate the best industries, markets, and acquisition candidates.

Do industry studies and competitor analysis. Also, identify and analyze key competitors, customers and suppliers. IMA examines major barriers to entry, exit or expansion. We look for opportunities and threats, economic and demographic trends, and political and regulatory factors. Finally, we check out competitive forces and industry outlooks.

We conduct custom-tailored merger and acquisition conference presentations and seminars.

For more information on how to cash out for the most profit, **call 612-541-4803** or write: Bob Bergeth, International Mergers and Acquisitions, Suite 219, 326 South Broadway, Wayzata, MN 55391.

INDEX